SOUND FIGURES OF MODERNITY

Sound Figures of
Modernity

German Music and Philosophy

Edited by

JOST HERMAND

and

GERHARD RICHTER

THE UNIVERSITY OF WISCONSIN PRESS

The publication of this book was supported by grants from

William F. Vilas Trust Estate

Wisconsin Alumni Research Foundation (WARF)

The University of Wisconsin Press
1930 Monroe Street
Madison, Wisconsin 53711

www.wisc.edu/wisconsinpress/

3 Henrietta Street
London WC2E 8LU, England

1   3   5   4   2

Printed in the United States of America

Library of Congress Cataloging-in-Publication Data
Sound figures of modernity: German music and philosophy /
edited by Jost Hermand and Gerhard Richter.
p.   cm.
Includes bibliographical references and index.
ISBN 0-299-21930-5 (cloth: alk. paper)
1. Music—Germany—Philosophy and aesthetics.
2. Music and literature.
I. Hermand, Jost.   II. Richter, Gerhard.
ML3845.S6833   2006
781.1′7—dc22   2006008595

CONTENTS

ACKNOWLEDGMENTS

The essays gathered in this book, with the exception of Samuel Weber's contribution, first were presented as papers at the international conference "Elective Affinities: German Music and Philosophy," the 36th Wisconsin Workshop, jointly organized by Jost Hermand and Gerhard Richter at the University of Wisconsin–Madison in October 2003. All of the texts have been substantially revised and expanded for the present volume. In addition to the speakers whose essays appear here, moderators from the University of Wisconsin's Departments of German, Musicology, and Philosophy, along with a lively multidisciplinary audience, helped to make the three days of the conference a success. Joan Leffler's unfailing grace and unparalleled efficiency once again proved invaluable to the organization and execution of the event. Special thanks also are extended to the University of Wisconsin Anonymous Fund, the Trustees of the William F. Vilas Estate, the Wisconsin Alumni Research Foundation, the DAAD Center for German and European Studies at the University of Wisconsin, the Deutsche Forschungsgemeinschaft, and the University of Wisconsin's Department of German, all of whom furnished material support for the conference or for the present volume. The editors also would like to thank the staff at the University of Wisconsin Press and the two anonymous reviewers of the manuscript.

An earlier German version of Lydia Goehr's essay appeared in *Dialektik der Freiheit: Frankfurter Adorno-Konferenz 2003*, ed. Axel Honneth (Frankfurt am Main: Suhrkamp, 2005). Portions of David Farrell Krell's essay were included in his *The Tragic Absolute: German Idealism and the Languishing of God* (Bloomington: Indiana University Press, 2005). Finally, a German version of Samuel Weber's contribution first appeared in *Narben des Gesamtkunstwerks*, ed. Richard Klein (Munich: Fink, 2001).

SOUND FIGURES OF MODERNITY

I

German Music and Philosophy

An Introduction

JOST HERMAND and GERHARD RICHTER

> Therefore art stands in need of philosophy that interprets it in order to
> say that which it cannot say, whereas art is only able to say what it says
> by not saying it.
>
> Theodor W. Adorno, Ästhetische Theorie

Sound Figures

Any thinking about music will always have come too late. The future
perfect tense of this construction specifies the temporal situation in
which the project of theorizing music necessarily occurs, namely, in a
time that is out of joint. Like the grammatical future perfect, music's
being is neither fully present nor fully past nor merely in the future, but
rather is lodged in that temporal space of which one can only ever say
that it will have been. This is so because music unfolds in time, even as
time, and vanishes for good with the last notes of its performance. Even
in an age in which music can be recorded, archived, and infinitely reproduced by a plethora of technical devices, this phenomenon persists.
Music comes into its own in time, exists and formally generates itself in
time, and thematizes, as one of its central concerns, the very experience
of time. If the time in which music takes place, that is, the time that belongs to music, gives music over to time while, at the same time, setting
time to music, then any philosophical engagement with music must
come to terms with the out-of-jointness of the time that affords us both

3

the pleasure and the intellectual possibility of thinking music as a variously modulated leitmotif.

Unlike literary writing, painting, or other aesthetic practices, music leaves behind no immediate material traces. Rather, it is coextensive with its own performance regardless of whether the time and space of that performance are shared by a listener. To think about music, therefore, is to engage the notion that music exists in and for itself, as a potential or executed performance of figures and sounds that, strictly speaking, have no need of a witness. As Walter Benjamin reminds us in 1923, "nowhere does a consideration of the receiver prove fruitful for the cognition of a work of art. . . . No symphony [is directed toward] its circle of listeners."[1] Benjamin's observation reenacts the epistemo-critical shift from an aesthetics of intentionality and of affect anchored in an examination of the subject's response to an artwork, to an aesthetics of form concerned with an artwork's formal criteria of beauty and the critical judgments that it may sponsor independent of any particular subject's response. At the same time, the transitory nature of the representational traces that traverse an aesthetic structure defy the hermeneutic attempt to arrest the meaning of that structure.

If a special affinity does, in fact, exist between music and philosophy, then the tenor of that relationship necessarily is modulated by the fundamental tensions permeating every aesthetic form and saturating music in medium-specific ways. In other words, the pleasure derived from a work of art, especially a musical one, although certainly open to analysis, will raise the question of art's raison d'être once any attempt is made to understand that work by means of the precepts of reason alone, whether the attempt is made merely with an eye to its *illustrative* function vis-à-vis this or that philosophical or political agenda, or in a totalizing attempt to translate aesthetic form and its irrational pleasures into a rational system of concepts. Benjamin's friend, Theodor W. Adorno, illustrates this conundrum in his *Aesthetic Theory* as follows: "When one asks a musician if music is a pleasure, the reply is likely to be—as in the American joke of the grimacing cellist under Toscanini—'*I just hate music.*'" The following dilemma then emerges: "Whoever enjoys artworks concretistically is a philistine; expressions such as 'a feast for the ears' [*Ohrenschmaus*] give him away. Yet if the last traces of pleasure were extirpated, the question as to the purpose of artworks would be an embarrassment."[2] As such, any philosophical explication of music first of all must acknowledge that "art stands in need of philosophy that interprets it in order to say that which it cannot say, whereas art is only able to say what it says by not saying it."[3] The challenge of remaining faithful to the difficulty of this task confronts any speculative analysis of musical aesthetics.[4]

The difficulty of speaking philosophically about music increases when one considers the proximity of music to discursive language and the attendant conceptual content that it simultaneously extends and withdraws. Does music *have* a language? If so, *is* it a language of its own? What kind of language is it? If it can be conceded that music is or has a form of language—and the jury among musicians and theorists of music alike remains out on this point—how would the language of music relate to the language of speculative thought, its grammatical categories and organizing principles, its logic and its vocabulary? In his "Fragment on Music and Language," Adorno argues that "music resembles language [*Musik ist sprachähnlich*] . . . in that it is a temporal sequence of articulated sounds that are more than mere sounds. They say something, often something human. The more sophisticated the music, the more penetratingly they say it. The succession of sounds is related to logic: there is right and wrong." He continues: "But what has been said cannot detach itself from the music. Music forms no system of signs [*kein System aus Zeichen*]."[5] Thus, although music and language share certain modes of signification that, broadly speaking, could be construed as belonging to the vast realm of textuality, the content of music cannot be considered as belonging to the temporal gesture of its performance and cannot be paraphrased without being erased. In its refusal to supply reliable hermeneutic access to its arrangements of acoustic signs, music singularly denies itself, if not to citation, then certainly to summary and paraphrase.

This refusal to be summarized or paraphrased should not, however, simply be regarded as a deficit, since it constitutes a triumph as well as a failure. The triumph resides in the musical artwork's insistence on remaining faithful to the difficulties that lie at the heart both of musical composition and of philosophical thought. In following this logic, we may recall Adorno's comments in *Negative Dialectics* when, apropos of his musical mentor Arnold Schönberg and the Second Viennese School, he writes:

> An experience that Schönberg noted with regard to traditional music theory is confirmed in the case of philosophy: one actually only learns

from it how a movement begins and ends, nothing about the movement itself, its course. Analogously philosophy would need first, not to turn itself into a series of categories, but rather, in a certain sense, to compose itself. It must, in the course of its progression, relentlessly renew itself, as much from its own strength as from the friction with that against which it measures itself; it is what happens in philosophy that is decisive, not a thesis or a position; its fabric, not the deductive or inductive single-tracked train of thought. Therefore philosophy is in essence not summarizable. Otherwise it would be superfluous; that most of it allows itself to be summarized speaks against it.[6]

Far from merely equating music with philosophy, Adorno here emphasizes the shared compositional form and meticulously constructed aesthetic elements that, in the most rigorous and liberating musical and philosophical works, mitigate against a freezing of their sounds and signs into an apparently fixed and scanable database of meaning capable of being expressed independent of the resistant rhetorical singularities of their forms. From this perspective, what the musical compositions of such figures as Beethoven, Gustav Mahler, and Schönberg share, or ought to share, with the philosophy of such thinkers as Marx, Ernst Bloch, and Adorno is a resistance to paraphrase and a refusal to play along with the commodity fetishism of regressive listening that characterizes capitalism and the ideology of lucidity that demands submissive transparency.

Genealogies of German Musical Aesthetics

Although such considerations may seem to situate our discussion firmly within the twentieth century, any contemporary philosophical reading of musical aesthetics must occur within the historical context of those multiply refracted genealogies that have fostered an awareness of music as a phenomenon worthy of speculative attention. The principal foundation for a document-based scholarly commentary on music was the invention of an Italian monk, Guido d'Arezzo, who, during the first half of the eleventh century, developed a system of musical notation based on a four-staff line enabling composers to record their works in manuscript form for the first time. Although music can be traced back to ancient times when its rhythms were used to synchronize the heart beats of tribal members during collective rituals, a significant aesthetics of music did not emerge until around 1800.[7] Even the Enlightened discourse of the eighteenth century had not considered the phenomenon of musicality worthy of sustained attention. In the area of vocal music, the expectation was that music would reinforce the semantic content of its corresponding text without imposing itself too noticeably as an autonomous form of artistic expression. In the area of instrumental music, the phenomenon of musicality was even more sorely neglected because, to many thinkers of the Enlightenment, the absence of words that could be channeled into accessible concepts made music largely superfluous, an empty ringing or, worse yet, a courtly form of diversion to be strenuously avoided by those hoping to achieve freedom from court and church ritual through rationally mediated truth.

Not until the period of Romanticism was instrumental music increasingly valorized as an intellectual form, and a theoretical discourse specifically devoted to an aesthetics of music began to take hold. Although he was the chief representative of a new form of instrumental music around 1800, Beethoven exerted a less pronounced influence on the development of a genuine aesthetics of music than did the writers and theorists affiliated with German Romanticism.[8] Their theoretical works engaged the idea of a pure or absolute instrumental music that, in its emancipation from the semantics of the word, was felt by many to exemplify both the nuanced rejection of a teleological form of Enlightenment and the highest expression of the aesthetic. In the wake of these developments, vocal music lost its primacy in Germany and was replaced by a plethora of chamber-musical and symphonic musical genres claiming for themselves a certain "subjective inwardness," as Hegel termed it.

Hegel's conjuncture of music and the subject with an eye toward establishing the systematicity of the aesthetic as a category of the Absolute emerges forcefully in the section of his *Lectures on Aesthetics* devoted to music. There, he writes: "The subject is gripped by this element [of sound] not merely according to this or that specificity or merely through a determined content, but rather is elevated into the work and put to work there according to its simple self and its spiritual being. For instance, in the case of striking, easily flowing rhythms, we feel like clapping the beat, and dance music even goes straight to our legs: in general, the subject is enlisted as *this* person."[9] For Hegel, music does not simply reflect or capture the subject through the performance of a specific acoustic content; it elevates the self into its very unfolding. In music, the essence of the self comes into its own; when listening to music, the self abandons itself to itself, hears itself as that which comes to itself by involuntarily abandoning itself to melody and rhythm. Music, as an aesthetic manifestation of Spirit, allows the self to move on its way to the Absolute at a pace and rhythm that the speculative discourses of abstract aesthetic systems hardly can match.[10]

That this trend toward regarding music as a paradigm of the individual subject was most pronounced in Germany hardly comes as a surprise, considering the specific cultural and intellectual episteme of Germany between 1800 and 1820.[11] After all, during that time the dissolution of the venerable Holy Roman Empire of the German Nation under the pressure of French conquerors left behind a volatile situation of ideological and cultural confusion largely characterized by a retreat into what Friedrich Engels termed "effusive misery." The most important reactions to this situation are arguably to be found in the various forms of a nuanced German Idealist philosophy (especially Hegel and F. W. J. Schelling) and in the Romantic valorizations of the imagination (above all in the works of Novalis, Friedrich Schlegel, Wilhelm Heinrich Wackenroder, and E. T. A. Hoffmann), tendencies that, in 1819, Arthur Schopenhauer attempted to condense into an aesthetic system in his main philosophical work, *The World as Will and Representation*. In this aesthetic system, Schopenhauer reserves for music the highest place in the hierarchy of the arts, in part because, thanks to its forces of internalization and inwardness, it involves the human subject less in the dark contingencies of the empirical world than do arts such as literature and painting, which should be considered more referential and "realistic."

The result of such speculative thinking was a collective belief in the inner elective affinity between music and philosophy, a conviction that remained vibrant in Germany far into the second half of the nineteenth century. Again and again, writers and thinkers in that country sought to emancipate both music—that is, instrumental music—and philosophy from empirical "shackles" and to elevate them to the realm of the merely abstract, even to the realm of the timeless Absolute. In the wake of these cultural trajectories, the following decades witnessed an almost perpetual generation of important new chamber-musical or symphonic works and philosophical treatises—all of which contributed to the image of Germany outside its borders as the country of composers and thinkers, while within Germany, largely because of the impact of Goethe and Schiller, the somewhat erroneous self-image as a country of poets and thinkers (the land of "Dichter und Denker") persisted.

Of the causal elements that contributed to this cultural-historical development, the following seem most salient to us: first, an insufficient anchoring of music among the German bourgeoisie in a country that, for the longest time, had neither a national capital nor a broad-based, liberal middle class; second, a weakly developed "bourgeois realism" in the arts at a time when this was the dominant artistic paradigm in other countries; and third, a consequent cult of the lonely, underappreciated genius or at least cultural outsider who appeals to his refined bourgeois aesthetic sensibilities by producing works of art that strive for the Absolute, whether in absolute music or in philosophical abstractions.

As a result, one self-consciously lonely man followed the next in nineteenth-century Germany, without any sustained avant-garde movements such as those in France or England. In the discursive realm of philosophy, the series begins with Schopenhauer and ends with Friedrich Nietzsche, while in music it begins with Franz Schubert and ends with Anton Bruckner, Hugo Wolf, and Gustav Mahler. Even the most significant German composer of operas, Richard Wagner, remained, for the longest time, a lonely and unrecognized man who ecstatically allowed the writings of Schopenhauer to suffuse him, permitted Nietzsche to praise him, and, finally, withdrew to his lonely temple of music in the small town of Bayreuth rather than perform his operas in Berlin, Hamburg, or even Frankfurt. Even he was not a societally oriented composer in the tradition of Giuseppe Verdi in Italy or Georges Bizet in France; instead, he was proud of his lonely greatness, albeit no longer in the older sense to be found in Idealism or the older forms of Romanticism. Viewed from this perspective, Nietzsche puts it well in the musical aphorisms of his 1878 collection *Human, All Too Human,* when he writes that music is always "at home" with those peoples "who have no 'society' but who have all the more individuals with a tendency toward loneliness, toward semi-dark thoughts and the veneration of everything unspeakable." Such people he calls the "actual musical souls."[12]

Concepts of this sort hardly lost their currency among the educated bourgeois circles of the late Wilhelminian age and even of the Weimar Republic. Striking in this regard are the influential musical theories of Arnold Schönberg, Thomas Mann, and Theodor W. Adorno, all of whom remained attached to the concept of an intimate elective affinity between music and philosophy and starkly opposed the tendency toward vulgarization occurring within popular music, which, around 1925, was becoming an ever more salient element of the culture industry. In his 1918 *Reflections of a Nonpolitical Man,* Mann even presented this affinity as one of the core elements of Germanness. During these years only the philosopher Bloch, in part because of his more explicit affinity to self-avowedly left-wing concepts of culture, attempted to identify specific utopian potentials in forms of popular music, while Adorno and others regarded "popular music" as a delusional misnomer, because the music being served was not really popular—that is, originating with the people—at all but rather strategically manufactured by marketing experts and sales strategists in the boardrooms and publicity departments of an administered world.

Even the time of exile between 1933 and 1945 brought no end to the elective affinity between music and philosophy. Above all, Schönberg, Mann, and Adorno—whose shared fate during that time brought them to Los Angeles—remained convinced of the notion that German culture had produced its purest flowers in these two realms. Schönberg, for one, taught only German music during these years and even suggested that, in spite of his Zionist leanings, his invention of the twelve-tone technique would secure for German music once again the respect of the world for a century to come. At the same time, Mann composed his novel *Doctor Faustus* (1944–47), in which he transformed the old figure of Faust from a tirelessly searching scholar into a composer to exemplify the simultaneous greatness and danger of what it means to be German. And Adorno submitted American popular music forms such as jazz and the music of Hollywood films to critical scrutiny in order to juxtapose them with Beethoven, Mahler, Schönberg, and Berg, who, for him, comprised the only significant composers.

While these three representatives of German high-cultural traditions held fast to their views and continued to engage the traditions associated with the proper names Schopenhauer, Nietzsche, and Wagner during the years immediately following World War II, another group of philosophers and composers whose left-wing political convictions also had necessitated emigration from Germany to escape persecution by the National Socialists made a decisive break with certain older concepts of musico-philosophical loneliness and a belief in the absence of societal embeddedness. This group included, above all, Ernst Bloch, Georg Lukács, and Hanns Eisler, who, after the war, did not settle in neutral Switzerland like Mann or return to the American Occupied Zone of West Germany like Adorno but rather opted for socialist countries such as Hungary and East Germany. While they too endorsed the concept of an elective affinity between music and philosophy, they were reluctant to suffuse this concept with ideas derived from Schopenhauer and Nietzsche, preferring instead in their interpretation of music to subscribe to the dialectical movement of thought informing Hegel's philosophy of history and transformed by Marx from an Idealist commitment to a materialist one.

With these two groups the old idea that music and philosophy are interconnected in such a way that music bestows an aesthetic core to philosophy while philosophy bestows greater speculative depth to music, had, for the time being, seemingly come to an end. So much so, in fact, that a certain "thinking with one's ears" appears to have outlived itself in the context of most current musical production (from techno to country, from Christian rock to death metal, from turntableism to karaoke), which is largely manufactured by corporate boards for the culture industry's consumers. In an age in which even marginality and otherness are readily cooptable as market commodities, it remains to be seen whether any compositional innovations in popular music will sponsor a transformative politics of the kind that Jacques Attali, in his 1977 meditation *Noise: The Political Economy of Music,* could still imagine, since the current paradigm of musical cooptation has less to do with what Adorno once described as the experience that the listening subject has when new music grows old and more to do with a brand of commodity fetishism that now seems to have come into its own, even and especially in the sphere of the acoustic.[13] And yet the very notion that certain artistic forms have come to an end is itself an integral and recurring element of philosophical aesthetics at least since Hegel.[14] To speak, therefore, of the elective affinity of music and philosophy as having come to an end is also to inscribe oneself in a discourse that at its core perpetuates what on the surface it claims to have erased.

German Music and Philosophy: Constellations and Case Studies

The rich conceptual and experiential links between music and philosophy—the echoes of what Adorno called *Klangfiguren,* or "sound figures"—resonate in a field of relations characterized by perpetual attraction and repulsion, presence and displacement, manifestation and deferral, identification and differentiation. This force field of relations becomes particularly significant in an aesthetic and philosophical modernity that ranges, roughly, from early German Idealism to the Critical Theory of the Frankfurt School. It is as though we, as sensitive readers of the relations between music and philosophy, were being asked to proceed like the critic in Benjamin's seminal 1924 essay on Goethe's *Elective Affinities* who "inquires into the truth, whose living flame continues to burn over the heavy logs of what has been and the light ashes of what has been experienced."[15]

As the flames of our search for truth burn over them, the ashes and heavy logs of the complex and often neglected relationship between music and philosophy can be seen as belonging to the realm of the un-dead. The contributors to this volume, each following Benjamin's critic in his or her own way, engage abiding concerns regarding the relation between the realms of aesthetic and intellectual experience. Tracing the political, historical, and philosophical trajectories of a long tradition in which German thinkers of modernity, to an extent unparalleled by any other national tradition, have taken recourse to music both as an aesthetic practice and as the object of their speculative work, the authors of the present volume reexamine the relation between German music and philosophy in such a way as to produce new insights into some of the most pressing issues in critical inquiry and cultural studies today. Focusing on the work of thinkers such as Schelling, Schopenhauer, Nietzsche, Bloch, Mann, Adorno, and Lukács in relation to individual composers such as Beethoven, Wagner, Schönberg, and Eisler as well as in relation to the problem of music as a discourse of representation, the essays seek to articulate how each field is altered, both culturally and conceptually, when one domain attempts to express itself in the terms defined by the other.

Lydia Goehr's far-reaching contribution fittingly explores the *Doppelbewegung,* or "double movement," that mediates between the spheres of music and philosophy. Taking as her point of departure the notion of elective affinity in relation to the figure of movement as it is portrayed in Goethe's novel *Elective Affinities,* she traces two specific trajectories through the German tradition of music and philosophy. Analyzing Adorno's suggestive mobilization of terms such as "affinity," "convergence," "mediation," and "unfolding"—all of which can be subsumed under the concept of *Bewegung,* or "movement"—Goehr argues that a thinking of *Bewegung* allows us to conceptualize the relation between music and philosophy in a more dialectically charged manner than conventional preoccupation with stable notions of time and temporality permit. She shows how Adorno's insistence on the fluid and elusive gestures of *Bewegung* enables him to transform certain elements of a classical German Idealist dialectic into a negative dialectic. Goehr then proceeds to observe the fluid and dynamic relation between music and philosophy—that is, a relation of non-identity that remains an affinity, even an affinity mediated by non-identity—through the prism of Adorno's concept of *Bewegung*, situating these concerns within the context of a philosophical history of musical aesthetics that includes the contested terrain staked out by such seminal figures as Hegel, Schopenhauer, and Hanslick.

Next, David Farrell Krell turns our attention to Schelling's overdetermined engagement with the origins of music and tragedy. Following closely the rhetorical maneuvers of such texts as *The Ages of the World*, published in 1811, he articulates the ways in which Schelling—in contrast to the later Nietzschean preoccupation with the notion of music giving birth to Greek tragedy—views ancient Greek cults as giving rise to music. Connecting Schelling's early *Philosophy of Art* and his late *Philosophy of Mythology*, Krell analyzes in unexpected ways the seminal role that the concepts of *Klang und Ton* play in a mythologically imbricated philosophical engagement with the sphere of musicality.

Goehr's analysis of Adorno's *Bewegung* and Krell's analysis of a mythologically inflected *Klang und Ton* both reverberate in Ludger Lütkehaus's reading of Schopenhauer's philosophy of music. Schopenhauer, he argues, valorizes music both in terms of an ontological specificity in which music is accorded the most esteemed position in a hierarchy of the arts and as an aesthetic form that has liberated itself from the reproductive iterations of conventional forms of mimesis. Attending to such texts as "Platonic Idea: The Object of Art" and "On the Metaphysics of Music" in *The World as Will and Representation*, Lütkehaus makes the case by situating Schopenhauer's metaphysics of music within the philosophical framework of his refractory metaphysics of the Will. For him, Schopenhauer's philosophy of music, which continues and radicalizes his metaphysics of the Will, is directed toward an emancipation and mobilization of dissonance, even as that same philosophy threatens to be undermined by an enharmonic confusion that falsely asserts the Will's reconciliation when it is in need of redemption instead.

Samuel Weber's incisive reading of Wagner's *Ring* tetralogy investigates the highly charged relationship between the work and the tradition of modernity out of which it arises. Turning to Benjamin's reflections on

Western modernity, the chapter meditates on Wagner's challenges to, and reconceptualizations of, the dreams of self-identity and individual self-presence that inform the tradition of the autonomous subject. According to Weber's excavation of the logic of ambivalence in Wagner's aesthetics of theatrical performance, the *Ring* exposes a certain dismantling of the Western metaphysical subject, a musical deconstruction that remains conscious of the impossibility of ever fully disowning the aesthetic conditions and epistemological commitments of its own narcissism.

Margaret Moore and Rebekah Pryor Paré argue that Nietzsche's philosophy of music provides fertile ground for a rereading of the particular relationship he posits between ethics and aesthetics. When reconstructing Nietzsche's critical engagement with the Christian and, for him, decadent legacy of Wagner's *Parsifal* in the context of Nietzsche's philosophical comments on music in *The Case of Wagner* and in *Ecce Homo*, the vexed and unexpected relationship that Nietzsche traces between moral concerns and the aesthetic specificity of music is illuminated in a new way.

In his essay on the first great twentieth-century philosopher of music, Gerhard Richter investigates the ways in which Bloch's insistence on reading the world as a text whose "singular and abiding question [concerns] its meaning to be excavated" radicalizes and fulfills itself in his articulation of the complex role of music in the process of making sense and interpreting meaning. Richter argues that Bloch's philosophy of music gestures toward the future possibility of a certain non-naive hopefulness inscribed in the Blochian "not-yet." He shows how the extensive section titled "Philosophy of Music" in Bloch's 1918 *Spirit of Utopia*, when situated within the context of the literary thought-images from his 1930 *Spuren* (Traces) and the larger network of his theoretical writings, reveals the unexpected logic by which two interconnected models of hopefulness—the music of dreams and the dream of music—propel Bloch's aesthetic and ethico-political commitments.

In their respective contributions, Beatrice Hanssen and Hans Rudolf Vaget each turn to seminal figures in Adorno's aesthetic orbit: Schönberg and Mann. Investigating a seemingly dissonant chord in Adorno's thought—a thought that, on the one hand, transforms the Hegelian system into a radical, materialist form of negative dialectics and, on the other hand, remains invested in the quasi-theological category of the Absolute—Hanssen subtly interprets Adorno's philosophy of music, which often focuses on the Second Viennese School, as departing from the traditional metaphysics found in classical music while, at the same time, remaining entangled in the metaphysical presuppositions it wishes to undo. Beyond merely developing a philosophy of music, Hanssen argues, Adorno's work stages the unfolding of the non-conceptual philosophy that is at the core of music. While Adorno focuses his negatively dialectical movements of musical thought on the work of Schönberg, especially the latter's *Moses und Aron*, his work holds out the promise of turning nothingness itself into a constitutive category, thereby tacitly generating an identity-based model of redemption that would be at odds with the undoing of music's metaphysical commitments. In a gesture that has been constitutive of much aesthetic thought since Hegel, Hanssen also considers the extent to which Adorno's dialectical mobilization of Schönberg's music echoes yet another end of art.

Elements of this analysis are corroborated by Vaget's intricate reconstruction of the uneasy relationship between Adorno and Mann with respect to musical theory. Although Adorno was Mann's chief musical adviser while the latter wrote the novel *Doctor Faustus* during his exile in California, Vaget posits that Mann maintained an attitude of friendly reservation toward his conceptual counselor, not least because the critical theory that Adorno was developing did not always, in Mann's estimation, take self-reflexive account of the ways in which the alleged philosophical and cultural supremacy of German music could be coopted for arguments that deduced a possible justification for German claims of historical leadership and political might. After all, it was the very connection between certain empirico-political mobilizations and supreme aesthetic production that *Doctor Faustus* had set out to dislodge.

Albrecht Betz and Jost Hermand, in the closing essays, also address such political dimensions of the elective affinities between music and philosophy. Betz's reconsideration of Hanns Eisler's engagement with Hegel's philosophy of music sheds new light on Eisler's compositional practice. Never having developed any philosophical system of music himself, Eisler nevertheless suffused his work with philosophical observations regarding the contemporary situation of music vis-à-vis the structures of its historical unfolding. Betz shows how for Eisler, in the final analysis, music could not be separated from the rational structures of thought that speak to the condition of exile, the abuses of the culture industry, and after 1945, the challenges of mediating between transgressive compositional practices and the cultural demands of an emerging East German state.

Hermand revisits questions of the mimetically concrete in musical aesthetics by turning to the often-neglected philosophy of music in Georg Lukács's aesthetics. Submitting to renewed scrutiny the chapter on music in Lukács's *Die Eigenart des Ästhetischen* (The Specificity of the Aesthetic), Hermand accounts for the ways in which Lukács, whose affiliation with realist and materialist modes of aesthetic presentation might appear to foreclose any serious engagement with the elusive sphere of instrumental music, develops a differently charged program of music's progressive potential. To this end, Lukács constructs a model of aesthetic concreteness that hopes to locate in music a socially and historically traversed aesthetic form hinging on a thinking of *"gedoppelte Mimesis."* This "double mimesis," or mimesis of mimesis, enables Lukács to understand music not as re-presenting objects and ideas that allegedly preexist in empirical reality but rather as presenting, in an indirect manner, the very idea and movements of a mimetic representation that nevertheless remain forever inaccessible to music. As a double mimesis, Lukács's project recoups from within the movements of instrumental music and the engagement with historical and ethico-political imperatives, which for most formalist critics simply were not to be found outside of a text. As Hermand argues, Lukács wishes to understand instrumental music not merely as resounding air, a pleasurable diversion, or a dazzling chess game with sounds but rather as an aesthetically specific form separate from other artistic practices such as literature and painting, the Hegelian and post-Hegelian condensation of a certain historical situatedness. Here, for all their differences, Lukács shares with Adorno the view that music and the listening subject can *never not* be in a situation, a situation that in principle can be described and analyzed—even to such an extent that the fantasies, preoccupations, and aberrations of an entire age promise to become audible in it.

Collectively, then, the essays in this volume show how the transparency of aesthetic artifacts and the putative straightforwardness of the discourses they sponsor can no longer be taken for granted. Through their engagement with the elective affinities between music and philosophy, the intersection of aesthetically arranged sounds with the stringent requirements of conceptual thought emerges as a privileged site, even as a critical model, for any such intervention.

NOTES

1. Walter Benjamin, "Die Aufgabe des Übersetzers," *Gesammelte Schriften,* vol. 4 (Frankfurt am Main: Suhrkamp, 1991), 9–21, here 9. Unless otherwise indicated, translations are the authors'.

2. Theodor W. Adorno, *Ästhetische Theorie,* vol. 7 of *Gesammelte Schriften* (Frankfurt am Main: Suhrkamp, 1997), 27.

3. Adorno, *Ästhetische Theorie,* 113.

4. Some of the ways in which this difficulty has successfully prevented an integrated theory of musical practice and philosophy from being developed are analyzed by Lydia Goehr, *The Imaginary Museum of Musical Works: An Essay in the Philosophy of Music* (Oxford: Oxford University Press, 1994).

5. Theodor W. Adorno, "Fragment über Musik und Sprache," in *Musikalische Schriften I–III,* vol. 16 of *Gesammelte Schriften* (Frankfurt am Main: Suhrkamp, 1997), 251–56, here 251.

6. Theodor W. Adorno, *Negative Dialektik,* vol. 6 of *Gesammelte Schriften* (Frankfurt am Main: Suhrkamp, 1997), 44.

7. For genealogical treatments of musical aesthetics, see Jost Hermand, *Konkretes Hören: Zum Inhalt der Instrumentalmusik* (Berlin: Argument, 1981); Edward Lippman, *A History of Western Musical Aesthetics* (Lincoln: University of Nebraska Press, 1992); Enrico Fubini, *Geschichte der Musikästhetik: Von der Antike bis zur Gegenwart* (Stuttgart: Metzler, 1997); and Christoph Asmuth, Gunter Scholz, and Franz-Bernhard Stammkötter, eds., *Philosophischer Gedanke und musikalischer Klang: Zum Wechselverhältnis von Musik und Philosophie* (Frankfurt am Main: Campus, 1999).

8. A sustained discussion of Romantic musical aesthetics is offered by Carl Dahlhaus, *Klassische und romantische Musikästhetik* (Laaber: Laaber Verlag, 1988).

9. Georg Wilhelm Friedrich Hegel, *Vorlesungen über Ästhetik III,* vol. 15 of *Werke* (Frankfurt am Main: Suhrkamp, 1986), 155.

10. For nuanced discussions of Hegel's analysis of music as part of his dialectical system, compare further Heinz Heimsoeth, "Hegels Philosophie der Musik," *Hegel-Studien* 2 (1963): 161–201, and more recently, Herbert Schnädelbach, "Hegel," in *Musik in der deutschen Philosophie: Eine Einführung,* ed. Stefan Lorenz Sorgner and Oliver Fürbeth (Stuttgart: Metzler, 2003), 55–75.

11. An attempt to trace the elusive relationship between music and changing notions of German identity is made in the collection *Music and German National Identity,* ed. Celia Applegate and Pamela Potter (Chicago: University of Chicago Press, 2002). For a recent analysis of the question of the "subject" as it relates to nineteenth-century German music, see Michael P. Steinberg, *Listening to Reason: Culture, Subjectivity, and Nineteenth-Century Music* (Princeton, N.J.: Princeton University Press, 2004).

12. Friedrich Nietzsche, *Menschliches, Allzumenschliches II*, vol. 2 of *Kritische Studienausgabe*, ed. Giorgio Colli and Mazzino Montinari (Munich: Deutscher Taschenbuchverlag; Berlin: de Gruyter, 1999), 621.

13. Jacques Attali, *Noise: The Political Economy of Music,* trans. Brian Massumi (Minneapolis: University of Minnesota Press, 1985), originally published in French in 1977. More recent treatments of the relationship between music and cultural politics are gathered in *The Cultural Study of Music: A Critical Introduction,* ed. Martin Clayton, Trevor Herbert, and Richard Middleton (New York: Routledge, 2003).

14. For recent studies concerning the discourse of the end of art since Hegel, see Alexander García Düttmann, *Kunstende: Drei ästhetische Studien* (Frankfurt am Main: Suhrkamp, 2000); and Eva Geulen, *Das Ende der Kunst: Lesarten eines Gerüchts nach Hegel* (Frankfurt am Main: Suhrkamp, 2002). For a meditation on discourses of the end more generally, compare further Jean Baudrillard, *The Illusion of the End,* trans. Chris Turner (Stanford, Calif.: Stanford University Press, 1994).

15. Walter Benjamin, "Goethes Wahlverwandtschaften," in *Gesammelte Schriften,* vol. 1 (Frankfurt am Main: Suhrkamp, 1991), 123–201, here 126.

Doppelbewegung

The Musical Movement of Philosophy and the Philosophical Movement of Music

LYDIA GOEHR

Was bedeutet die Bewegung?

Goethe/Marianne von Willemer, *Suleika*

When Charlotte asks Eduard on one of those evenings at home to explain to her what is meant by the word "affinity"—*die Verwandtschaft*—she clearly irritates him by interrupting his performance. Eduard has long enjoyed reading aloud in company, even if it is, as it has been of late, one of those more technical books of science. In his deep, melodious voice, he likes to unfold the thought in his own time, pausing and pacing, surprising and consoling, where he sees fit. He doesn't want his company to know what will happen next and certainly not the ending before he's reached it. He most dislikes it, therefore, when someone looks over his shoulder, as Charlotte is now doing, to read alongside him. "If I read to someone, isn't it just as if I were explaining something orally?" he rebukes his wife. "The written or printed word takes the place of my own feeling, my own heart; and do you think I'd bother to talk if a small window were placed on my forehead, or on my breast, so that the person to whom I wished to tell my thoughts or feelings one by one would already know in advance what I was aiming at? When someone reads over my shoulder, I always feel as if I were being torn in two parts."[1]

Eduard is willing to explain the term anyway, this metaphor as he calls it, which so confuses Charlotte. With the help of the captain, he describes the natural affinity with which different elements are drawn or adhere to but also repel or react to one another, as if each were choosing its own particular arrangement: *Wahlverwandtschaft*. Eduard speaks of chemistry and physics; the captain, too, of how affinity or cohesiveness can be seen in liquids with their tendency to form into round shapes— falling water drops or little balls of quicksilver or molten lead. At the same time, they all hear a description of human relations. They know they are playing with analogies; they each see the double meaning of the term. Elements and persons: each compelled to spring into activity to form novel and unexpected constellations, a lively movement that disturbs each along the way but will eventually reach a final resting place. Here is a principle whose movement cannot be predicted in advance.

Charlotte wants to believe she knows how things will turn out: she doesn't always need to look over Eduard's shoulder. But how can she really know what is meant when she finds herself much more than a mere observer of the story? No real understanding is acquired independently of the experience; everyone participates, the captain explains, and experience takes time to unfold. What unrest will Charlotte then feel when she finds herself drawn, as she quickly is, to the captain, or when, days later, she notices that Eduard has taken up reading love poems again and is allowing the beautiful Ottilie to read alongside him? He even pauses longer than needed to avoid having to turn the page before Ottilie is ready. Ottilie prefers to read herself rather than trust the word of another, and yet though this obviously interrupts Eduard's reading, he no longer objects. With Ottilie he doesn't feel torn; after all, sometimes *Verwandtschaft* means a "meeting of minds." And so, too, is this seen when Eduard and Ottilie play music together. When Charlotte plays with Eduard she always has to adjust her tempi to keep up with him. With Ottilie the situation is different: she somehow learns the piece exactly to mirror his mistakes. This is a stronger affinity perhaps, an exceedingly pleasant experience, yet out of their union materializes a new piece—entirely with the wrong tempo.

The Aim

Goethe's novel—from which I drew my own telling of the story— enfolds a description of its central principle—*Wahlverwandtschaft*—into a performance of Eduard's reading aloud. It shows the movement inherent in the principle as well as the movement of its coming to be understood. This is not surprising: the novel, it has often been remarked, has the style of a recitation or "unfolds inside the categories of the 'storyteller.'"[2] As in Goethe's novel, my essay is also about a *Doppelbewegung*, about two sorts of movement brought into special affinity. Inspired by Goethe but focusing on the work of Theodor W. Adorno, this essay tracks the particular affinity between philosophy and music in the German tradition.

When writing about philosophy and music, Adorno uses the terms "affinity" *(Verwandtschaft and Affinität)*, "convergence," "mediation," and "unfolding." He prefers these terms to the more traditional terms "analogy" and "metaphor." He refers often to Goethe's novel. Arguing for a dynamic language of *becoming* to replace the static language of *Being*, he speaks both of philosophy and of music as dynamic *modes of conduct*. He works out his preferred schema through the general notion of movement—*Bewegung*. (Henceforth, I shall mostly use the German term to show its prevalent use.) Adorno believes that this notion can do more work, and more important *dialectical* work, than the more commonly used notions of time and temporality.[3] When late in his life he argues in Darmstadt with composers (Stockhausen, Boulez, and Cage) about the concept of time, he assumes for his own argument the broader vantage point of *Bewegung*.

Adorno employs the notion of *Bewegung* throughout his musical and philosophical writings to show the difference between the earlier German Idealist dialectic and his own preferred negative version. He uses it to work out an affinity between Hegel and Beethoven as well as to develop themes of lateness and aging. He uses it to explain why, as he often says, dissonance is the truth about harmony, disorder the truth about order, and, one may add, movement the truth about rest. He uses *Bewegung* further to describe the form and expression of both music and philosophy. He takes the idea of unfolding a thought in philosophy as seriously as the idea of unfolding a theme in a musical composition. The idea that one should read dialectical philosophy as if it were written with expressive markings is no mere rhetoric; nor is it a way to render philosophy (merely) an art. On the contrary, Adorno uses *Bewegung* to keep philosophy and music in a mutually productive relation, but in anything but a *static* relation of *identity*.

Although this essay describes Adorno's use of *Bewegung*, its attention does not remain solely there. From the outset, it recounts a story in the

more general history of musical aesthetics. By moving backward through
the figures of Hanslick, Schopenhauer, and Hegel, this story situates
Adorno's use of the concept in a broader historical set of debates.

The Term

The term *Bewegung* has an extensive application going back to the
pre-Socratic philosophers. In music it is used to refer to the motion and
tempi of sounding events through time and space, for example, to the
horizontal and vertical structures provided by rhythm and counterpoint. It is connected with clocks and timing, pendulums and metro-
nomes. "Ziehet, ziehet, hebt! / sie bewegt sich, schwebt!" (Pull, pull, lift!
It's moving, floating) writes Schiller in *Das Lied von der Glocke* (1797). Normally when we speak of *Bewegung,* we assume that something moves or
that something is being moved. Yet in music we speak of the forms as
being *in* movement or as being *of* pure temporal movement, because, although tones endure through time, no tone moves literally across space.

From a different perspective, the term *Bewegung* conveys the idea of
music as embodied dance: movement as "metakinetic." When Adorno
once described a Beethoven symphony as embodied, it is evident that
he was thinking less about the ontological embodiment of an artwork in
a physical object than about the musical work as a living body in performance. "The relationship of the symphony to dance may be defined
as follows: if dance appeals to the bodily movements of human beings,
then the symphony is the [kind of] music that itself becomes a body. . . .
The symphony moves, stirs 'itself'; stands still, moves on, and the totality of its gestures is the intentionless representation of the body. . . . This
corporeal nature of the symphony is its social essence: it is the giant
body, the collective body of society in the dialectic of its moments."[4]
What a moving body admits, as a symphony admits, is a broad commitment to development and change. In contemporary theory, *Bewegung*
appears most often in relation to sport and dance. However, when used
in music it underscores also the ontological and social necessity for a
work to be performed and heard: a work considered in the process of its
own (dialectical) unfolding.

Although he is not the first, Adorno uses the term *bewegt* at least twice
to name movements of his own compositions.[5] The term is not redun-
dant. (After all, all music moves; how can it not move?) Of course, the

term conveys the particular sense of energy and speed with which his movements are to be played. In this context too it is worth noting that whereas in English, French, and Italian, the terms "movement," *mouvement,* and *movimento* refer to the distinct parts of a musical work—a symphony in four movements—the German term for the same is *Satz.* This term stems from *Gesetz* (law, principle, rule) and even more from *setzen* (putting, setting, i.e., composing), but where the division of a work into discrete *Sätze* (movements) follows a modern analogy between music and language whereby, according to Heinrich Christoph Koch's *Musikalisches Lexikon* of 1802, the term "designates each individual part of a musical work that has for and in itself a complete meaning."[6] What remains in German, as in the other languages, however, is the use of "movement" terms—also called tempi and character terms, such as "largo," "allegro," "presto"—to mark the different sorts of *Sätze.*

Bewegung is used further to refer to the *modification,* following Rousseau, of our passions or emotions: our agitations, excitements, and stirrings.[7] In music, as in the other arts, it shows particular ranges of human gestures and expressions. In addition to Lessing's path-breaking discussion of expressive movement in his *Laokoon* (1766), a documented English use from the 1770s notes the "rise and fall, the advance and recess . . . in the different parts of a building, so as to add greatly to the picturesque of a composition."[8] In this use, as in *Laokoon, Bewegung* occurs within a particular art as well as between the arts, as demonstrated through the significant metaphorical exchange of their respective terms.[9]

Bewegung is further employed to capture the movement of thought—of thinking in process *(Gedankenbewegung).* In ancient philosophical texts, one may follow the movement and mediation of thoughts or propositions through syllogistic logic and dialectical reasoning. This usage is not so far removed from other ancient and also modern usages, where we read of the linear or cyclical patterns or vibrations of the celestial and earthly bodies. Kant thus speaks of the Copernican Revolution in terms of *Himmelsbewegung* (the movement of the heavens) in the context of reconfiguring his own metaphysical system. Merleau-Ponty's phenomenological existentialism depends significantly upon his view of intentionality explored through the terms of the *mouvement* of both body and thought: intentionality as embodied thinking in movement.

Across the board, *Bewegung* captures the dynamics of history as well as evolutionary passages of nature. We speak also of moves in a chess game, of the movement in the stock market, of moving staircases, moving pavements, and, of course, of moving pictures—about which the most perfect comment is made in Tennessee Williams' *The Glass Menagerie* in a conversation between Jim and Tom.

JIM: What are you gassing about?
TOM: I'm tired of the movies.
JIM: Movies!
TOM: Yes, movies! Look at them—. . . All of those glamorous people—
    having adventures—hogging it all, gobbling the whole thing up!
    You know what happens? People go to the movies instead of moving.
    Hollywood characters are supposed to have all the adventures for
    everybody in America, while everybody in America sits in a dark room
    and watches them have them! Yes, until there's a war. That's when
    adventure becomes available to the masses! Everyone's dish, not only
    Gable's! Then the people in the dark room come out of the dark room
    to have some adventures themselves—goody, goody! It's our turn now,
    to go to the South Sea Island—to make a safari—to be exotic, far-off!
    But I'm not patient. I don't want to wait till then. I'm tired of the movies
    and I am about to move![10]

Finally, there is a political meaning, originating in the early 1800s, used to refer to the German movement, to the Catholic movement, and, later, as recorded in 1885, to student movements, about which it was once claimed that whereas Oxford is the home of movements, Cambridge is the home of men.[11] Since then, there has been the historical or authentic performance movement, the phenomenological movement, the fascist and workers movements, the feminist movement, and the student movements of the sixties. Of course, not everything that claims to move actually does move or moves in the right way. Hence Adorno always points to the tendency in a movement that promotes a new style, a new performance practice, or a new politics to fall or degenerate into ideological or collective stasis.

In philosophy, politics, and the arts, the concept of *Bewegung* makes little sense unless it is used in relation to positive and negative notions of resting, waiting, ending, suspending, pausing, and stopping. These notions are connected to others: establishing, congealing, sterilizing, stabilizing, and solidifying. Adorno employs all these terms to describe what he takes to be the rigidifying and reifying tendencies of ontology or metaphysics (in his critique of Heidegger), or of music (in his critique of serialism and *Neue Sachlichkeit*), and of politics (in his critique of totalitarianism).

The Concept

"Up to now, in the investigations of music's essence and effect, the concept of *movement* has been noticeably neglected; yet it seems to me that it is the most important and fruitful." So wrote the Viennese music critic and thinker Eduard Hanslick in 1854 in his canonic text *Vom musikalisch-Schönen*.[12] However, though he could not have made the point more explicit, the concept continues in large measure to be neglected. Hanslick is partially to blame: he embeds his favored concept in an account that overly obscures it.

In his recent *Aesthetics of Music*, the British philosopher of music Roger Scruton notices the neglect of the concept and partially blames Hanslick too. The shared observation leads Scruton in a direction different from my own and different from Adorno's. As Scruton correctly sees, Hanslick unfolds his concept of *Bewegung* within an overly anxious account of metaphor. Scruton largely dispenses with that anxiety. "In hearing sounds," he writes in summary of his own account of moving metaphor,

> we may attend to them in the way we attend to pictures, on the lookout, or listen-out, for imaginative perceptions. There then arises the peculiar double intentionality that is exemplified in the experience of metaphor: one and the same experience takes sound as its object, and also something that is not and cannot be sound—the life and movement that is music. We hear this life and movement in the sound, and situate it in an imagined space, organized, as in the phenomenal space of our own experience, in terms of "up" and "down," "rising" and "falling," "high and low." . . . Music is the intentional object of an experience that only rational beings can have, and only through the exercise of imagination. To describe it we must have recourse to metaphor, not because music resides in an analogy with other things, but because the metaphor described exactly what we hear, when we hear sounds as music.[13]

In the text omitted from the quoted passage (indicated by the ellipsis), Scruton suggests that it would not be wise to move too quickly toward phenomenological accounts, as suggested by Sartre and Merleau-Ponty, or into Schopenhauer's metaphysics to explain the movement inside music, simply because the foundations of these theories are too "dubious." Other contemporary philosophers of music have been similarly skeptical and have confined their accounts as best they could to accounts of metaphor.[14] Adorno too is skeptical of these metaphysical views but worries, first, that by retreating too far from them, one might lose something from the concept of *Bewegung* one actually needs and, second, that by tying the concept too closely to an account of metaphor, one might obscure its independent import.

From a broader perspective, Scruton employs the concept of *Bewegung* to develop a firmly principled, securely grounded, and normatively significant metaphysics in support of the harmonious development of music and the human soul. Within this project, he attributes the interruptions to, and unrest in, the development to the ruin and relativism of culture. Here Scruton and Adorno find common ground: Adorno also sees culture's ruin (and ruins) in terms of the interruptions and unrest in the history of harmony. However, rather than using the concept of *Bewegung* to place philosophy and music safely on the side of the harmonious soul, he uses it to expose the dialectical movement of history. He writes: "Every self-righteous appeal to humanity in the midst of inhuman conditions should be viewed with the greatest suspicion. There are no words for the noble, the good, the true and the beautiful that have not been violated and turned into their opposite—just as the Nazis could enthuse about the house, its roof resting on pillars, while torture went on in the cellars."[15] In strong contrast to the approach adopted by Scruton, Adorno finds no philosophical safety in using harmony to sustain in the modern world what he believes have become false or deceptive political conceptions of the good. Adorno always uses *Bewegung* as a dialectical or doubling concept in the service of philosophical and political critique. Hence the title of this essay: *Doppelbewegung.*

Hanslick

Hanslick articulates the objective conditions for a musical aesthetics to meet the standards of natural science. He names chemistry, mathematics, and physiology in particular. His aim is more Goethean than positivistic: "Ariel bewegt den Sang / In himmlisch reinen Tönen"—which means that though Hanslick sees in music what he sees in chemistry, namely, "natural connections" and "elective affinities" between the elements, he also notices, following Goethe, that the affinities are "strange" and "mysterious."[16] "All musical elements stand to one another, according to the laws of nature, in secret connections and elective affinities."[17]

What Hanslick means by the mystery in music is fairly simple and oft repeated: music's affinities are to be understood in terms of the autonomous relations between musical elements. They follow artistic and aesthetic principles or laws appropriate to music as a fine or beautiful art. They are not reducible to the laws or principles of any other science or art. However, they are almost impossible to describe. Only in Ariel's song, in the pure listening experience of music itself, are we adequately provided the evidence of the mysterious movement we seek.

Hanslick separates music's beauty from a traditional, subjectivist feeling theory. Feelings aroused in listeners by music neither constitute nor account for music's beauty nor stand in any essential relation to its meaning. "The beauty of a musical piece is specifically musical, that is, inherent to the tonal relationships without reference to a foreign, extramusical arena of ideas."[18] He turns his attention to "the music itself." He finds, following Kant, a musical object of purely aesthetic contemplation and imagination and, following Hegel, the unfolding of a specifically or purely musical idea *(Gedanke)*. The musically beautiful lies in the notes in compositional arrangement, and in nothing else. Music's content—*Inhalt*—is just its "tönend bewegte Formen."[19]

What Hanslick writes before and after he enters this celebrated but untranslatable phrase into his account should lead his readers to think that he is deeply concerned with its middle term—the term *bewegte* used to suggest forms—in movement—through the medium of tones.[20] However, in the subsequent reception of his theory, the middle term is increasingly suppressed by the terms between which it is sandwiched. In the development of musical formalism, more attention has been given to the structured arrangements of sounds—the tonal forms—than to the *Bewegung*. Of course, no formalist ever denies that tonal forms "move," but they do restrict the meaning of "movement." Compelled by Hanslick's separation of musical forms from the subjective arousal of feeling and emotion, they think it correct to separate, within the concept of *Bewegung*, music's more intangible aesthetic potential from the objective fact that tonal forms move in time. The term *bewegt* is accordingly interpreted to capture just the "motion" generated by music's rhythm and temporal sequence. Formalist theories of rhythm and meter abound in the literature, and they are productive. Still, in my view, there has been a loss in the concept of *Bewegung*.[21]

Hanslick inadvertently encourages this loss. However, he is more reacting to traditional accounts of musical beauty than prescribing a

strict formalism for the future. When he divorces musical forms from
the subjective arousal and representation of emotions, be they emotions
conceived in general or particular ("joy" or "this particular feeling of
joy"), he does not intend thereby to separate the forms from their expressive or aesthetic potential. He intends only to assert a separation
where in previous theories he sees a collapse. Hanslick uses the term
Bewegung both because it is widely used in earlier, enlightenment theories of musical meaning and because it can capture the double truth that
music is a temporal art and an art par excellence of lived experience or
expression. Music moves and it moves us, but it does *not* move us by
arousing or representing everyday feelings.

Hanslick wants to account for music's ability to move us aesthetically
entirely in terms of music's ability to move itself, to move fast and to move
slow, he writes, to rise and swell in a thousand shades. He speaks of
music as an audible *kaleidoscope*, full of tension, dynamics, and contrasts.
Bewegung, so the argument goes, is the only element that the actual music
shares with our emotional states. However, that shouldn't encourage us
to seek in music a portrayal of those states. To develop a thought that
Goethe offers in his color theory, Hanslick argues that tonalities, chords,
and timbres each have their own moral or emotional characters or associations (ecstasy at A-flat major, melancholia with the key of B minor),
but this should not lead us to conclude that a work in which we find such
elements just then exemplifies, represents, or portrays this string of characters. On the contrary, in a given work, the isolated correspondences
or symbolisms are *suspended* in favor of the "law" or "movement" of the
work itself. A work follows or unfolds a purely musical logic, a logic of
form or arrangement that cannot, strictly speaking, be *translated* into any
other language—of emotion, character, or concept.[22]

Hanslick argues that in music's *Bewegung* alone lies music's beauty
and expression. "For its alleged purpose, music has no other means
other than via the analogy of movement and the symbolism of tones."[23]
Any other sort of appeal lies outside music's proper domain. And yet a
problem is lurking in the analogy of movement and symbolism of tones,
as Hanslick describes it in this next, most decisive passage:

> "It is extraordinarily difficult to describe this autonomous beauty of the
> art of tone—the specifically musical. That music has no prototype in
> nature and expresses no conceptual content means that it can be talked
> about only through dry technical determinations or in poetical fictions.
> Its realm is in fact 'not of this world.' All the fanciful descriptions,

characterizations, or paraphrases of a musical work are either figurative or erroneous. What in every other art is still description is in music already metaphor. Music wants finally to be grasped as music and understood only from the perspective of itself and enjoyed in and for itself."[24]

Obviously Hanslick cannot and does not want to dispense with metaphor even in a philosophical treatise. But he constantly worries that a necessary use of metaphorical language that remains tethered to music's movement will too often fall into poetical inexactness. Preventing this fall is the hardest task of all.

After Hanslick, it is the threat of *inexactness* that seems most to have encouraged the later, scientifically inclined formalists to confine their attention to the "drier" movements of musical form. All this accomplishes, as previously noted, is to narrow the concept of *Bewegung* to its most technical and least aesthetic use. When other theorists then judge these formalists to have become too restrictive, they take the obvious course, namely, to reintroduce the full aesthetic and metaphysical dimensions of *Bewegung* into the account. But, in doing so, they also make the theory of metaphor more central. As with Scruton, the two tasks are accordingly combined, with the consequence that the singular importance Hanslick assigns to the concept of *Bewegung* is overshadowed by the need to explain how music moves through metaphor.

The Transition

In this essay, I isolate the concept of *Bewegung* from the account of metaphor to retrieve the former's full potential. To that end, I return to the philosophical uses of this notion prior to Hanslick's. If Hanslick is reacting to the feeling theories predominant in enlightenment aesthetics, he is doing so by drawing also on the philosophers of Romanticism and Idealism who develop an aesthetics of absolute music. The terms of that development are well documented; less so, however, is the role given to *Bewegung* to connect absolute music to a metaphysics of the Absolute. In this context, and this is the crucial transition in my own argument, the concept of *Bewegung* plays as significant a role in shaping philosophy's conception of itself as it does in shaping an understanding of music.

In the following sections, I accordingly summarize the views of two key but contrary figures: Schopenhauer and Hegel. In the matter of *Bewegung*, Schopenhauer gives pride of place to music, Hegel to philosophy. Schopenhauer, like Hanslick, relies on a commitment to analogy and metaphor; Hegel does not. Schopenhauer has long been known as "the musician's philosopher"; Hegel has never been renowned for his philosophical interest in music.[25] Yet arguably, with the focus on *Bewegung*, Hegel's philosophy demonstrates the deeper affinity to music.

Schopenhauer

In Schopenhauer's account, music is a temporal and expressive art, an art of pure unfolding that, though expressive, nonetheless expresses no definite emotion or concept. It is expressive but not expressive of, and expressive in purely musical terms. Yet, contra Hanslick, what makes the expression purely musical depends less for its explanation on the *Bewegung* of the tonal forms per se and more on the *Bewegung* of the world Will. Drawing on a Pythagorean and Platonic employment (as well as on certain strains of Indian philosophy), Schopenhauer sees the world in terms of a Will in movement, a blind Will of active drives, urgings, and strivings. The world, he claims, is equally embodied music as embodied Will.[26]

Music stands to the Will not as a copy or representation but as its unmediated embodiment. It bypasses the world of individuated emotions and any mediating Platonic Ideas. It stands above and beyond all the other arts. If, then, we are tempted to say that music expresses the different emotions at all, we should say it expresses them at best "in themselves"—abstractly, universally, or essentially—as pure form without matter. But if, more exactly, we speak less about expressing emotions and more about music's movement, then all we need say is that, as pure temporal process—as pure *Bewegung*—music tracks the emotional course of the world, of our selves, only from the "innermost" perspective.

That music is so immediately related to Will leads Schopenhauer to articulate the deep Romantic paradox of describing music in a necessarily inadequate philosophical language. How can a language that is essentially conceptual, as philosophy must be, grasp music's inexpressible (nonconceptual) movement? This question concerns less the difficulties of translating one language into another than the notion that, with its inexpressible significance, its being the unmediated expression of Will, music has a purer metaphysical import than does even philosophy itself.

Whereas Leibniz maintains that music is "an unconscious exercise in arithmetic in which the mind does not know it is counting," Schopenhauer claims that "music is an unconscious exercise in metaphysics in which the mind does not know it is philosophizing."[27] What value can a metaphysics that proceeds unconsciously possibly have? The same epistemological value apparently as does a pure aesthetic experience, when, according to Schopenhauer, that experience makes us most aware of the Will's dynamic pull precisely by momentarily releasing us from that pull.

If music is embodied Will, then to provide a perfectly accurate and complete description of music is to provide a description also of Will. "[W]hoever has followed me this far," Schopenhauer thus writes, "will not find it so very paradoxical when I say that, supposing we succeeded in giving a perfectly accurate and complete explanation of music which goes into detail, and thus a detailed repetition in concepts of what it expresses, this would also be at once a sufficient repetition and explanation of the world in concepts, or one wholly corresponding thereto, and hence the true philosophy."[28] To the extent that Schopenhauer describes music in its concrete form, he does so through a relation of *repetition* and *parallelism*, to demonstrate how, in its full melodic, harmonic, and rhythmic complexity, music *matches* each and every movement of the Will. Hence: "[I]n the whole of the ripienos that produce the harmony, between the bass and the leading voice singing the melody, I see the whole gradation of the Ideas in which the Will objectifies itself."[29]

Yet Schopenhauer always reminds us that when we describe music from the perspective of the world as representation, we are employing only an indirect language of *analogy*. For music expresses not the represented phenomenon but only its inner nature seen from the perspective of Will. Whereas Schopenhauer employs the term "analogy," Hanslick uses "metaphor." Whereas Hanslick worries about fantastical falls into inexactness, Schopenhauer puts his hope in the possibilities of perfect analogy.

Indeed, with far less anxiety than Hanslick, Schopenhauer believes his metaphysical scheme will bring philosophy and music into a clear parallelism—through complete and accurate description—thereby overcoming the necessary fact of indirection. Is he right? Or to put the question more pressingly, does his own philosophy successfully repeat or parallel music's essential *Bewegung*? Thomas Mann, for one, seems to think it does when he describes Schopenhauer's metaphysical work as reading like the symphonic movement of a musical work: "I have often called his great work a symphony in four movements."[30] However, I think Mann's observation is too quick. Despite his profound interest in music, Schopenhauer's own philosophy remains quite static, in part because of his tendency to treat the Will more in the static Kantian terms of an unknowable *Ding-an-sich* than as a force essentially in movement. Only with the stress clearly given the latter would one judge his philosophy as being itself essentially in movement. To be sure, he uses the term *Bewegung* pervasively to highlight the dynamic tensions in all the arts, from architecture to music. He also describes human and animal bodies in their willed actions and physical movements as well as the moving constellations of heavenly and natural bodies. In other words, he draws on the long history of the concept's most common uses. But he still seems to absorb the concept of *Bewegung* into a metaphysics in which the Will's "thingness" is finally accorded more metaphysical significance than its "movement." If I exaggerate, I do so to introduce a single assertion, namely, that, despite the priority he gives to music, he does not seek to correlate—nearly as much as many of his contemporaries do—the movement of music and the movement of will into the conduct—*die Verhaltensweise*—of his own philosophy.

Hegel on Music

In this respect, Hegel differs from Schopenhauer. Hegel makes *Bewegung* a central concept *in* his philosophy *and* a self-conscious concept *of* philosophy's operation. Though Hegel does not use music's movement only as his model, he does take seriously the rhythm of his philosophy. Conceived partly in musical terms, dialectical rhythm stands at the core of his work, from its beginning to its end. What he sees in philosophy's movement he then sees in music's. Or when he chooses to speak about music in his lectures on the fine arts, he seeks exactly the type of *Bewegung* he has already identified for his dialectics as a whole.

Only once in his remarks on music (recorded by his student Hotho) does Hegel mention an affinity to his work on logic, which means to the dialectical *Bewegung* of the Concept *(Begriff)*. In other terms, he introduces into these remarks not only *der Begriff der Bewegung* (the concept of movement) but also *die Bewegung des Begriffs* (the movement of the concept). The doubling-up here is important: if one does not notice it, one tends to think that Hegel is only inheriting, which he largely is, all the

usual thoughts about the art of music as a pure language of subjectivity or human feeling. For Hegel music is such a language but its operation follows a decidedly dialectical logic: the necessary movement of
dissonance—contradiction, opposition, unrest—within an overall harmonic structure. In his lectures on fine arts, he explains that already in
his *Science of Logic,* he developed

> the concept as subjectivity, but where this subjectivity, as an ideal trans-
> parent unity, is lifted into its opposite, i.e., into objectivity; indeed, as
> purely ideal, it is itself only one-sided and particular, and retains
> contrasted with itself something different and opposed to it, namely
> objectivity; but it is only genuine subjectivity if it enters this opposition
> and then overcomes and dissolves it. In the actual world too there are
> higher natures who are given power to endure the grief of inner opposi-
> tion and conquer it. If now, as a form of art, music is to express both the
> inner meaning and the subjective feeling of the deepest things, e.g. of
> religion and in particular the Christian Religion in which the abysses of
> grief form a principal part, then it must possess in the sphere of its notes
> the means capable of representing the battle of opposites. These means
> it gains in the so-called dissonant chords of the seventh and ninth.[31]

However, in *Science of Logic* itself, he develops more than a concept of
subjectivity; he also explains something of what he means by movement
in music, when, in a passage on the concept of "elective affinities" he
sees the correlation, as Hanslick sees it, between series or rows of music
and chemical elements. This is a remarkable passage and not well
known, so I quote it at length:

> The expression *elective* affinity used here [as well as] the terms *neutrality*
> and *affinity* . . . refer to the *chemical* relationship. For a chemical sub-
> stance has its specific determinateness essentially in its relation to its
> other and exists only as this difference from it. Furthermore, this spe-
> cific relation is bound up with quantity and is at the same time the re-
> lation, not only to a single other but to a series of specifically different
> others opposed to it. The combinations with this series are based on a
> so-called affinity with *every* member of the series. . . . It is, however, not
> only in the sphere of chemistry that the specific relation is represented
> in a circle of combinations; the individual note, too, only has meaning
> in relationship and combination with another note and with a series of
> others. The harmony or disharmony in such a circle of combinations
> constitutes its qualitative nature which is at the same time based on
> quantitative ratios; these form a series of exponents and are the ratios of

the two specific ratios which each of the combined notes is in its own self. The individual note is the key of a system, but again it is equally an individual member in the system of every other key. The harmonies are exclusive elective affinities whose characteristic quality is equally dissolved again in the externality of a merely quantitative progression. What . . . constitutes the principle of a measure for those affinities . . . (whether chemical or musical . . .) are [therefore] elective affinities between and in opposition to the others.[32]

In Hegel's view, the purely instrumental stratum of music is a purely temporal language of "subjective inwardness." It is also a language of *double negation*. It cancels out, first, its spatial situation, its stability in persistent material and, second, its own sounding-out in time. The first negation allows this sounding stratus to exist as pure movement, as pure sensuous vibration. It moves through itself or through its material in transitional patterns of tension, discord, resolution, and rest. The second negation cancels out its own assertion of becoming. The sound vanishes or annihilates its objective existence in the moment it asserts it: a tone is heard and then it is gone.[33]

With its double negation, music as a sounding art is the mode of expression most adequate to the inner life, the self, experienced *in* its own pure movement *as* pure movement. In this sense, music is pure self-expression, expressive of itself alone and, by mediation, expressive of the self. Within Hegel's overall dialectical history of the arts, it has the status of a Romantic art in second place following poetry. (Between purely instrumental music and poetry lies Hegel's beloved space for opera.) In its particular movement, music not only matches, through a "sympathetic harmony," the dialectical movement of the conscious self, but it does so to make explicit to the self its own movement. Moving through feeling, music's sounding stratum negates its mediation of the objective world to allow the self to experience itself (as pure negativity) in "its own formal freedom." The sympathy between music and self is premised here on a relation not of "analogy" or "repetition" but of *mediation*. Music's patterns mediate the self's formal freedom. Through the unfolding of these patterns, the freedom or inner life of the self is made intelligible to the self. Although participating in the unfolding of music's movement is only one way the self comes to know itself, it is indispensable to the self's coming to know itself in a particular way.

For Hegel, music and the self both dialectically engage the flow of time. The self first moves to time's flow by constantly interrupting that flow. It constitutes itself in time but becomes conscious of itself just at the moment of reflective withdrawal. The self exists neither as "an indeterminate continuity" nor in "unpunctuated duration." Rather it becomes conscious of itself by concentrating on momentary experiences from which it then withdraws back into itself. In the movement between its "self-cancellation," when it "becomes an object to itself," and the return to itself, it achieves "self-awareness."[34] Similarly music's movement is significantly more than sounds merely moving in time: it involves also a dialectical unfolding. Music achieves its identity through a successive or "temporal dispersal of its moments," through a course in which the moments relate to one another in backward and forward directed patterns, in flowing and interrupted, melodic and contrapuntal movements, such that the patterns surpass the individuality of the individual moments.[35]

It is important to repeat that music and the self stand not merely in a parallelism but in a relation of mediation. Thus music "takes" the sphere of inner sensibility or the abstract comprehension of the self "for its own." So taken, that comprehension is transfigured into purely musical form. However, the transfigured form does not leave behind what it transfigures: rather, it "draws" or "carries" it along as it draws or carries us through the movement of music. In other words, the movement of our inner life becomes known to us through the movement of music, in the act of our engaging with music as listeners.

Neither Hanslick nor Schopenhauer would disagree. Schopenhauer claims almost the same thing; Hanslick certainly absorbs many of Hegel's claims. But what sets Hegel's view apart is his emphasis on the mediation and transfiguration made possible by the concept of *Bewegung*. For, with this emphasis, Hegel has to neither resort to what in the most anxious moments looks like an almost compensatory language of metaphor nor apologize that his philosophical description in any way distances us from music.

Put otherwise, it is in and through mediation that music's purely musical but dialectical movement and thought's purely conceptual but dialectical movement are made inextricably to interact. Thus in music as in the movement of concepts, not all that is given is given at once: the movement, the passage, is indispensable. Although, as Hegel writes, "the true concept is an inherent unity, it is not an immediate one. Split internally and falling apart into contradictions on the way, it eventually resolves itself."[36] So, too, with music's eventual moment of resolution, when the harmony eventually "goes beyond" the "dissonant" chords, which present themselves to the ear along the way as "nothing but a contradiction." Hegel thus concludes: "Only this movement as the return of the identity to itself is what is simply true."[37]

"Das Wahre ist das Ganze" (The true is the whole), Hegel elsewhere famously declares.[38] Yet because in German *ganz* connotes *vollständig* (completed) as well as *ungeteilt* (indivisible), in English, when Hegel says "the true is the whole" he means that "the true is the completed." For him, truth is just *the completion of a movement,* be it the movement of the self, of a concept, or of a song. The movement of *Geist* (Spirit) is the absolute method of cognition.[39]

Hegel on Philosophy

Hegel once remarked that when a law or principle becomes too general, it runs the danger of losing its significance. The same is surely true of *Bewegung* if one employs the concept to capture the dialectical movement of everything and anything indiscriminately. To avoid this danger, Hegel works out his dialectical system through the mediation between abstract or universal principles, general laws and their specific, particular, and concrete determinations.[40] The mediations are neither static nor fixed but rather track the historical unfolding of *Geist.* He employs the concept of *Bewegung* to capture the passage of Absolute *Geist* from its first to its final stages of completion.

Recognizing that *der Begriff der Bewegung* (the concept of movement) is both the explanatory concept for the system and a concept within the system, he does what the Greek philosophers did earlier, namely, conceives of the *Bewegung* of *Bewegung* as *Selbstbewegung.* Self-movement is the *formal character* of the activity of *Geist* through all its manifestations; it cannot, therefore, be treated as a fixed or unalterable first principle. Following Aristotle, Hegel writes that nature is purposive activity, and "purpose is what is immediate and *at rest,* the unmoved which is also *self-moving;* and as such is Subject. Its power to move, taken abstractly, is *being-for-itself* or pure negativity. . . . The realized purpose, or the existent actuality, is movement and unfolded becoming, but it is just this unrest that is the self."[41]

In the preface to his early *Phenomenology of Spirit,* from which the preceding quotation is taken, Hegel writes also of the form and manner by which to unfold (philosophical) truth, of how philosophy brings things to light without ever being at rest until its end. He writes of progressive development, of the time of birth and death, of ceaseless activity, of working things out, of traveling one's path, of temporal process and periods of transition. He writes also of science as a morphogenetic process of cultural development and of transformation as part of the scientific enterprise.

Along the way, Hegel warns specifically against the formalist danger of repetition, where a concept or idea assumes the appearance of movement but actually remains stuck in the same place. In preference to *cold or shapeless repetition,* a monochrome formalism, he describes a *constructive unfolding* through which a concept moves and changes through its assertions of sameness and difference. To this movement he connects another, that bearing on the necessary role the subject plays in establishing objective truth. He rejects the idea of a static and fixed subject position from which fixed knowledge of a fixed world can be gained. The subject acquires knowledge only through its movement. In its abstract form, the subject starts out, as music does, from a place of pure and simple negativity, a "non-place" from which it propels itself into action. It sets factors into opposition, breaks up and differentiates between things, all in its process of becoming. It comes to know itself by becoming an Other to itself. It gradually returns to itself in self-knowledge. Hegel describes the process as twofold: each assertion asserts a position and assumes an opposite or negation; in the end the contradiction is resolved.

Inherent to philosophy's movement is the act of *defamiliarizing the familiar,* for what is familiar, Hegel claims, is not *properly* known. In a movement of "cancellation," each thought or concept needs to be turned back on itself for its truth to be expressed. To extend the point: when philosophy rests content with the familiar, it declines into a deadly dogmatism whereby philosophical truth is reduced to an apparently fixed and final, but presumably not properly known, set of propositions. Philosophers, he explains, tend too quickly to believe they have found certainty or safe resting places on the way.

Toward the end of his preface, Hegel describes the rhythm of dialectics. One description, here the first, is clearly more dialectical than the other. "The conflict between the general form of a proposition and the unity of the Notion which destroys it is similar to the conflict that occurs in rhythm between meter and accent. Rhythm results from the floating center and the unification of the two. So, too, in the philosophical proposition the identification of subject and predicate is not meant to destroy the difference between them, which the form of the proposition expresses; their unity, rather, is meant to emerge as a harmony."[42] Second, Hegel insists that in the process of philosophical thinking one ought neither to wander off nor to interrupt the movement. One sure way to break philosophy's rhythm is to float off into figurative presentations, into foreign ideas, or into associations and reflections that have no bearing on the thought's internal logic.[43] With this instruction, certainly Hanslick would agree. For what could be better than concentrated philosophical reading brought into kinship with concentrated musical listening?

I have discussed Hegel in two parts to highlight an affinity between his conceptions of music and philosophy. I did this to anticipate my reading of Adorno, who follows closely along Hegel's tracks. Yet emphasizing the particular affinity between music and philosophy does not preclude finding other affinities. After all, even Hegel's descriptions of dialectics are drawn significantly from developmental conceptions of science and history, and his mention of rhythm is drawn as well from poetry as from music. Adorno recognizes these other affinities, too, but to the affinity between philosophy and music he accords an extraordinary importance. Following the tradition described here, music, conceived as a language of pure form and no concept, stands at the most extreme point of difference from philosophy, conceived as a language of all concept and no form. Adorno asks what each can now borrow or learn from the other. Where and how might these extremes of language meet? His answer lies with the concepts of *Verwandtschaft* and *Bewegung*. To understand why Adorno gives pride of place to music in his conception of philosophy and to philosophy in his conception of music, one must consider his use of these two concepts both to drive and sustain his dialectical critique.

No Exit

Adorno shares with Hegel the fear of stasis and cold repetition but refuses that which dictates Hegel's movement the most, the teleological drive of absolute *Geist*. Hegel brought dialectics to an end, but to a false and authoritarian end, so Adorno argues, in the Prussian state.[44] Though Adorno speaks of endings as well—in music, art, philosophy, and politics—they are negative endings brought about through catastrophic decay, degeneration, and defeat. Endings are not metaphysical triumphs over history nor achievements or completions of movement. They are metaphysical expressions of historical loss.[45]

For Adorno a completed movement is not now *das Wahre* (the true) but rather *das Unwahre* (the untrue or the false). Maintained as *das Wahre*, the claim sustains in modernity only a desperately dangerous illusion of freedom and happiness in what has become an *almost* gapless or *almost* fully administered society. Between Hegel and Adorno lies the *Bewegung* of history—the dark and displacing dialectical movement of enlightenment. The historical difference has consequences as much for what music can be as for what philosophy can now be. Hence, also, my own earlier pitting of Adorno against Scruton to show the basic difference between their accounts. Recall that both ask whether harmony in music and/or in philosophy is still possible. Scruton thinks so; Adorno does not. Scruton claims that his answer depends on getting metaphysics right before engaging in cultural analysis. Adorno claims the two are inextricably interwoven. What was once possible versus what is now possible is a complex question within Adorno's philosophy as opposed to the literally consequential role Scruton claims it plays in his, according to which (Scruton writes) from a proper metaphysical understanding of the ordering of sound one can reach a proper cultural understanding of the ordering of the soul.[46]

Adorno criticizes Hegel for giving the "nonconceptual, individual and particular" negligible roles.[47] Favoring the overall achievement of *Geist* expressed by the universal, the general, the shared, the necessary, and the beautiful, Hegel fails to recognize "the temporal core" of truth.[48] Intending to retrieve this temporal core to dialectics, Adorno seeks significance where Hegel does not, in the "non-fixed" and the "non-posited," or, much under the influence of Walter Benjamin, in the traces, remainders, and remembrances of the historical present. "All music-making is a recherche du temps perdu," Adorno writes. "This is the key to the dialectics of music up to its liquidation."[49] Or elsewhere: "One can no longer claim that only the immutable is truth or that the mobile or transitory is [just] appearance, or [simply] that there is a mutual indifference between temporality and eternal ideas."[50]

Whereas Adorno believes that Hegel passes "through and beyond" negation in order to achieve resolution in identity and harmony of spirit, he seeks for his own dialectics the *on-going* movement of negation (thus my emphasis given just above to the word "almost"). He says the on-going movement is the only way left to break through the world's contemporary deceit. To break *through* that deceit is not, however, fully to break *out* of it. For Adorno there is no absolute exit or ending. Thus, in his *Minima Moralia,* he argues that "[n]egative philosophy, dissolving everything, dissolves even the dissolvent." To dissolve something is not to dismiss it. It is to hold it in suspension, to preserve it at a critical distance. To distance it is to defamiliarize its familiarity, as a way, following Hegel, to let its truth be seen. Still, the point is not to leave the good in place and to discard the bad; that is not feasible. It is, rather, to keep the movement moving, the negative thinking in the process of being thought. Thinking, this train of thought continues, neither begins from a fixed starting point nor ends with a "pure liberation" from an antagonistic society. He concludes accordingly: "As long as domination reproduces itself, so long as the impure element reemerges even in the dissolving of the dissolvent: [then] in a radical sense no [final or absolute] leap is made at all."[51]

It is sometimes claimed that although Adorno denies the final leap, he still absolutizes the negative within his system just as others absolutize the positive, and thus, like the other theorists, he brings the dialectical movement to a halt. Adorno is aware of the criticism. To avoid allowing his negative dialectic movement to terminate in hardened declarations of absolute nihilism or nothingness, he makes conscious gestures toward possibility and hope, usually in the last move of his argument. The gestures are neither blind nor pure; they carry with them all the feelings of loss and decay that have moved the arguments preceding them. Sometimes he writes of gestures of hope not fully hiding the despair, sometimes of the "grayness of despair" that cannot appear unless set against "the scattered traces of color."[52] Either way, he is methodologically interested in the double character of the final thought. "The way negative dialectics breaks through its hardened objects is via possibility," the thinking of something different.[53]

Adorno often speaks of "knots," of dramatic knots, structural knots, and Gordian knots. At least once he takes his model from the music of Anton Webern, but is unfortunately in this case no more specific about the music.[54] What knots convey is the double character of a final thought or a thought along the way: the sense of a thought's standing firm, of the argument's having hit upon the right constellation, or of an ending having tied the movement up, but also the sense of its being possible to untie the conclusion, to begin the thinking anew, of their being a moment of freedom or possibility contained even in an argument that initially seemed only to lead to death. Thinking might come to a halt, Adorno argues, but (at best) the *need* to think continues.[55]

Late in life Adorno writes that in a final move ("in einer letzten Bewegung") dialectics must turn "even against itself."[56] Although in such a move one is allowed to think the absolute, the absolute remains in bondage to the thought that cannot rid itself of its conditioning. There is no "stepping out" of thought. As much as we want it to be so, a negation of a negation issues no unconditioned positive. Dialectical thinking coerces us into thinking it does, just as modern society coerces us. We want our thought to rest comfortably with the world. But if the world is untrue, our thinking should do everything to resist this want. In this resistance, in our *not* stopping the thought, we are given the only (negative) form now for our hope.

Adorno finds this hope expressed in the last moment of Goethe's novel, in an interpretation he borrows from Benjamin. At the end of *Die Wahlverwandtschaften,* the lovers, Eduard and Ottilie, "rest side by side. Peace hovers above their resting place, serene angels of common likeness look down at them from the vault, and what a charming moment it will be when in time to come the two awake together."[57] In his own interpretative essay, Benjamin writes: "The more deeply emotion understands itself, the more it is transition; for the true poet, it never signifies an end," from which he concludes both for his own essay and for Goethe's: "Only for the sake of the hopeless are we given hope."[58] Adorno now reiterates this gesture in the last line of one of his own essays, written in this case about the last scene of Goethe's *Faust:* "Hope is not a memory that is held on to, but the return of something that has been forgotten."[59]

For Benjamin, given the movement of the argument as a whole, this hope is inseparable from the fact of Ottilie's having lost, having starved, having become mute, having retreated almost into nothingness.[60] Adorno repeats the gesture again when he argues that his own negative dialectics contains "practically nothing" anymore of the traditional metaphysical content of truth: "presque rien," he then adds to recall, he says, a modernist musical motif. What comes to an end comes, as with Ottilie, to a diminuendo. Negative dialectics tends toward the smaller, the quieter, and the micrological, indeed, toward "the smallest transitions of thought."[61] Adorno is still thinking about Goethe, only this time, alongside Benjamin, about the parable of *New Melusine's box.* Benjamin makes the point first: "Whereas the characters of the novel

[*Die Wahlverwandtschaften*] linger more weakly and more mutely, though fully life-sized in the gaze of the reader, the united couple of the novella disappears under the arch of a final rhetorical question, in the perspective, so to speak, of infinite distance. In the readiness for withdrawal and disappearance, it is bliss that is hinted at, bliss in small things, which Goethe later made the sole motif of 'The New Melusine.'"[62]

If "knots" bring Webern's music to Adorno's mind, then "the smallest things" or "the smallest cells" remind him of Alban Berg, at least when he writes of Berg's music that it dissolves to a minimum, "virtually in a single note."[63] As in Goethe's novel, the significance of the final note depends on the entire movement that precedes it. In the smallest cells and transitions we thus hear something quite new, since each revokes its own structure in the overall movement of becoming. The cells resist "solidifying." Like the dissolving of the dissolvent, they put themselves forward only to turn back on themselves. What is the point of this dialectical *Doppelbewegung*, as Adorno here describes it? To reject the final (Hegelian) positing of "ein musikalisches Etwas"—a final or hardened musical "something" that falsely assumes the character of Being.[64]

Affinity

"Affinity," according to Adorno, "is the point [or peak] of a dialectics of enlightenment."[65] It has the double character of enlightenment's thinking, both of identity thinking and of dissonant or resistant thinking. To find affinity with something is to identify with it, to desire to become it, to mirror it, to tolerate it. The less one feels the affinity, the more ruthlessly one seeks it: an affinity *elected*. But the spell is broken by the very fact of choice or election, that is, when one realizes that it was one's own hand—the subject's hand—that established the identity with the Other in the first place. Affinity, in Adorno's view, is as much about difference as about identity. A drop of water seen under a microscope shows as much commotion as stillness. Under a microscope, the drop begins to teem with life, for even though our "stubborn, spellbinding gaze" tries to focus on a firmly delineated object, the object remains "frayed at the edges."[66] Elsewhere Adorno writes about kaleidoscopes not to support the production of cold arrangements or empty variations, as kaleidoscopes can often do, but as part of his constant search for ways and means to resist the compulsion to achieve identity.[67]

Adorno employs the concept of affinity to explain the relationship between music and philosophy. Affinity is a lively and complex relation that keeps its relata in movement. And to keep things in movement is the point of his negative dialectics. Philosophy and music, he thus argues, share less their form or forming process than a particular mode of conduct *(Verhaltensweise)* that prevents (at best) a loss of movement. This requires further elucidation.

What distinguishes music's form is its sensuous unfolding of tones through time; what distinguishes philosophy's form is its movement of thought and concept. Yet each nonetheless yearns for what the other has. This is the basis of their affinity: philosophy yearns for music's immediacy as music yearns for philosophy's articulated meaning. Neither succeeds (at best) in becoming the other. In their mutual failure to become the other lies the success of their yearning. But they cannot give up the yearning; not to seek what the other has is to accept a much too narrow conception of their own possibilities. Thus, yearning for each other, music is brought into contact with conceptual meaning and philosophy with expression in such a way—the way of mediation—that each gains something thereby.

For one thing, to yearn *to be* another thing or *to want* what the other has are ways of expressing the deep *need* that one thing has *for* another. In writing about musical works, Adorno likes to stress the fact that they are enigmatic. Their enigmatic meanings are grounded entirely in their technical procedures and in the particular constellations of their materials. In this sense, musical works are their *tönend bewegte Formen.* Yet because their meanings are enigmatic or concealed, they call for decipherment or interpretation. Here is their *need* for philosophy. Although philosophical interpretations articulate the meanings in concepts, however, they should not be reductive. Something more than the conceptual articulations must be retained: something of the works' so-called mimetic or aesthetic comportment. As the principle of affinity demands, philosophical interpretation attempts something, and must attempt something, that succeeds by not completely succeeding—a *schwebende* (suspended or floating) condition of holding back from fully conquering or subsuming under its concepts the object of its attention. How, indeed, do interpreters hold back from conquering the object of their attention? In part by not treating music solely as an object (or "work") but also as a medium or mode of experience.

Adorno is touching here on the old and familiar problem of how one interprets a musical work in a language foreign to it. However, unlike many of his predecessors, he argues (with Benjamin) that interpretation aims not at a perfect correspondence or translation but rather to reveal something in the work that the work itself cannot directly show, what he often calls the work's (mediated) social or historical truth content. That which lies already mediated by the work's sensuous musical language must, he contends, be mediated a second time by philosophical reflection.[68] Philosophical reflection brings aspects of the work to articulation that the work by itself cannot. Whereas Schopenhauer conceives of music as an unconscious exercise in metaphysics, Adorno argues for music's unconscious writing of the world's history. But about what does music unconsciously write? About nothing: there is no simple aboutness. Music does not directly offer a picture of a social or historical situation, as suggested, say, when we claim that Beethoven's *Eroica* is *about* the Napoleonic Wars. What music writes or rather offers is the kind of knowledge that can be drawn from the *Bewegung* of our concepts. From the philosophical interpretation of a musical work, in other words, we can learn something about the dialectical movement of our concepts.

What is true of philosophical interpretation is true of other kinds of interpretation as well. Despite his allegiance to the *Werktreue* ideal, Adorno rejects a *buchstäblich* (literal or word-perfect) allegiance based on a cold or unconstructive repetition. Reading a score or performing or listening to a work stands to the work as philosophical interpretation stands to the work, as bringing out something (hitherto) unseen. Certainly the work is tracked as the same work throughout all these activities, but these activities are meant also to do *something more*. More than once Adorno (not very plausibly) criticizes the pianist Arthur Schnabel for playing Beethoven's music like a positivist, for failing to bring out the music's tensions, for overstressing the melody, for failing to reveal anything of its dialectical potential.[69] What is the point of playing Beethoven *not* like a positivist? To challenge what the very concept of a musical work claims most, namely, not actually to need its interpretation or performance. A dry, cold, or perfectly correct performance of a work—a positivist performance—is a performance that has fallen too dangerously under the authoritative spell of the work-concept.[70]

Under its absolutist development around 1800, the work-concept increasingly allowed its instances, the works, to assume the self-confident and self-sufficient appearance of being fixed, final, and fully composed. To bring out a work's tensions through a performance or a philosophical interpretation is a way to challenge this absolutist claim. Activities of "reproduction" (as performance, listening, or experience) should dialectically reveal aspects of a concept that the concept itself conceals behind its own false assertion of a work's autonomy; in this sense, the activities must surpass their own tendency merely to reproduce. Here, for Adorno, is dialectical activity at its best, namely, understanding reproductive activities as turning musical (or indeed social) practice against itself—as in the Hegelian movement of a concept—as a way of preserving the movement of that practice against the ever-threatening stasis of its governing concepts. To perform or interpret a musical work is to see the work as participating in the enlightenment dialectic of freedom's relation to authority. To see a *particular* work participating in a *particular* way in this dialectic is to read the enlightenment dialectic at a *particular* historical stage.

Adorno thus often describes the ability of works to "point beyond" themselves, to point beyond their own ability, uniqueness, and particularity. To be sure, works unfold according to their internal forms, but they also participate in unfolding the work-concept, the concept of music, of art, and so on. "Overstepping" their particularity is one way of capturing the mediation of concepts, how works can be read as ciphers of music's history and practice in dialectical movement. Adorno also describes the sedimentation of a tradition and the history of musical materials working on and within the works. Yet, although he speaks this way, he always looks at the works *from the inside out*, so as not to overstep their uniqueness altogether. Like Hegel and Hanslick, he insists that to interpret a musical work demands that one follow entirely and *without distraction* its unfolding structure.

To sustain the claim, Adorno rejects the idea that when we interpret a work we feel as if we thereby become distanced from it. In fact, we move closer, for interpretation, even social or philosophical interpretation, demands that we turn our gaze not outward but inward and deeply into the work's details. Neither interpretation nor performance should be regarded as imposing a schema of concepts on a work. For such activities are the means by which something concealed in the work is brought to expression. On one occasion Adorno thus turns his attention to a specific detail in a specific work in order to make both the musical and the philosophical point. Interestingly, again, the concealed aspect bears on the work's expression of possibility, of hope. "When, just before the close of the first movement of Beethoven's sonata *Les Adieux,* an evanescently fleeting association summons up in the course of three measures the sound of trotting horses, the swiftly vanishing passage, the sound of disappearance, which confounds any effort to pin it down anywhere in the context of the phrase, says more about the hope of return than any general reflection would on the essence of the fleetingly enduring sound."[71]

Reading Hegel

"Canonic for Hegel is Goethe's statement that everything perfect points beyond its own kind."[72] Thus writes Adorno to suggest that if a musical work can point beyond itself, so too can a philosophical work or thought, since each bears an "elective affinity" to the other. Stated otherwise, if music calls for philosophical decipherment, then philosophy, at least of certain types, calls for music's expression. Why should philosophy call for music's expression? Again, to keep itself in movement, to fight against its own isolating tendency toward hardening, stasis, or congealment.

Constellation must resist becoming a system, even in philosophy. Adorno writes, "Everything does not get resolved; everything does not come out even."[73] Dialectics is not a matter of wrapping things up neatly. But apparently Hegel, according to Adorno, tries to do exactly this; in the end he makes his dialectic too systematic and thereby strips its mobility from its movement. Adorno attributes the error to Hegel's attitude toward language as increasingly becoming "sovereignly indifferent." The language becomes doctrinaire. How, then, can one overcome the authoritative character of the texts? By treating them as one would a musical text, as hermetic or in need of decipherment.

Although or precisely because Hegel betrays his own (early) commitment to keep the dialectical or rhythmic movement of his texts in motion, Adorno argues that one should read his later works against their own authoritative grain. Only then would their movement be retrieved. Carrying the thought further, he notes first that, as was customary for the times, Hegel's texts were not in fact fully written out but were written rather as if only to be "read aloud" (recall Goethe's novel). It was also customary for the texts to be accompanied by keywords, words that functioned as expressive markings functioned in music.[74] Adorno concludes that one should read Hegel's texts "by describing along with him the curves of the intellectual movement, by playing his ideas with the speculative ear as though they were musical notes." One should "float along," let oneself be borne by the current of the thoughts and not forced to linger. And yet one should also "develop an intellectual slow-motion procedure" or "slow down the tempo" when the thoughts become cloudy, but never so much as to lose their motion.[75]

Adorno criticizes Hegel more than once for having underestimated the mimetic character of a concept, the *Nichtbegriffliches in dem Begriff*, which is to say, the expressive, concealed, unarticulated aspect of a concept's meaning that yet brings a concept or a name *in touch* with an object. If the mimetic or aesthetic character is underestimated in the concepts, so too is it in the texts. Accordingly, Adorno demands that a philosophical text resist its own static impulse and release, as in music, its dynamic side. Hegel's texts should "murmur and rustle" as great music murmurs and rustles, for philosophy "is allied with art in wanting to rescue, in the medium of the concept, the mimesis that the concept represses." Too often, Adorno complains, Hegel behaves like Alexander with his Gordian knot. Cutting rather than untying the knot, Hegel "disempowers the individual concepts, and uses them as though they were the imageless images of what they mean." Hence one should hold onto the Goethean "residue of absurdity" in Hegel's philosophy of absolute spirit.[76]

Hegel and Beethoven

Adorno often argues for a special affinity between Hegel's logic and Beethoven's composition. "The central categories of artistic construction are translatable into social ones," he explains in this crucial passage.

> The affinity with that bourgeois freedom-movement, which rushes through his [Beethoven's] music, is that of the dynamically self-unfolding totality. In allowing the movements to follow their own law, as becoming, negating, confirming themselves and the whole without glimpsing to the outside, they come to resemble the world whose forces move them; they do not do it by imitating the world. For this reason, Beethoven's standing toward societal objectivity is more that of philosophy—the Kantian in some points and the Hegelian in the decisive ones—than that of the ominous mirroring posture: society in Beethoven is recognized *without concepts, not painted* (my emphasis).[77]

In the specific use in Beethoven's music of a "reprise," Adorno finds just that sort of return and reminiscence that reminds him, so he says, of Hegel's logic. In Beethoven's "highly organized music" he says that he discovers a "multidimensional" movement that moves "forward and backward at the same time." The principle of temporal organization apparently *requires* this because dialectical time can be articulated only "through distinctions between what is familiar and what is not yet familiar, between what already exists and what is new." As with Hegel, therefore, one "has to know a whole movement and be aware retrospectively at every moment of what has come before."[78]

And yet, if Adorno sees in Hegel's philosophy a tendency toward absolutism and authority, then surely he recognizes the same in Beethoven's music. Indeed he does. Still, in Beethoven he hears also the formal movement of absolutism's undoing. This leads him to conclude of some of Beethoven's works, and especially of his later, more fractured ones, that they therefore carry more dialectical truth than is found in Hegel's philosophy. In fact, he even goes on to suggest that Beethoven's works put Hegel's idea that "das Wahre ist das Ganze" to the test, because, as great works of art, the works show what "identity" considered as a *completed whole* really is, namely, only the appearance *(Schein)* or product of construction.[79]

To see philosophy and music standing in an elective affinity is thus to see each as mediating and being mediated by the other. For this reason, they stand in a relation to each other that far surpasses "mere analogy." Here is Adorno's anti-Schopenhauerean strike, a strike against "an ominous mirroring posture" (as the first quotation in this section put it), a strike against a static picturing relation. The history of music is not merely analogous to the history of philosophy, as Schopenhauer assumes; it is, for Adorno the same history. "What Hegel called the unfolding of truth is the same in the movement of both."[80] Adorno speaks too of philosophy and music coinciding, which is to say that, though they travel by "qualitatively different" means, they converge *in* truth.[81] Again the point is not to assert an identity between philosophy and music, but only to assert an affinity based on their both shared and particular (same and different) dialectical movements.

Adorno always stresses affinity, convergence, and mediation over analogy and metaphor to sustain within philosophy and music the shared possibility of cognitive transformation. Dialectics demands not movement per se but transformational movement. Musical movement is not merely the movement of tones through time; music (at best) moves in such a way as to bring about a transition in musical-social-philosophical (conceptual) understanding. Philosophical argument likewise moves (at best) in such a way that concepts confront themselves through the movement of their particular instances.

In general, by "critique" Adorno thus understands not the philosophical activity whereby one merely describes or comments on what is in the music, as if all a work's aspects are to be treated neutrally on a level. There is no such thing as the philosophy *of* music if by this we mean that philosophy stands as the established method by which to capture the musical object. Philosophy and music stand, rather, in a mutually informing relationship such that the activity of performing and interpreting conceptless musical works comes to tell us something about the social and historical tensions implicit in our concepts. What it tells us is made explicit by philosophy or critique. Critique makes explicit, in each and every one of its movements, the convergence and kinship of music and philosophy.[82]

It should be added, however, that Adorno does not seek just any kind of movement or antagonism in his conception of critique, only the kind that performs the desired dialectical work. Thus of Beethoven's early work Violin Sonata in C minor, opus 30, he claims that even though it is a work of the highest genius, its "antagonism" is "still *unmediated.*" Its arrangement is "set out only in splendid contrast, like armies or pieces on a chessboard, that at most collide (like atoms) in a dense developmental sequence." And yet, by contrast, in Beethoven's *Appassionata*, Adorno finds an "affinity" to Hegel's philosophy just where "the antithetical themes are at the same time identical in themselves."[83]

It is of course most tempting here to criticize Adorno for making the movements of music and philosophy match and, furthermore, mirror his own dialectical aims. The criticism is legitimate only if one assumes that his descriptions of movement are literal. They are not: within a negative dialectic the interpretations are not made so much for the sake of descriptive accuracy as they are offered "figuratively" and "drastically" at the extremes (to keep alive the entire spectrum of meaning and possibility). Who would ever really believe that there is only a Hegelian dialectical movement in Beethoven's music? The question, therefore, is what Adorno is unmasking by his "descriptions." The answer lies in his claim that the concept of *Bewegung* can and should be used dialectically to resist the tendency in all thought and in all music — even in his own — toward a deadly and disciplined stasis. Everything turns, here, on how much a reader wants or wants not to hear in the movement of Adorno's own dialectic.

Pent-Up Time

That he is constantly thinking against the grain of identity thinking does not lead Adorno to underestimate the role of momentary stops and pauses. On the contrary: he writes about moments of stillness, suspension, and standstill as well as repose, equilibrium, and compression in the overall moment of music and thought. In the natural beauty of romanticism, he thus observes that the "natural and historical elements interact in a musical and kaleidoscopically changing fashion." However, in this kaleidoscopic arrangement, the natural beauty shows its history of movement suspended or punctuated by its pregnant moments of becoming (following Lessing), of explosions (following Goethe), and of dialectics coming to temporary standstills (following Benjamin).[84] For example, of the first movement of Beethoven's *Pastoral* he notes that the repetition is not, as it *sometimes tends* to be (as he claims) in Stravinsky, "the outcome of a repetition compulsion" but instead "a relaxation, a letting go." "The bliss of dawdling" he adds to capture this marvelous sense of suddenly staying still: "Dillydallying as Utopia."[85]

The Greek musicologist Thrasyboulos Georgiades once noted though we say that a work's first note depends on its last, as the last on its first, the dependence is sustained entirely by the movement that occurs between. However, this movement achieves a special character in the listening experience of music: the illusion of "pent-up time," namely, that between the first and the last note no time has really passed at all.[86] Adorno refers to this argument to underscore the separation of *musical* from *empirical* time, to explain the *double character* of a work's aesthetic movement. To become absorbed by a work's aesthetic movement is to break out of empirical time. And yet—and this is a typical dialectical step—one cannot break out altogether. "Music cannot do without empirical time." Thus, our absorption might bring the musical movement to a standstill, it might make us feel as if the movement all happened in an instant, but what is captured in that instant is the work's entire movement. Thus, to conclude that the movement really had been captured in this instant would be to surrender to the illusion. To not surrender would contrarily be to recognize the double character of the experience, that is, that the pent-up or timeless character of the aesthetic experience of music cannot do without the empirical time in which it unfolds.[87]

If a work as a whole can be experienced *as if* in a single moment, then, in reverse, a single moment or detail of a work can beg for the entire work to be heard. Drawing again on the work of Benjamin, Adorno takes from chapter 13 of part 2 of Goethe's *Die Wahlverwandtschaften* a piece of a single line that gains luminosity, he says, only by virtue of the whole: "Like a star hope fell from the heavens."[88] Benjamin himself claims he is following Hölderlin in identifying this line with the caesura of the work, when the embracing lovers seal their fate.[89] Once more Adorno adapts the thought to music: "Many measures in Beethoven sound like the sentence in *Elective Affinities:* 'Like a star hope fell from the heavens.'" Think, he continues, of the "Adagio of the Sonata in D minor, op. 31, no. 2. It only requires playing the passage [bars 27–38] first in context and then alone to be able to recognize how much its incommensurability, radiating over the passage, owes to the work as a whole. The passage becomes extraordinary because its expression is raised above what precedes it by the concentration of a lyrical, humanized melody. It is individuated in relation to, and by way of, the totality; it is product as well as suspension."[90]

Bewegung versus Time

Adorno writes about the history of music's dialectical movement to criticize the regressive tendencies of contemporary music (of the fifties and sixties). Influenced by Ernst Lewy's essay on lateness and aging in Goethe, he separates the dialectical potential of *late style* from the *aging* of new music.[91] He finds a preferred late style in Beethoven and Mahler but aging in the music of Boulez, Stockhausen, and Cage, though he is quick to add that lateness and aging are intertwined. Accordingly there is the tendency to age also in Beethoven and the tendency of lateness in Cage. Furthermore, in his critique of contemporary music, he notes that he does not want to judge the music according to traditional categories but on its own terms. However, on its own terms (despite the sometimes genius the music displays) he sees a loss of dialectical potential. He shows this loss by reading the composers' claims for their new music against their own grain. He then reads the loss as having always been possible in the tradition stemming back through Schönberg, Wagner, and Schubert, to that first Beethovenian moment. This is Adorno's way of reading the past through the present and the present through the past: in terms entirely provided by the formal dialectical *Bewegung* of enlightenment's history.[92]

Adorno might have compared Beethoven's early or middle undialectical works to the undialectical works of contemporary music. However, for the purposes of critique, he instead uses Beethoven's late and most "dialectical" works against them. Thus, in Darmstadt in 1961 he pits Beethoven's dialectical use of the "reprise" against the use within what he describes as a fully rationalized, serialist work. What the reprise shows in Beethoven is the possibility of dialectical movement: "the feeling of something extraordinary having occurred earlier,"[93] but this is not shown in the serialist works. That this is not shown, however, results less from any intrinsic misuse of the reprise than from broader changes in the concept of time. Temporal interrelations are reduced to static repetitions; transformational movements of the kind once heard in Beethoven are no longer evident. With the loss of immanent dynamics is a loss of tension, and with a loss of tension, the New Music shows its age.[94]

The notion of aging recalls Goethe's remark that aging is a gradual stepping back from appearance. Goethe reflects on beauty and nature's laws, whereby in a flower's full bloom or at the physical peak of human existence beauty appears at its best.[95] Like Goethe, Adorno sees the gradual movement toward decay, disintegration, and dissociation. In Beethoven's late works he sees what he describes as a paring or peeling away of sensuous appearance, a renunciation of material. But he thinks too that the spirit remains in these works "as if the whole world of sensuous appearance were reduced in advance to the appearance of something spiritual."[96]

For contemporary music, however, his description is different: there is retreat from appearance altogether, a retreat without the possibility of spiritual remainder. Adorno rejects as false the claims he hears regarding the new immediacy, spontaneity, and naturalness of contemporary sounds: the return to nature. In rejecting aesthetic appearance, contemporary composers are not stepping closer to nature or spirit; they are only stepping further away. Again, Adorno partially blames the problem on their rejection of the very category of aesthetic time. A stepping back from aesthetic time is a stepping back from aesthetic appearance, and a stepping back from aesthetic appearance amounts to a rejection of the very possibility of art. Art cannot do without appearance.

Although, he thus argues, Stockhausen acknowledges Bergson's distinction between *temps espace* and *temps durée,* a distinction that has kept separate aesthetic from empirical time, the composer nonetheless collapses the distinction in the actual production of his totally organized works. From this, however, Adorno does not conclude that Stockhausen has completely erased music's relationship to aesthetic time, only that the relationship has been broken, which therefore leaves open the possibility of its mending.

Comparably, Adorno credits Stockhausen for offering a most advanced articulation of "wie die Zeit vergeht" (how time passes)—*in theory*—but then criticizes him for reducing the actually produced works to static entities. With their fully stipulated electronic scores and their fully stipulated realizations, the works are effectively reduced to singular or identically repeatable events. The performances leave or show no remainder in or of the works. From the works are thus removed the possibility (via the performances) of their dialectical undoing. Rather than destroying the work-concept, which is allegedly part of the contemporary project, the performances only meet its regressive or authoritative demand, by reconfirming the work's claim to be self-sufficient and complete. "Seamless" or "gapless," Adorno concludes, the total works submit to the totalitarian tendencies of identity thinking.

Adorno thus judges contemporary music's employment of the concept of time against the condition of dialectical *Bewegung.* He regards time as having become immobile and the musical score as having lost its fluidity or "informality"—to pick up his own preference for what he describes (following Heinz-Klaus Metzger) as *musique informelle.* He writes accordingly that this music has become too formed, but at the cost of form's mobility: "the material and compositional principles" no longer mediate each other; they simply "remain alien." Reduced to mere kaleidoscopic arrangements of elementary particles, the elements of pitch and duration no longer dialectically move in aesthetic time but rather just merge under the general and undifferentiated heading of time.[97] And yet, Adorno adds, there has always been this tendency toward the unification of time in music's history—since Beethoven, with the development of the work-concept. Given the movement of the concept of enlightenment, the tendency has always been there to move toward the mechanical and the technological; reified rationality was always implicit.

Adorno connects the same tendencies to what he describes as the weak ego development of reified collectivities and contemporary political movements. He reads Cage's proclamations on chance, in accordance with the Zen Buddhist movement, as expressions of, and compensations for, a collectivity of weak egos. Such egos may think they are claiming control, but they are really relinquishing it every time they submit their thinking to the regressive myth of spontaneity and nature.

Wherever possible, Adorno articulates the argument for *Bewegung* to articulate the regressive tendencies of contemporary society. He offers no more succinct example of his claim than this extreme statement:

> Many a contemporary composer is praised for his "dynamism." In the world of machines, which we insult when we compare that sort of music with it, it is a matter of moving masses of material or people. But musical dynamism is ideologically a law unto itself: nothing is moved, and why the only visible purpose, that of the work of art, should be achieved by means of movement for its own sake, remains a mystery. For this reason it is inevitable that movement should soon turn out to be mere pseudo-motion in the static structure of this "dynamic" music in which nothing that occurs is forced to change. They are all running on the spot like soldiers on the parade-ground. If you really want to dismantle humanity, you should at least try to find more intelligent excuses.[98]

The Last Move

Adorno's criticisms sometimes feel backward looking, nostalgic, and conservative. This impression misses at least their intended point. He does not argue for a return to a golden age. There has never been one. He also recognizes the genius or brilliance of the composers he most strongly criticizes. His purpose is only to unravel the false rationalizations he thinks he can identify in the present and thereby retrieve what in the present has been forgotten or cast aside. He is concerned with the recognition of the hidden and the shadowed, with the acknowledgment of what history has made into ghosts. In other terms, his apparent conservatism is counteracted by dialectical critique every time he uses the present to show the tendencies of the past. As he himself argues, the dangers felt in the last note are already implicit in the first, even if one cannot, from the first note, predict what will happen. History is as much about contingency as it is about determinate patterns. At the same time, he takes a moment in history, the catastrophic moment of Auschwitz, from which to articulate the terms of his negative dialectics. What he always looks for in philosophy and in music is how to destabilize their inherent tendencies toward social order, not because order is always bad but because it can be very bad and he is not inclined to ignore this fact.

From the point of view of what I wanted to show most in this essay, it is worth repeating that Adorno is obviously neither the first nor the last to seek in philosophy and in music a way to think about politics and history, but he does stand significantly apart from many others in having brought philosophy and music into so close an affinity, and in having used the Hegelian *Begriff der Bewegung* to sustain this relationship. Taking this concept as seriously as he does, he begs the interpreters of a most German history of philosophy and music to read and keep rereading that history against its grain. In this essay, I try further to contribute to this field by rereading the history of the philosophy of music with a focus specifically on *Bewegung* separated from its link to the better-known theories of analogy and metaphor.

Putting these two final paragraphs together I would like to end simply by writing what is most obvious, that Adorno was always unrelenting in his critique. Without doubt, there were moments when he was justified in being so; at other times, one cannot help but feel that he went too far or further at least than we are willing to go now. Sometimes his commitment to dialectical *Bewegung* got in the way of his musical listening. But if, on the other hand, "it's your conscience that leads you to make such remarks" Charlotte would have responded, then one need not worry so much. For it is always good "to take a look at ourselves and give due thought to the meaning of . . . words" such as "elective" and "affinity" in this connection.[99] It is the looking at ourselves, when we do not meet our own humanist ideals, that most motivated Adorno to think the way that he thought.

NOTES

1. These opening paragraphs are drawn from pt. 1, chaps. 4 and 8 of Goethe's *Elective Affinities*, ed. David E. Wellbery, vol. 11 of *Collected Works*, trans. Victor Lange and Judith Ryan (Princeton, N.J.: Princeton University Press, 1988), 109–17 and 130–32 (translation from p. 112 is modified).

2. The reference to the recitation comes from Georg Simmel; the reference to the storyteller comes from R. M. Meyer, as recorded by Walter Benjamin in his essay "Goethe's *Elective Affinities*," in *Selected Writings*, vol. 1, 1913–1926, ed. Marcus Bullock and Michael W. Jennings (Cambridge, Mass.: Harvard University Press, 1996), 330.

3. On the difference between movement and time from Aristotle to Derrida, see Kai von Eikels's "Die erste Figur: Zum Verhältnis von Bewegung und Zeit," in *de figura: Rhetorik-Bewegung-Gestalt,* ed. Gabriele Brandstetter and Sibylle Peters (Munich: Wilhelm Fink Verlag, 2002), 33–50.

4. Theodor W. Adorno, *Beethoven: The Philosophy of Music,* trans. Edmund Jephcott (Stanford, Calif.: Stanford University Press, 1998), 116 (translation modified).

5. See the first movement of Adorno's *Two Pieces for String Quartet,* op. 2 (1924/25) and of *Six Short Orchestra Pieces,* op. 4 (1929).

6. H. H. Eggebrecht, ed., *Brockhaus-Riemann Musiklexikon,* s.v. "Satz" (Mainz: Schotts, 1979), 444 (my translation); from Koch's *Musikalisches Lexikon* (Frankfurt, 1802/R, 2/1817).

7. J. J. Rousseau, "Mouvement," in *Dictionnaire de musique,* vol. 5 of Œuvres Complètes (Paris: Gallimard, 1995), 913–14.

8. Robert and James Adam, *Works in Architecture,* preface 3 note (London, 1773–78), recorded in *Oxford English Dictionary,* s.v. "movement."

9. For a most useful discussion of *Bewegung* in the visual arts, see Herbert Molderlings's "Film, Photographie and ihr Einfluss auf die Malerei in Paris um 1910: Marcel Duchamp-Jacques Villon-Frank Kupka," in *Wallraf-Richartz-Jahrbuch* (Cologne: Verlag M. Dumont Schauberg, 1975), 247–86.

10. Tennessee Williams, *The Glass Menagerie,* ed. Robert Bray (New York: New Directions, 1999).

11. From *Pall Mall,* 1 Dec. 1885 4/1, in *Oxford English Dictionary,* s.v. "movement."

12. "Der Begriff der *Bewegung* ist bisher in den Untersuchungen des Wesens und der Wirkung der Musik auffallend vernachlässigt worden, er dünkt uns der wichtigste und fruchtbarste," *Vom Musikalisch-Schönen: Ein Beitrag zur Revision der Ästhetik der Tonkunst* (Wiesbaden: Breitkopf & Härtel, 1966), 27 (all translations of Hanslick's text are my own).

13. Roger Scruton, *The Aesthetics of Music* (Oxford: Oxford University Press, 1999), 96.

14. Cf. Peter Kivy's work on "how music moves" (us), e.g., in his *Music Alone: Philosophical Reflections on the Purely Musical Experience* (Ithaca, N.Y.: Cornell University Press, 1990), 146–72. See also his "Movements and 'Movements,'" in *New Essays on Musical Understanding* (Oxford: Oxford University Press, 2001), 168–83, in which he argues that though there are movements, as in the four movements of a symphony, and though there are musical movements linked perhaps to social or political developments, there is no good reason to think that "spectator music" of the kind suitable for absolute music should be expected to influence social movements, even if, granted, a certain aspect of its expressiveness, when joined to program or text, might have a social influence

(182). With more than a touch of Hanslickean anxiety, Kivy, here, as in much of his work, defends a philosophical account of music's purity.

15. Written in 1960 with an explicit allusion to Goethe's *Wilhelm Meisters Lehrjahre* ("Mignon's Song") "Kennst du das Haus? Auf Säulen ruht sein Dach" (Knowest thou the house? On pillars rests its roof); quoted in "Music and New Music," trans. R. Livingston, in *Quasi una Fantasia: Essays on Modern Music* (London: Verso, 1992), 265.

16. Quoted verse from Goethe, *Faust*, 1.1.4239.

17. Hanslick, *Vom Musikalisch-Schönen*, 64 and 72.

18. Hanslick, *Vom Musikalisch-Schönen*, September 11, 1891, preface (vi).

19. Hanslick, *Vom Musikalisch-Schönen*, 59.

20. In thinking about the translation of this most distinctive phrase, one needs to ask why Hanslick chooses so poetic a construction; why does he not use more straightforward phrases such as *tönende* or *bewegende* or *bewegliche Formen*?

21. For a study that is part survey and part new and original treatment of these topics, see Christopher Hasty's *Meter as Rhythm* (New York: Oxford University Press, 1997). Moving beyond traditional limitations, it places contemporary thinking about rhythm, meter, and time against a broad musical, philosophical, and historical background. Roger Scruton also sets his account against more traditional accounts as offered, say, by Victor Zuckerkandl and L. B. Meyer.

22. Adorno adopts a remarkably similar argument against Rudolf Kolisch's "Tempo and Character in Beethoven's Music." Kolisch's piece appeared in *The Musical Quarterly* pt. 1, 29, no. 1 (Apr. 1943): 169–87; pt. 2, 29 N (July 1943): 291–312. Adorno's response to Kolisch (in the form of a letter, dated Nov. 16, 1943) appears as an appendix, text 7, in Adorno's *Beethoven*, 179–81. It argues against the positivistic or mechanistic construction of "types": "this knowledge must be concrete and must yield overarching connections through the movement of one particular moment to another, and not through establishing general features [characteristics or types]."

23. Hanslick, *Vom Musikalisch-Schönen*, 29.

24. Hanslick, *Vom Musikalisch-Schönen*, 62.

25. Cf. the conclusion to Herbert Schnädelbach's chapter "Hegel," in *Musik in der deutschen Philosophie: Eine Einführung*, ed. Stefan Lorenz Sorgner and Oliver Fürbeth (Stuttgart: J. B. Metzler, 2003), 75: "So kann man sagen, daß Hegel auch heute noch zu den unbekannten Musiktheoretikern der Vergangenheit gehört" (Thus one can say that Hegel still even today belongs to the [group of] unknown music theorists of the past).

26. Schopenhauer writes about music in *The World as Will and Representation*, 2 vols., trans. E. F. J. Payne (1819; reprint, New York: Dover, 1958 and 1969). The remarks here are almost entirely drawn from Section 52 of vol. 1, 252–67 and chap. 39 of vol. 2.

27. Schopenhauer, *World as Will and Representation*, I, 264.

28. Schopenhauer, *World as Will and Representation* I, 264.

29. Schopenhauer, *World as Will and Representation* I, 258.

30. Thomas Mann, "Schopenhauer," in *Essays of Three Decades*, trans. H. T. Lowe-Porter (New York: Knopf, 1947), 394.

31. Georg Wilhelm Friedrich Hegel, *Hegel's Aesthetics*, trans. T. M. Knox, vol. 2 (Oxford: Clarendon Press, 1975), 928 (translation modified).

32. Hegel, *Hegel's Science of Logic*, trans. A. V. Miller (Amherst, N.Y.: Prometheus Books, 1989), 355.

33. Hegel, *Aesthetics*, 890 and 897.

34. Hegel, *Aesthetics*, 914.

35. Hegel, *Aesthetics*, 928.

36. Hegel, *Aesthetics*, 928.

37. Hegel, *Aesthetics*, 928.

38. Hegel, *Phenomenology of Spirit*, trans. A. V. Miller (Oxford: Oxford University Press, 1977), 11. "Das Wahre ist das Ganze. Das Ganze aber ist nur das durch seine wesentlich Resultat, daß es erst am Ende das ist, was es in Wahrheit ist; und hierin eben besteht seine Natur, Wirkliches, Subjekt oder Sich-selbstwerden zu sein." Hegel: *Phänomenologie des Geistes, Hegel-Werke*, Frankfurt, Suhrkamp, 1970, vol. 3, 24.

39. Cf. Hegel's *Science of Logic*, preface, section 9. "This spiritual movement which, in its simple undifferentiatedness, gives itself its own determinateness and in its determinateness its equality with itself, which therefore is the immanent development of the Notion, this movement is the absolute method of knowing and at the same time is the immanent soul of the content itself."

40. The concrete mediation in Hegel's view is precisely what Hanslick finds lacking when he rejects Hegel's theory in the last paragraphs of his treatise. There he criticizes Hegel for finding in music a generalized expression only of a non-individualized *Inneres* (inwardness) that overlooks and thus seriously underestimates the particular, formal activity of the composer (*Vom Musikalisch-Schönen*, 173). This leads Hanslick (unlike Adorno, who similarly criticizes Hegel) to reject the dialectical approach altogether.

41. Hegel, *Phenomenology of Spirit*, 12.

42. Hegel, *Phenomenology of Spirit*, 38.

43. Hegel, *Phenomenology of Spirit*, 35–36.

44. Theodor W. Adorno, *Negative Dialektik*, ed. Rolf Tiedemann, vol. 6 of *Gesammelte Schriften* (Frankfurt am Main: Suhrkamp, 1966), 38 (hereafter cited as *GS*). See also E. B. Ashton's translation, *Negative Dialectics* (London: Routledge, 1973), 27.

45. For another discussion of historical loss in modernism, see Michael Theunissen's *Negative Theologie der Zeit* (Frankfurt am Main: Suhrkamp, 1991).

46. Scruton writes: "I have begun from first principles" that "should lead at last to a philosophy of modern culture"—from "the ordering of sound" to "an ordering of the soul" (Scruton, *Aesthetics of Music*, ix).

47. Adorno, *Negative Dialektik*, 8.

48. Cf. Adorno, *Aesthetic Theory*, trans. Robert Hullot-Kentor (Minneapolis: University of Minnesota Press, 1997): "Hegel arrests the aesthetic dialectic by his static definition of the beautiful as the sensuous appearance of the idea" (51). Also "Hegel fails to recognize this [art's impulse to objectify the fleeting, not the permanent] and for this reason, in the midst of dialectics, fails to recognize the temporal core of art's truth content" (219, translation modified).

49. Theodor W. Adorno, *Zu einer Theorie der musikalischen Reproduktion*, ed. H. Lonitz (Frankfurt am Main: Suhrkamp, 2001), 228 (my translation).

50. "Daß das Unveränderliche Wahrheit sei und das Bewegte, Vergängliche Schein, die Gleichgültigkeit von Zeitlichem und ewigen Ideen gegen einander, ist nicht länger zu behaupten, auch nicht mit der verwegenen Hegelschen Auskunft, zeitliches Dasein diene vermöge der seinem Begriff innewohnenden Vernichtung dem Ewigen, das in der Ewigkeit von Vernichtung sich darstelle." Adorno, *Negative Dialektik*, *GS* 6, 354; *Negative Dialectics*, 361 (translation modified).

51. Theodor W. Adorno, *Minima Moralia: Reflexionen aus dem beschädigten Leben*, *GS* 4, 280; *Minima Moralia. Reflections from Damaged Life*, trans. E. F. N. Jephcott (London: Verso, 1974), 245 (translation modified).

52. Adorno, *Negative Dialectics*, 377–78. This thought actually forms part of a critique of Schopenhauer's nihilism, against which Adorno quotes the last line of Benjamin's essay on Goethe's *Die Wahlverwandtschaften*, which I discuss later in this essay.

53. Adorno, *Negative Dialektik*, *GS* 6, 62 (my translation).

54. References to knots and dialectical knots are scattered throughout Adorno's writings. Clearly he is drawing on a prevalent use of this idea and phrase in German Idealism, from Hegel to Kierkegaard (cf. *Aesthetic Theory*, 171). For the mention of Webern within a discussion of the relation between the universal and the particular in the movement of concepts, see *Aesthetic Theory*, 181 ("So wird bei Webern die allgemeine musikalische Form der Durchführung zum 'Knoten' und büßt ihre entwickelnde Funktion ein. . . . [*GS* 7, 270]). On the subject of knots and on the problem of beginning and ending contemporary artworks, see *Aesthetic Theory*, 102.

55. On metaphysics as a need and yearning, see Adorno's lectures in *Metaphysics: Concept and Problems*, ed. Rolf Tiedemann, trans. E. Jephcott (Stanford, Calif.: Stanford University Press, 2001), and especially chapters 11 and 12 on *Bewegung*. One route by which Adorno returns to Goethe's notion of affinity is via Schelling's *Philosophy of Nature*.

56. Adorno, *Negative Dialektik*, 406.

57. Translation of Goethe's final lines modified.

58. Benjamin, "Goethe's *Elective Affinities*," 349, 356.

59. Theodor W. Adorno, "Zur Schlußszene des Faust," in *Noten zur Literatur*, vol. 11 of *Gesammelte Schriften*, 138 (my translation); but cf. *Notes to Literature*, trans. Shierry Weber Nicholsen, vol. 1 (New York: Columbia University Press, 1991), 120.

60. Stanley Corngold develops this theme of muteness in his "Genuine Obscurity Shadows the Semblance Whose Obliteration Promises Redemption: Reflections on Benjamin's 'Goethe's *Elective Affinities*,'" in *Benjamin's Ghosts: Interventions in Contemporary Literary and Cultural Theory*, ed. Gerhard Richter (Stanford, Calif.: Stanford University Press, 2002), 154–68.

61. All these claims appear in the final section of his *Negative Dialectics* (*GS* 6, 399). Compare also Adorno's earlier remark that "Die Gestalt des Denkens als innerzeitlicher, motiviert fortschreitender Bewegung gleicht vorweg, mikrokosmisch, der makrokosmischen, geschichtlichen, die in der Struktur von Denken verinnerlicht ward," *Negative Dialektik*, *GS* 6, 63. "The form of thought as motivated progressive movement in time microcosmically resembles from the start the macrocosmic, historical movement internalized in the structure of thought." Benjamin also often employs the term "diminuendo."

62. Benjamin, "Goethe's *Elective Affinities*," 333.

63. The distinction here is not so sharp, for in relation to Webern, too, Adorno speaks often about the brevity of his music and of its "fury of disappearance." "Anton von Webern," *Sound Figures*, trans. Rodney Livingstone (Stanford, Calif.: Stanford University Press, 1999), 94.

64. Theodor W. Adorno, *Alban Berg: Master of the Smallest Link*, trans. Julianne Brand and Christopher Hailey (Cambridge: Cambridge University Press, 1991), 39. For the other reference to "Doppelbewegung" see Adorno's discussion of Hegel and the double, aesthetic and empirical, historical character of art (*GS* 7, 180 and *Aesthetic Theory*, 118).

65. Adorno, "Affinität ist die Spitze einer Dialektik von Aufklärung," *Negative Dialektik*, *GS* 6, 266–67; *Negative Dialectics*, 270.

66. Theodor W. Adorno, "Skoteinos, or How to Read Hegel," in *Hegel: Three Studies*, trans. Shierry Weber Nicholsen (Cambridge, Mass.: MIT Press, 1999), 133. In the terms of social theory, Adorno explores "the subject's hand" in terms of social labor. Borrowing from Marx, he criticizes Hegel for not having seen society's *Bewegung* in the material terms of human and social labor. Hegel, he writes, went astray in allowing "the quintessence of movement," i.e., "the absolute," to become identified with "the reconciled life, the life of the pacified drive" that no longer recognizes either the deficiency of or the social labor that has gone into producing the illusion of reconciliation in the first place ("Aspects of Hegel's Philosophy," in *Hegel: Three Studies*, 32).

67. Adorno, *Negative Dialectics*, 156–57. Adorno mentions the kaleidoscope again in reference to Hanslick (*Aesthetic Theory*, 197).

68. Cf. Adorno, *Aesthetic Theory*, 358.

69. In his draft of Beethoven, Adorno remarks on Schnabel's "over vivid rendition of sung melodies" (127), and in *Aesthetic Theory*, on his nominalistic attempt always to replace the indeterminate "expressivo" with a specific thing expressed (104–5).

70. To make a comparable point Adorno also argues that in an over faithful performance, "the performance sounds like its own phonograph record. The dynamic is so predetermined that there are no longer any tensions at all. The contradictions of the musical material are so inexorably resolved in the moment of sound that it never arrives at the synthesis, the self-production of the work, which reveals the meaning of every Beethoven symphony. What is the point of the symphonic effort when the material on which that effort was to be tested has already been ground up?" "On the Fetish Character of Music and the Regression of Hearing," translated and reprinted in *Theodor W. Adorno: Essays on Music*, ed. Richard Leppert (Berkeley: University of California Press, 2002), 301 (*GS* 14, 31–32).

71. Adorno, *Aesthetic Theory*, 358 (translation modified).

72. Theodor W. Adorno, "The Experiential Content of Hegel's Philosophy," in *Hegel: Three Studies*, 66.

73. Adorno, "Skoteinos," 109–10.

74. Adorno, "Skoteinos," 109–10.

75. Adorno, "Skoteinos," 123–24. For a more musicological perspective, cf. Leo Treitler's "Beethoven's 'Expressive' Markings," specifically for a discussion of the relation between the movement of music, thought, and language. In *Beethoven Forum* 7, ed. Mark Evan Bonds (Lincoln: University of Nebraska Press, 1999), 89–111.

76. Adorno, *Hegel: Three Studies*, 51 and 89, quoting the poet Rudolph Burchardt, "Ich habe nichts als Rauschen" (used by Adorno as an epigraph for his essay "Skoteinos").

77. Adorno, *Beethoven*, 43 (translation modified).

78. Adorno, "Skoteinos," 136.

79. Cf. Adorno, *Beethoven*, 13–15.

80. Adorno, *Aesthetic Theory*, 222; see also Adorno, *Beethoven*, 37: "Herein lies the real coincidence with Hegel: from the standpoint, their relationship can be defined as one of logical unfolding, *not* of analogy."

81. Adorno, *Aesthetic Theory*, 358. In Adorno's work, "Konvergenz" carries less the connotation of *converging on*, if this means "reaching" truth, as if we have gotten somewhere final, than the *meeting in truth*.

82. Adorno offers a most difficult statement, which, though almost untranslatable, brings together many of the themes with which this essay is concerned.

He begins in a Goethean mode by noting the deep relation between theory and experience, a relation established by their intertwined or doubled mode of conduct. For this shared mode of conduct, the elective affinity, he finds a certain movement of consciousness essential, a movement that makes the interaction between theory and experience dynamic, conflicted, and deeply dialectical. Finally, he concludes that it is the dialectical *Bewegung* between the two that makes his own notion of critique possible. Thus, he writes: "theory and mental experience need to interact. Theory does not contain answers to everything; it reacts to the world, which is false to the core. What would be free from the spell of the world is not under theory's jurisdiction. Mobility is of the essence of consciousness; it is not an accidental feature. It means a doubled mode of conduct: an inner one, the immanent process that is the properly dialectical one, and a free, unbound one like a stepping out of dialectics. Yet neither functions merely as disparate. The unregimented thought has an elective affinity to dialectics, which as criticism of the system recalls what would be outside the system; and the force that liberates the dialectical movement in cognition is the very same force that rebels against the system. Both attitudes of consciousness are linked by criticizing each other [as in critique], not by compromising" (*Negative Dialectics*, 31, translation modified).

83. Adorno, *Beethoven*, 48.

84. Cf. Adorno, *Aesthetic Theory*, 71.

85. Adorno, *Beethoven*, 244.

86. Adorno, *Beethoven*, 118–19. This idea is offered in a critique of the radio symphony, which tends, Adorno says, to neutralize and level out differences in the composition for the sake of comfortable electronic transmission.

87. Cf. Adorno, *Aesthetic Theory*, 137–38 and 85: the "movement at a standstill is eternalized in the instant, and what has been made eternal is annihilated by its reduction to the instant." To put Adorno's argument again in a broader context, it is worth recalling a small article titled "Zeitraffer, Zeitlupe, und der Raum" (Accelerated time, decelerated time, and space) by Adorno's colleague Ernst Bloch. Here Bloch offers a descriptive richness to the idea of something's being "pent-up." He describes the uncanny quality of time's having been "snatched up" and stretched, of its suddenly lapsing, of its being reduced, of its reaching a "diminuendo," of its achieving moments of compression and blissful suspension. In part Bloch's point, like Adorno's, is to shift the attention from everyday experience to the aesthetic experience of works of art, of music, and, in Bloch's case especially, of opera. It is no coincidence that Bloch also finds a paradigmatic expression of time's ability to accelerate and decelerate in the *Zeitlupe* of the box in Goethe's "New Melusine." In part he intends to demonstrate not just the contribution of space but that of time too, in matters of magnitude and diminishment, in the Goethean/Kantian experience of the dynamic sublime. (Adorno is also concerned with the dynamic sublime.) In

opera—Beethoven, Wagner, Verdi—Bloch also finds particular moments of intensity: like Adorno, he argues that in pregnant or uncanny moments, one sees "the totality of a world in the process of coming to itself." Ernst Bloch, *Literary Essays* (Stanford, Calif.: Stanford University Press, 1998), 482–86.

88. "Die Hoffnung fuhr wie ein Stern, der vom Himmel fällt." Goethe's line reads: "Die Hoffnung fuhr wie ein Stern, der vom Himmel fällt, über ihre Häupter weg."

89. Benjamin, "Goethe's *Elective Affinities*," 354.

90. Adorno, *Aesthetic Theory*, 187–88 (translation modified). Bars are indicated in Beethoven, 184, in a text titled "'Beautiful Passages' in Beethoven."

91. Ernst Lewy, *Zur Sprache des alten Goethe: Ein Versuch über die Sprache des Einzelnen* (Berlin: Verlag bei Paul Cassirer, 1913). Cf. Theodor W. Adorno, "Beethoven's Late Style," in *Beethoven*, 187 and 192.

92. Cf. "Vers une musique informelle," in *Quasi una Fantasia*, 269–322. Cf. also his "Über statische und Dynamik als soziologische Katergorien" (1961), in *GS* 8, 217–37.

93. Adorno takes another approach to Beethoven's use of the reprise in his book *Mahler*, trans. Edmund Jephcott (Chicago: University of Chicago Press, 1992), 94. Here he criticizes Beethoven for using the reprise in a way that meets the idealist demand for final identity. Mahler is now the figure, for Adorno, in whose music one may find not a return of what has been but rather a (Proustian) expression of the "irrecoverability" of lost time. This passage is relevant also because it mentions the problem in new music of how one brings a composition to an end.

94. Cf. "The Aging of the New Music," trans. Robert Hullot-Kentor and Frederic Will, reprinted in *Theodor W. Adorno: Essays on Music*, ed. Richard Leppert (Berkeley: University of California Press, 2002), 187–88.

95. Johann Wolfgang von Goethe, *Maximen und Reflexionen*, no. 1345 (Weimar: Verlag der Goethe-Gesellschaft, 1907), 279.

96. Adorno, *Beethoven*, 188.

97. Cf. Adorno, *Aesthetic Theory*, 23–24, 178–81; "Vers une musique," 285, 295–98, and 312.

98. Adorno, "Motive," in *Quasi una Fantasia*, 14.

99. Goethe, *Elective Affinities*, 115–16.

3

Brazen Wheels

F. W. J. Schelling on the Origins of Music and Tragedy

DAVID FARRELL KRELL

> You, Kant, always get what you want.
> Hedwig, in *Hedwig and the Angry Inch*

> Who that has heard a strain of music feared then lest he should speak extravagantly any more forever?
> Henry David Thoreau, *Walden*

One of the most striking passages in the 1811 printing of F. W. J. Schelling's *Ages of the World* concerns the origin of music, an origin not without tragic overtones. The passage is reminiscent of Hegel's famous remarks on "Bacchic tumult" in his analysis of "the religion of art" in the *Phenomenology of Spirit*.[1] Schelling's 1811 text exhibits a great number of corrections and emendations, and one feels compelled to reproduce them, inasmuch as they show how diligently he worked on this passage, trying to get it right. The context of the passage is Schelling's discussion of the burgeoning *life* that springs *volens nolens* from the *ground* of the divine essence; even what seems outside or beneath that essence—and to be outside the divine essence is to verge on nonbeing—is bursting with autonomous life. The ground of God, which is somehow *in* him but not *of* him, is riotous with life, insane with life (Note that curly braces indicate words crossed out while square brackets indicate additions.):

> Not for nothing did the ancients speak of a divine madness. [, which they attribute to the poet and to every other person in whom a power becomes manifest that works more effects than it can grasp. Thus] {For thus} we also see the visible [already becalmed] nature, {which is but

the extrinsic image of the inner nature,} in such a way that when nature approaches the spirit, it becomes increasingly tumultuous. For it is true that all things of nature find themselves in a state that is devoid of contemplation; yet those creatures that pertain to the final period of struggle between scission and unification, consciousness and consciouslessness, we see wandering in a state similar to that of drunkenness, and {as it were} [as though] driven by [devastating] madness. Not for nothing is it said that the chariot of Dionysos is drawn by lions, panthers, tigers. For it was this wild tumult of inspiration, into which nature was plunged {by virtue of} [by] the inner view into its essence, that was celebrated in the primeval cult of nature among intuitive peoples, with their drunken festivals of Bacchic orgies. [as though thereby to lament the demise of the old and pure things of nature.] In contrast to that we find [the terrific pressure of the contractive force,] that wheel of incipient {nature} [birth] turning crazily on itself, and the {powerful} frightful forces of circular motion [working from within], symbolized in that other terrifying display of primitive ritual custom, to wit, insensate, frenzied dancing, which accompanied the terrifying procession of the mother of all things, seated on the chariot whose brazen wheels resounded with the deafening clamor of an unrefined music, in part hypnotic, in part devastating.[2] (42–43)

Divine madness and the madness of the things of nature—these two intimately related forms of devastating madness—are the themes of the passage. Madness, enthusiasm, and intoxication. Dionysos appears in the text as the god of verdant life, of ivy and vine, of sap, serum, and wine. Yet his companion animals—panther, tiger, and lion, the great cats—lend the reference a foreboding quality. Excessive life is dangerous. Schelling is no doubt thinking of the Corybantic dancers, the subject of a long quotation from Johann Georg Hamann that he cites in his 1809 *Philosophical Investigations into the Essence of Human Freedom*.[3] However, whereas in 1809 the Corybantic rites of self-emasculation served Schelling's polemic against modern Cartesian philosophy, which with its mind-body split mutilates science and philosophy, here the allusion occurs in the context of a discussion of the divine essence itself. The Corybants, of which the whirling dervishes are distant descendants, dance the inner strife of essence. Their terrifying rites, which require them to throw their severed organs against the statue of the Great Mother as her brazen car clatters by, suggest something quite specific about the divine father's suffering and pain, to which Schelling's 1811 printing of *The Ages of the World* is most sensitive. If later on in the nineteenth century, with

Nietzsche, music will give birth to Greek tragedy, the most savage of ancient Greek (or "Oriental") cults will, prior to that, in Schelling's philosophy, give birth to music. Schelling's text continues:

> For sound and tone [*Klang und Ton*] appear to originate solely in that struggle between spirituality and corporeality. Thus the art of music alone can provide an image of that primeval, incipient nature and its motion. For its entire essence consists of a cycle, taking its departure from a founding tone, and, after an incredible number of extravagant sallies, returning to that beginning point.[4] (43)

Klang und Ton play an important role in Schelling's lectures on the philosophy of art, held at Jena in 1802–3 and repeated in Würzburg in 1804–5.[5] After examining Schelling's *Philosophy of Art*, I will turn to a very late text, the 1842 *Philosophy of Mythology*.[6] For about halfway through that text, the wagon of the Great Goddess clatters onto the scene once again and is discussed in some detail. I will therefore have to advance from Schelling's 1802–3 *Philosophy of Art* to his 1842 *Philosophy of Mythology* before coming to any conclusions about music and tragedy as discussed in the 1811 draft of *The Ages of the World*.

Absolute Mythology

Nothing could be more surprising than the importance of music in the 1802–3 aesthetics, inasmuch as *language* and *light* are as omnipresent there as they will be many years later in Hegel's aesthetics. Both the preeminence of the eye among the other sense organs, the eyes over the ears, and the preeminence of speech among all possible objects for the hearing ears make us wonder whether music can truly occupy a position of importance here. Is there not too much necessity—rather than freedom—at work within the porches of one's ears, which funnel into us all the tocsins and toxins of the world? In a text that begins by asserting the importance of *absolute freedom* for the system—the freedom exercised by the all-dominating eye, assisted by the all-dominating logos—one is surprised by Schelling's acknowledgment of the invasive power of sound and tone, the pulsions of musical rhythm, melody, and harmony.

Schelling's lectures on art continue to celebrate the identity philosophy—the philosophy of the absolute—that followed directly in the wake of the 1800 *System of Transcendental Idealism*.[7] For identity philosophy, philosophy as such is the science of the absolute, that is, of the totality of ideal determinations and levels of potency in the universe, taking as its point of departure the absolute identity or absolute indifference of opposites (366–67). Philosophy is concerned with particulars—particulars such as art—only "to the extent that the particular takes up the whole of the absolute into itself and presents it in itself" (367). Yet philosophy also, and above all, concerns primal images, *Urbilder,* and one of these primal images is music. Music appears already in the introduction to the lecture course as "nothing other than the primal image of rhythm in nature and in the universe itself" (369). Also appearing early on in the introduction is the art of tragedy. Among the particulars of poesy, the introduction tells us, is tragic drama: "Drama = synthesis of the universal and the particular" (371). Allow me to focus here on the primal images of music and tragic drama.

Schelling's lecture course unfolds in two main stages: first, a "general" part, which considers the construction of art as matter and as form; second, a "particular" part, which treats of various art forms in terms of their ideality and reality. The general part, proceeding through a series of seventy-five theses (marked by section [§§] numbers), seeks to establish that "the absolute, or God" is the beginning and the end of the philosophy of art. God, as absolute, is infinite affirmation of self, absolute identity and totality, perfect eternity, absolute freedom and necessity, and absolute indifference (§§13–14; 380). The very possibility of a relation of so particular a matter as art to the absolute may seem strange, and Schelling's "preliminary determination" of art is anything but clear: "Philosophy is immediate presentation of the divine; art is immediately the mere presentation of indifference as such (this, the fact that indifference [*Indifferenz*] alone constitutes the counter image [*das Gegenbildliche*]. Absolute identity = primal image)" (381). Even when we recall that *Indifferenz* is not carelessness but a prior point of nondistinction among eventual oppositions and dualities, it is hard to imagine that indifference could be anything other than tone-deaf and iconoclastic. Yet in a telling synthesis of the two halves of Kant's third *Critique,* Schelling declares that "in the ideal world philosophy comports itself to art as in the real world reason comports itself to the organism" (§17; 383). Matters nevertheless take an unexpected turn when the unification of the universal and the particular is described as the production of *images* of divinity—in real terms, the production of *gods* (§28; 390). Art is essentially polytheistic, and mythology comprises its essential stuff.

Most divine about the gods of myth are their charming limitations. Not surprisingly, Schelling's favorite example of charming limitation is Venus Aphrodite. She is never more divine than when she satisfies Paris's lust for Helen and so, quite demurely, precipitates a war. No doubt we all wish her a bit more circumspection. "But then she wouldn't be the goddess of love anymore; no longer would she be an object of our fancy, for which the universal or absolute in the particular—in the bounded—is supreme" (393). We do not reason with Aphrodite; we fancy her. Even when Aphrodite is least herself, for instance, when she becomes that incompetent warrior whom Diomedes handily wounds, so that Athena can mock her—Aphrodite must have pricked herself with a golden brooch while she was disrobing, says Athena—and Zeus can feel constrained to tell Aphrodite to stick to what she's good at, which is lovemaking, she is utterly divine. In other words, precisely as an object of derision and playful laughter, Venus Aphrodite exhibits to the fancy of humankind what it means to be a god (394). Primal images answer to the fancy, *die Phantasie*, alone. (We will therefore have to revert to this faculty—to *Phantasie*—at the end.) To Xenophanes' complaint that the Homeric gods are often unethical, Schelling replies that whereas human beings need ethicality, gods do not. For they are "absolutely blessed" (§32; 396). Indeed, later in the course (420), he will say that ethicality, "like sickness and death," is something that "befalls mortals alone."

To be sure, less charming limitations of the gods are displayed in mythology, and Schelling does not shy from them. The relatively perfect images of the Olympians can appear "only after what is purely formless, dark, and monstrous is suppressed" (394). For the formless dark is precisely that which causes us "to remember eternity, the first ground of existence [*den ersten Grund des Daseyns*]" (394). These words are familiar to us from the treatises of 1809 through 1815, though we may be surprised to find them in such an early text. Mythology, which recounts the oldest fables, tales that had intrigued Schelling since his school days, would be nothing without Hesiodic Chaos, nothing without the Titans and their mother, gloomy Night:

> As the common seed of gods and human beings, absolute Chaos is Night, or Gloom. The first figures that the fancy causes to be born of Night are also shapeless. A world of unformed and monstrous figures must founder before the milder realm of blessed and lasting gods can enter on the scene. In this respect too the Greek poems remain true to

the law of all fancy. The first births that result from the embraces of Ouranos and Gaia are still monstrous—they are hundred-armed Giants, mighty Cyclopes, and savage Titans. These are births in the face of which the begetter himself is horrified: he banishes them to the concealment of Tartarus. Chaos must once again swallow its own births. Ouranos, who keeps his progeny in hiding, has to be suppressed [*verdrungen*]. The dominion of Kronos begins. Yet Kronos too swallows his own children. Finally, the kingdom of Zeus commences, but here too not without antecedent destruction. Jupiter has to free the Cyclopes and the hundred-armed Giants so that they can help him battle Saturn and the Titans. And only after he has conquered all these monsters and the final progeny of Gaia, the mother who is angered by the wretchedness of her own children—that is, only after he has defeated the heaven-storming Giants and the monster on whom Gaia squanders the final ounces of her strength, namely, the Typhon—do the heavens clear: Zeus takes unchallenged possession of a cheerful Olympus. In place of all these indeterminate and formless divinities arise determinate, well-wrought figures—in place of old Okeanos, Neptune, in place of Tartaros, Pluto, in place of Helios the Titan, the eternally youthful Apollo. Even the oldest of all the gods, Eros, whom our archaic poems allow to originate simultaneously with Chaos, is born once again as the son of Venus and Mars, thus becoming a well-outlined, perdurant figure. (394–95)

It bears repeating that *die Phantasie,* active imagination, or the fancy, serves as the faculty of primal images. Thesis 31 asserts: "The world of the gods is an object of neither mere intellect nor reason; rather, it is to be grasped solely by the fancy" (395). Fancy "is thus intellectual intuition in art" (395).

These primal images are beautiful, Schelling assures his listeners, even if the particulars depicted in them arouse revulsion or invite ridicule. Limping Hephaistos, hirsute Pan, obese Silenos, the not-so-heavenly host of frolicking fauns and satyrs, even if they are "inverted ideals" and serve as a source of unconquerable laughter, are beautiful (398–99). The Parcae too, who spin and cut the thread of our lives, are beautiful. It is as though Schelling were already thinking what Nietzsche will insist on in *The Birth of Tragedy from the Spirit of Music,* namely, that *schön* and *Schein* are the same word. Primal images shine, even in the night: "—Night and Fate, the latter holding sway *over* the gods, just as the former is the mother of the gods, are the dark background, the concealed and mysterious identity from which they all have proceeded" (400).

Although Dionysos plays no role in the 1802–3 course, Eros certainly does. For the gods are absolutely procreative. Thesis 36 reads: "The relation of dependence among the gods can be represented in no other way than as reproduction" (405). Speculative polytheology pursues theo*gony,* and theogony is divine. It is absolute, in spite of the talk of dependence. Indeed, sexual reproduction "is the sole kind of dependence in which the dependent remains nonetheless absolute in itself " (405). For the future philosophy of scission *(die Scheidung)* and languor *(die Sehnsucht),* such an assertion is essential—even if it expresses a mystery rather than explains a state of being. If fancy cannot resolve the enigmas that loom before it, it nevertheless does not evade them by calling on the ruses of reason.

Schelling has little to say about Orphism and other mystery religions (though see 421), however much they will become important for his later work, for example, in "The Divinities of Samothrace." His passing remarks on Persian and Hindu myths, the latter exuding "an atmosphere of languor and lust" (423), lead all too quickly to a more detailed treatment of Christian mythology, if that is not a misnomer. For, in a sense, mythology fails altogether in Christianity, inasmuch as the Christ enters on the scene to bring antiquity to a close.[8]

Schelling will of course return to the theme of mythology when tragedy is the art form under discussion. Meanwhile, we need only note that the kind of artistic *genius* that conforms to a philosophy of the absolute is one that seeks to in-form *(ein-bilden)* the finite by means of the infinite— the art of sublimity (§§63–65; 460–61). Yet the return to mythology is in a sense already accomplished when Schelling defines Chaos as "the grounding intuition of the sublime," an intuition that is part and parcel of "the intuition of the absolute" as such (465). In transition to the second half of the lecture course, where particular art forms are to be delineated, speech and language are once again emphasized (482). We hear once again the voice intoning its soulful plaint, the voice that resounds in Rousseau's *Essay on the Origin of Languages, in Which Melody and Musical Imitation Are Discussed* (485). One suspects that any discussion of music will quickly deteriorate, becoming what it usually is for philosophers, namely, an opportunity to get the logos going—a conceptual logos whose categories will banish the art of music to the lowest rung on the ladder of the arts and trump tragedy as well. Kant and Hegel will always have fomented this suspicion on our part. Yet with Schelling things are different. In the final lines of the theoretical part of the 1802–3 course,

Schelling criticizes Kant's treatment of music as "subjective" and "vague" (487). He has no need to mention Hegel, at least not yet.

The *Klang* of Music

Music begins with sound, *der Klang*, which Schelling defines as the informing of the finite by the infinite as indifferent—*mere* sound (§76; 488). Such informing both occurs *in time* and expresses through sonority the cohesion and density of bodies *in space* (489). Sound is ultimately produced by the magnetism that constitutes, in Schelling's view, the very substance or in-itself of the universe (489). Further, in every sound we hear concordant tones—octaves and dominants—and even sympathetic tones at the very limits of audition (490). Schelling is clearly the original thinker of that thought, which Hegel makes so famous—to the effect that sonority expresses the first interiority of nature as spirit: Schelling calls *Klang* "nothing other than the intuition of the soul of the body [*Körper*]" (490).

Music expresses the real unity of objects in the world, yet it does so in successive time, which itself is the principle of self-consciousness in the subject (491). In other words, music exhibits the enormous synthesizing power that Western philosophy normally reserves for cognition. Music binds unity and uniformity with multiplicity and the manifold and does so precisely as rhythm: "Rhythm belongs among the most remarkable mysteries of nature and art; no discovery seems to have been more immediately inspired in humankind by nature itself" (492). One beat on a hollow log means nothing. Repeat that beat and you get regularity, periodicity, and tact. Following the beat, human beings count unconsciously, and the work of an entire group of laborers gets done in cooperation and with pleasure; rhythm liberates human beings from their subjugation to successive time by making fortuitous time *necessary* time—and this simply by *keeping* time (493). Rhythm is therefore not merely the initial aspect of music to be discussed. It is what transforms mere sound into music, beyond all mere noise and reverberation. *"Rhythm is the music in music,"* Schelling avers, allowing the mere repetition of the word *music* in this tautology to be the distant drummer for synthetic thought (494).

Modulation of tones (not merely in the modern sense of a shift in key signature, but in the sense of any recognized change in pitch) constitutes the next step. Modulation of tones adds *qualitative* difference to the *quantitative* difference of rhythm. When one thinks of tones as themselves a rhythm of pitched sounds—and Schelling here seems quite close to the later concept of sound waves—modulation is, of course, no more than an elaboration of the music in music (495).

Melody is the third unity, harmony the fourth. Yet before engaging in a discussion of harmony, Schelling describes in broad strokes the dimensions opened up by the unities of rhythm, tone, and melody: music as rhythm is "reflexion and self-consciousness"; music as modulation of tones is "sensibility and judgment"; music as melody is "intuition and the imagination" (496). Harmony will prove to be the coexistence of all of these, a kind of "breadth" expressed vertically on the musical staff. Because the three fundamental art forms are music, painting, and the plastic arts, and because rhythm is the music in music, we may anticipate that modulation of tones is a painterly quality, while melody is a form of plastic art—and Schelling's thought does indeed double back on itself (or double *forward* on itself) in this way throughout the lectures. Already we hear echoes of his famous pronouncement concerning architecture, namely, that it is "frozen" or "concrete" music (577, 593).

Because rhythm is the music in music, it is, when thought "in absoluteness," the "whole of music" (495). It is this that makes the music of the ancients so powerful. A sublime simplicity characterizes it—at least in our surmise of it, inasmuch as no one now living has ever heard it. Carefully avoiding a commitment to either side of the most famous dispute in the history of modern music, that between melody (Rousseau) and harmony (Rameau), Schelling turns to the sublimity of ancient Greek choral odes, the pulsing odes that Aeschylus and Sophocles composed for their plays. True, we know little about how they were performed. Yet we may be certain that later Christian choral hymns, with their plodding beat, are but a bloodless shade of the ancient chorals (497). Although Schelling's discussion is truncated here, we may be certain that he will return to the matter of choral odes when he takes up the art of Greek tragedy.

Schelling continues to discuss melody and the transformation of unity into a multiplicity and harmony as the arrangement in breadth, so to speak, of multiplicity into a unity—melody being a succession of tones, harmony their coexistence (498). Yet he is careful not to allow harmony to appear as merely the latest and most refined of musical dimensions. For, to repeat, even in a single tone there is a harmony of

concordant and sympathetic tones. Nevertheless, Schelling is prepared to identify rhythmic music as music that satisfies "hearty affects,"
whereas harmonic music better expresses "striving and languor" (500).
Sophocles produces plays of pure, necessitous, driving rhythm, whereas
Shakespeare, with his complex plots and subplots, is a master of counterpoint and harmony.

Schelling is unable to abandon the subject of music without referring to Pythagoras, Kepler, and the hallowed tradition of the "music of
the spheres." Music is the expression of pure motion (502): "Now for the
first time we can establish firmly the supreme meaning of rhythm, harmony, and melody. They are the first and the purest forms of motion in
the universe, and, intuited as real, they are the manner in which material things can be equal to ideas. On wings of harmony and rhythm, celestial bodies hover. What we call centripetal and centrifugal forces are
nothing but that—this rhythm, that harmony. Elevated by those same
wings, music hovers in space in order to weave an audible universe out
of the transparent body of sound and tone" (503).

Looking back (to the thing itself), or ahead (on the path of Schelling's thought), to the contractive and expansive forces of essence in the
preworldly past, we may say that God, or the absolute, is experiencing
the push and pull of primal rhythm and primal harmony as such. The
beat of his own heart pulls him inward, perhaps, and causes him to spin
on his own axis and to focus on his own sphere of interest; meanwhile,
harmony expresses the pull of other spheres, other axes, and the primal
rhythm of the heart is interrupted by a kind of languorous exertion.
That, at least, is one image. A different image would be that of the
mother of all things, transported on the rhythmic clatter of her rimmed
wheels. Those wheels, and their well-centered axle, appear to be what
the entire modern world yearns for: Schelling says that in our time we
are generally subject to the centripetal force, since we have long suffered
from dispersion and are "yearning to find the center"—*Sehnsucht nach dem
Centrum* is his phrase (504). Perhaps there is some truth in both images.
Perhaps music is this maddening interplay of centripetal rhythms and
centrifugal harmonies. Music appears as both the most closed of all the
arts, as though grasping at the still shapeless figures of Hesiodic Chaos,
and the most unbounded art, as though soaring in and as pure motion itself (504). Music is the first potency of nature. Everything depends on
how we hear it: it is either the highest and most universal or the deepest
and most earthbound of all the arts.

The *Klang* of Painting and the Plastic Arts

We must now hurry through many theses and many pages of the lecture course—on painting and the plastic arts—in order to take up one genre of poetry, to wit, tragic drama. We are doing so at the urging of the brazen wheels. Even so, however, there are moments when we have to pause, as at the moment when Schelling compares light to sound and the movement of physical bodies with developed sound, that is, music. Oddly, sound is thought here as *Indifferenz,* nondifferentiation: "Sound [*der Klang*] is nothing other than the indifference of soul and body. Yet it is this indifference only to the extent that it lies in the first dimension. Wherever the infinite concept is absolutely bound up with the thing, such as in a celestial body, which even as finite is still infinite, there orig-inates the inner music of the movements of the stars; wherever it is only relatively bound up with the thing, there sound originates, sound being nothing other than the act of reinstantiating the ideal in the real; thus sound is the appearance of indifference after both have been torn out of this indifference" (508).

Though much in this comparison of visible light to audible sound resists our understanding, even after repeated reading and study, Schel-ling's conclusion is clear: "Sound is thus the indwelling or finite light of corporeal things; light is the infinite soul of all corporeal things" (508). Presumably, when mere sound becomes music, the objects that reflect or radiate infinite light are already in motion.

Echoes of sound and music—however finite they may appear to be at first—continue to resound in Schelling's account of visibility, as when he calls drawing "the rhythm of painting" (520), or when he compares chiaroscuro—itself the painting in painting—first to harmony (538), then to rhythm (540). If the limitation of music seems to be that it ex-presses the merely formal "coming-to-be" of things, *das Werden,* whereas painting, for example, represents those things as having already become (542), one must wonder whether insight into the *process* of becoming should ever be made to stand in the shadow cast by any given repre-sented thing. In other words, whereas music, painting, the plastic arts, and poetry seem to take their places in a hierarchically ordered system, the very *becoming* of the system seems to occupy Schelling's attention first and foremost, hence all the fore- and backshadowings. To the extent that Schelling is an archeological thinker, rather than a teleological one, and to the extent that he will always prefer a good story to an apparently sound argument, he remains a musical thinker.

The special relation of architecture to music has already been mentioned. Architecture, like music, strives to return to the anorganic realm of pure elements (§107; 572). Hegel for that reason thought it crude; Schelling thinks it high art. Yet the parallel between the art of music and that of architecture is sometimes disconcertingly detailed: Schelling compares the three classical columns of architecture—the Doric, the Ionic, and the Corinthian—to, respectively, rhythm, harmony, and melody (§117; 591). He suggests, or at least implies, that the "architecture" of the ancient Greek lyre, the tetrachord, reflects the fact (which he has learned, presumably, from Rousseau's *Dictionnaire de musique,* which Schelling cites earlier in his lecture course, at 497) that the oldest musical system of the Greeks knew only four tones in an octave, the base tone, the *tonus major,* the fifth, and the octave. So far, so good. Yet he also speculates that this in turn has an influence on the dominance of *triglyphs* in monumental architecture (393–94). At all events, plastic art is taken to be "the accomplished in-formation [*Einbildung*] of the infinite into the finite" (§125; 617), so that plastic art at its best embodies the *sublimity* that is also characteristic of harmonic music. Strangely—and Schelling leaves this without much comment—the informing of infinity into finitude confronts human mortality, as though every bas-relief and every freestanding sculpture were a funerary monument: "Plastic art represents the supreme touching of life by death" (618).

The word for "touching" here, *Berührung,* suggests a contact and contiguity of indeterminate intimacy. Two objects can "touch" each other; so also can one hand "touch" an object; or two hands can "touch" each other. How does death "touch" life in plastic art? Schelling notes what he calls the "mix" of life and death in the universe, but he passes quickly by; he is reminded of the mix once again when discussing an ancient sculptural group devoted to the subject of Niobe and her slaughtered children. Schelling does not cite a specific work here, although the context suggests Phidias. At all events, an ancient statue of Niobe and her dying children, a group that apparently also shows the figure of Death, elicits from Schelling one of the very few references to death and dying in his lectures on the philosophy of art. Schelling writes, in words vaguely reminiscent of what Hölderlin is writing (in his "Notes" to Sophocles' plays), precisely in that same year, 1803:

> All life rests on the connection of something in itself infinite with something finite; life as such appears only in the juxtaposition of these two. Wherever their supreme or absolute unity prevails we find, viewed relatively, death—yet precisely for that reason once again we find supreme

life. It is, generally speaking, the work of plastic art to present that supreme unity; for that reason, absolute life appears, when art shows it in derivative images, already in and of itself, and also when compared with the appearance, as death.[9] In the "Niobe," however, art itself has betrayed this secret by presenting supreme beauty in death, and the calm that pertains to divine nature alone, but is unattainable for mortals, is achieved only in death, as though to suggest that the transition to the supreme life of beauty has to appear, in relation to the mortal, as death. (625)

The passage raises a number of questions without answering them. How can the connection of infinite and finite ever appear in "supreme or absolute unity"? How can it be precisely *death* that appears in that *absolute* unity, viewed *relatively?* And how, even when viewed relatively, as death, do we "for that reason once again find supreme life"? What has "Niobe" to do with this juggling of concepts—the sort of dialectic that Schelling, when he is at his best, spurns? Finally, one must wonder whether it is to this figure of death in the (as yet unidentified) "Niobe" group that Hölderlin is referring when he writes in his "Notes on Antigone" that the god has to appear "in the figure of death" *(in der Gestalt des Todes)?*[10]

Schelling appears to be describing an actual sculptural group depicting Niobe and her slaughtered children, one in which either an allegorical figure of Death or a stunning representation of a dead child appears. To repeat: perhaps when Schelling refers to the "supreme beauty in death," he merely means to characterize the beauty of the child who is no longer struggling but is sculpted in the perfection and finality of death. The group Schelling appears to be describing is reminiscent of ancient vase decorations, which were often used as inspirations for sculptural groups in late antiquity and the Renaissance.[11] The Uffizi Gallery in Florence (in room 42, the "Niobe Room") possesses such a sculptural group, which represents Niobe and her children along with a Psyche ("Psyche Tormented") and a number of other figures—and it may well be to this group that Schelling is referring. The Niobe group in the Uffizi, attributed to Scopas, rather than Phidias, and dated from the second half of the fourth century BCE, was unearthed in a vineyard near the Lateran Hill in Rome in 1583; the sensational discovery was brought to Tuscany in 1770, where from 1790 to the present day it has been on display. As for Psyche, "Psyche Tormented," with her hand outstretched in an effort to resist the oncoming threat, she stands as a symbol for the entire room. Psyche, we recall, appears as a winged sprite or "butterfly" figure in ancient vase decorations.[12] Such a "soul" in flight from the body could readily be taken as an allegorical depiction of Death. In *Propyläen*, the journal edited by Goethe at the turn of the nineteenth century, we find a detailed discussion by Johann Heinrich Meyer of Scopas's Niobe and her children.[13] Meyer also refers to Psyche and to the butterfly image of the soul (445). Yet Meyer is clearly struck above all by the sculpture of the youngest son of Niobe, a figure of death that Meyer praises as particularly beautiful (432). "The Dying Niobean" is supine, his trunk and torso supported by the sculpted pedestal, his legs extended and slowly coming to rest on the (imagined) earth. The youth's head is stretched back and down, his right arm obscuring the face. There is doubtless still tension in the figure; death has not yet supervened. And yet the tension produces no effects of struggle. Properly speaking, then, the boy is not yet sculpted in death, as we asserted earlier; he has not yet expired, is not yet an allegory of Death. It is the *process* of dying, which is to say, the terminal *life* process, that is depicted in such a godlike way here. The Uffizi's Niobe room, incidentally, is designed in such a way that "The Dying Niobean" is the first object one sees on entering the room, and it is the image around which visitors to the room even today linger for the longest time.

For the moment, however, Schelling prefers to gaze on the statues of the immortal gods, the Olympians. He praises "the supreme equilibrium and most profound calm" in their facial expressions (622). Only two emotions show through: the activity of thought that—in human beings, at least—furrows the brow, and "pleasure and desire, which draw the gods out of themselves" (623). Again, Schelling passes quickly by, failing to note that the conflict of centripetal and centrifugal forces, represented in furrowed brow and flared nostril, is quite sufficient to shatter divine equanimity. The word *Indifferenz* (§131; 623) now takes on a strangely modern, psychological sense: the god is said to be indifferent to pain and suffering. Even Prometheus, "the primal image of all tragic art" (623), suffers not pain but righteous indignation. "Thus in the figures of the gods no expression can be seen which, in and of itself, would show that the inner equanimity has been disrupted [*aufgehoben*]" (623). Zeus does not grimace in pain—at least not in statuary. Which leaves unexplained only that statuette of a grinning, lascivious, triumphant Zeus carrying off the boy Ganymede—one of the prize possessions of the Archeological Museum of Olympia, not mentioned by, and probably unknown to, Schelling. It is not an image of "indwelling indifference" or "contentment," much less "inner equanimity" (624). Schelling's own analyses of plastic art often do not ring true; they fail to harmonize with his own absolute mythology. The Schelling of 1802–3 has a way to go.

We ourselves are advancing to the theme of tragedy, where Zeus may fare differently, but we will pause to make general remarks about dialectic and narrative in Schelling's 1802–3 lecture course. The theses (§§) themselves are always formulated with dialectical conciseness and precision. These axiomatic propositions of absolute philosophy are interrupted, however, by addenda or remarks that often go on for pages. These more discursive pages contain the heart of Schelling's concerns, however. They are the pages on mythology, music, and poetry. As the theses become more dispersed in these pages, and as the addenda expand, we begin to see what by 1811 Schelling himself will thematize, namely, the superiority of narrative and even fable over dialectic. In 1802–3 there are hints of this. One notes, for example, Schelling's enthusiastic description of Goethe's *Wilhelm Meisters Lehrjahre* (1795) as a manifold of narrations, each rhythmic in its prose, the whole constituting a compendium of epic, lyric, dramatic, and even mythic forms (674–75; 681–82). In short, in the 1802–3 aesthetics we witness the subtle victory of discursive thought over axiomatics, even if discursive thought risks dispersion. Wherever dialectic remains victorious, it is merely a sign that an issue cannot yet be faced—an issue such as that of human mortality or divine desire. Only the old stories revive what most challenges Schelling's thinking, the oldest fables arising from the preworldly time of Chaos. Tragedy will prove to be the genre that presents the ancient *mythoi* most tellingly.

The *Klang* of Tragic Language

In preparation for his account of the arts of speech *(Rede)* and language *(Sprache)*, among which tragedy will hold pride of place, Schelling reminds us of the "principal propositions" of his philosophy of the absolute: "The universe . . . is divided into two sides, which correspond to the two unities in the absolute. In the one, observed *for itself*, the absolute appears merely as *ground* of existence, for it is that in which it configures its eternal unity into difference. In the other, the absolute appears as *essence*, which is to say, *as* absolute. For, just as there (in the first unity) the essence is shaped into form, here, by contrast, form is shaped into essence. There form is dominant, here the essence" (630).

Even though the terms will shift slightly by 1809, the problem will not budge—the problem as to how the two unities may themselves be united in what must be, after all, one absolute. There is something about the tumultuous life in the ground of existence that resists total absorption and assimilation into the essence. As long as that resistance prevails in the ground, there is no absolute but absolute tragedy.

In the turn to speech and language, Schelling stresses *poiēsis,* the creation *(Erschaffung)* of things. The ancient Romans called this *natura rerum,* which Schelling translates as "the birth [*Geburt*] of things" (631). The reminiscence of Lucretius, and from Lucretius back to Empedocles (not Epicurus), is essential here, and we will soon pursue it: the creation of things in *poiēsis* has less to do with the divine Word than with the struggles of the earth. However, for the moment, we will move quickly through Schelling's account of poesy as lyric, epic, and dramatic poetry, in order to reach the summit—tragedy.

Schelling begins by recalling the importance of absolute sound *(Klang)* in his system. "Sound = pure in-forming of the infinite into the finite" (635). Language completes the long development of sound by becoming the "stuff" of the infinite as such. "Matter is the Word of God that has gone into the finite. This Word, which still announces itself in sound through an entire range of differences (in variation of tone), and which is still anorgic in the sense that it has not yet found the body that corresponds to it, finds that body now in language" (635). In the identical way that flesh tones reflect all the different colors of the spectrum, speech is the "stuff" that restores all differential tones and sounds to indifference. Speech is the glorified flesh of the Word, luminous and transparent aural matter. When rhythm informs such matter, rhythm being "the talking art" (636), poetry is born. If poetry is not sung, that is, if its spoken word falls back on the "elementary tones" of natural speech, its syllables can nevertheless be stressed (637). Lyric poetry arises. All that needs to be observed concerning lyric poetry in the present context is that it expresses passion *(Leidenschaft).* Schelling appears to forget for the moment the role that the passions play in mythology and also in tragedy; he appears to forget the possible disruption of the equanimity of the gods in passion. He offers the following definition: "Passion in general is of the character of the finite, or of particularity, as opposed to universality" (641). Schelling's later philosophy will remember the shortsightedness of that definition. (And, speaking of forgetting, it is interesting to note that the divine Sappho is missing altogether from Schelling's account of lyric poetry.) Schelling does note that modern lyric poetry almost universally takes love as its theme; he also notes that *elegiac* poetry, whether ancient or modern, "sings of languor satisfied no less than of the stings of unrequited love" (660). Among modern elegies, Schelling singles out Goethe's *Roman Elegies* for praise: "These elegies sing of the supreme stimulation of life and pleasure" (661), as though languor *(die Sehnsucht)*, life, and pleasure were more than merely finite matters.

The fundamental characteristic of epic poetry is that it is indifferent to time. Because the eventual outcome of every epic adventure is guaranteed, no matter how toilsome it may have been, for instance, to build the walls of Rome, time passes episodically and without genuine tension (650). Necessity and freedom never enter into real opposition in epic, and even if Odysseus and Aeneus are buffeted and bumped about, they will wend their way home for sure, whether that home is old or new. Epic hexameter is the representative meter: its iambs are ultimately indifferent to time and can linger or move on, as the rhythm of the episodes dictates (653). Epic is unthinkable without the mythic background (654); yet epic poems themselves do not develop in any way the mysteries concealed in mythology.

Drama and in particular tragic drama differ profoundly from epic in this respect. Drama reflects "a higher identity" than either epic or lyric; it embraces both of these and is the "supreme appearance" of art, arriving last in the order of historical time (687). In dramatic poetry and especially in tragedy, the conflict between fateful necessity and freedom takes shape. Conflict alone enables necessity and freedom to show themselves as they are (689). Here we find full recognition of the fact that necessity, in Greek tragedy, always enforces ill *(das Ueble verhängt)*, and that freedom must voluntarily take on this dire necessity *(das Uebel übernimmt)* (691). *Das Üble, das Übel*, the origins of our "ill" and "evil," means both physical and moral evil. *Übelkeit* is nausea; *verübeln* is to take amiss, to blame. Tragedy deals with fateful necessity, and fate deals out ill. Notable here is the emphasis on victory as opposed to defeat—Pyrrhic victory, to be sure. The "essential aspect" of tragedy is that the actual strife between freedom and necessity ends in a double victory: both freedom and necessity "appear as both victorious and defeated at the same time, in perfect indifference" (693). Also notable is Schelling's grasp of a point made by Aristotle in his *Poetics*.[14] Aristotle insists twice in his treatise that even though tragedy touches on what is universal about humankind, its stories derive from a very few mythical households. In Schelling's words: "Aristotle adds . . . that ages ago poets had brought all sorts of fables onto the stage, although now, by *his* time, the best tragedies limited themselves to very few families, such as those of Oedipus, Orestes, Thyestes, Telephos, and those others to whom it befell either to suffer or to commit overwhelming things" (695). A small number of houses—the House of Cadmus and Labdacus, the House of Atreus—disclose a universe that is essentially tragic.

Schelling now offers a strange formulation of tragic conflict: "Thus we see that the strife between freedom and necessity is truly present only when necessity subverts the will itself, and freedom engages in a battle on its own turf" (696). One must ask whether this is not a formulation for Schelling's own future: the essence of human and divine freedom will ultimately be forced to surrender all discourse of voluntarism, taking up instead a discourse on the *Boden* or *Grund,* the soil, turf, or ground on which the struggle takes place. No philosophy will have prepared Schelling or anyone else for such a task. Schelling can reiterate that tragedy is the sublime art (699), but that now seems to mean, not that freedom is lifted up and purified of all dross *(erhoben/erhaben),* but that the vital ground of necessity will have become the object for thought. Not empirical necessity, Schelling insists, but *absolute* necessity, which cannot be grasped empirically (700). The gods themselves—in a world that appears to be divided between gods and mortals—stand under the sway of such a necessity. Mythology already tells us that. Yet how the gods themselves are to be engaged in tragedy—this question baffles Schelling. They cannot be mere heroes, nor can they rescue the hero or heroine from a necessity they themselves must suffer (702). Schelling ends his meditation on absolute necessity long before entertaining the possibilities that will drive his own later thinking as well as that of Hölderlin and Nietzsche. He remains for the moment far from the thought that tragedy implicates the gods themselves in demise and death, and that every hero and heroine from that small number of houses relates a part of the story of the sufferings of Dionysos, who is the new—and grimacing—Zeus.

Among the formal aspects of tragedy that Schelling discusses, we must pause to note only three, since they will prove to be important for the development of his—and others'—thoughts. First, tragedy is presentation of the necessitous, and as such is dominated by a constancy of plot itself deriving from the "pure rhythm" of its scenes (704–5). One must wonder whether Schelling's lucubrations on necessitous rhythm here have something to do with what Hölderlin—again, precisely during these years 1802–3—calls "counterrhythmic interruption," the famous caesura.[15] Nothing in Schelling's treatment of constancy suggests it, yet the attribution of the musical essence (rhythm) to the form of tragic drama is an attribution that Schelling and Hölderlin may have shared, no matter how far apart they had drifted in their personal lives. Second, Schelling notes the importance of the *chorus* in tragedy, as had Schiller before him. To the chorus fell "the determination of anticipating even what would be going on in the spectator, the movement within his deepest soul, both his being caught up and his being able to reflect, not allowing the spectator to be free even in this respect, and thereby captivating him utterly by means of the art" (706). Once again, one is reminded of what Hölderlin will see as the very purpose of caesura, namely, a simultaneous engagement in the entire sweep of the play and a reflection upon the play's representations *as* representation. Third, and last, Schelling affirms the importance of Aristotelian catharsis, taking it in a more refined sense than it is usually taken. At least in the plays of Aeschylus and Sophocles, catharsis is not the purging of pity and fear; rather, catharsis works on the soul of the spectator by purifying the passions (709). Tragedy seeks "to perfect them in themselves and to make them whole, not to eradicate and disperse them" (709).

So much for the 1802–3 *Philosophy of Art* on tragedy. Let us now advance forty years, to the end of Schelling's career, with the Berlin lectures on the *Philosophy of Mythology* of 1842–43, returning then to our original passage from the 1811 printing of *The Ages of the World,* obeying in all this the rhythm of the brazen wheels of the Great Goddess. Let us see whether our archaeology has dug up any useful artifacts and then come to a close.

Ironclad Necessity

Midway through his 1842–43 lectures in Berlin on the philosophy of mythology, Schelling begins to discuss the orgiastic cults—he needs to refer to them inasmuch as his absolute mythology culminates, according to his own view, in the mystery religions (351–52). He traces the multiple senses of *Orgiasmus,* including the Greek word for anger and rage *(Wuth, Zorn),* namely, *orgē,* as well as the original word for reaching out in desire, *oregō.*

Thus begins his confrontation with the Phrygian Mother, Kybele. She is the middle figure among the three great goddesses, Urania coming before her and Demeter after her.

She descends from the mountain, is herself a *katabolē*, in order thereby to become the very ground of the heretofore efficacious god (353). It is likely, given a reference that Schelling makes here, that Lucretius is the source for Schelling's entire description of the Great Goddess in her chariot (361). Lucretius interrupts his discussion in book 2 of *De rerum natura* of the original kinds contained within Mother Earth, a discussion heavily influenced by Anaxagoras and Empedocles (though not, Schelling says, Epicurus), with an account of the goddess herself:

Therefore she alone is called Great Mother of the gods, and Mother of the wild beasts, and genetrix of our bodies. She it is of whom the ancient and learned poets of the Greeks have sung, that seated in a chariot she drives a pair of lions, thus teaching that the great world is poised in the spacious air, and that earth cannot rest on earth. They have yoked wild beasts because any offspring, however wild, ought to be softened and vanquished by the kindly acts of the parents. And they have surrounded the top of her head with a mural crown, because embattled in excellent positions she sustains cities; which emblem now adorns the divine Mother's image as she is carried over the great earth in awful estate. She it is whom different nations in their ancient ritual acclaim as the Idaean Mother, and give her troops of Phrygians to escort her, because men declare that first from that realm came the grains, which they spread over the round world. They give her eunuchs, as wishing to indicate that those who have violated the majesty of the mother, and have been found to be ungrateful to their parents, should be thought unworthy to bring living offspring into the regions of light. The taut tom-toms thunder under the open palm, the concave cymbals sound around, horns with hoarse-echoing blare affright, hollow pipes prick up the spirits with their Phrygian cadences, martial arms show a front of violent fury, that they may amaze the ungrateful minds and impious hearts of the vulgar with fear through the goddess's majesty. Therefore, as soon as she rides through mighty cities, silently blessing mankind with unspoken benediction [*munificat tacita mortalis muta salute*], they bestrew the whole path of her progress with silver and copper, enriching it with bounteous largesse, and snow down rose-flowers in a shower, overshadowing the Mother and her escorting troop. Here an armed group, whom the Greeks name the Curetes, whenever they sport among the Phrygian bands and leap up rhythmically, joyful with blood, shaking their awful crests with the nodding of their heads, recall the

Dictaean Curetes, who are said once upon a time to have concealed
that infant wailing of Jupiter in Crete; when, boys round a boy in rapid
dance, clad in armor, they clashed bronze upon bronze in rhythmic
measure, that Saturn might not catch him and cast him into his jaws and
plant an everlasting wound in the Mother's heart. For this reason they
escort the Great Mother armed; or else because they indicate the com-
mand of the goddess that with arms and valor they be ready to defend
their native land, and to be both protection and pride to their parents.[16]

It is actually not a chariot that transports the goddess but a large
wagon with iron wheels. She is seated in the wagon with many empty
seats around her. It is as though she has come down from the mountain
to enthrone other gods, the gods to whom she will give birth. Her
pomp—again the word *Gepränge*—is replete with "sacred shuddering"
(voll heiligen Schauers). As she drives through the city, her route is strewn
with roses and the ores of iron and silver. She says nothing: *Munificat tacita mortalis muta salute* (1.325). If there is music here, it is *absolute* music.
Schelling writes:

> Thus she herself is silent whenever she surrenders herself entirely,
> quietly, to the god; meanwhile, in order to enhance the sacred mad-
> ness, or to anesthetize the final anxiety in the face of polytheism in this
> agony of consciousness, the tumult of a wild, lacerating music sur-
> rounds her in a whirlwind, excited by thundering kettledrums, shrilling
> cymbals, grating horns, and the piercing tones of the Phrygian pipes,
> the identical means that we employ nowadays in order to transpose into
> a state of unawareness the warrior who is about to go off to his cruel
> death struggle.[17] (325)

New here is the soldier. His appearance is surprising at first, since
1842 is not 1848, nor 1871, nor 1914. Yet we recall that the original Curetes were armed, and that it was their swords and shields that provided
the first percussion section. New too are the horns, rough sounding.
New, finally, is the opening fantasy of this passage, in which the Great
Goddess silently surrenders to the old, stern star god. The last time we
saw her, she was requiring the god to surrender something to her. Yet
here too the Galli (mentioned in the freedom essay of 1809, at 7:401) are
not absent—those emasculated priests, who "in the tumult of fanatical
frenzy mutilate themselves, merely in order to repeat on themselves the
god's emasculation" (363). Such self-mutilation and emasculation,
Schelling insists, perhaps to our surprise, is the typically Greek way of
saying what the Phrygians portray as a less violent transition to the

feminine Urania—although, as Schelling concedes, the Phrygians too have their Attis. However, let us move back several decades to Schelling's first draft of *The Ages of the World*, in order then to come to a conclusion.

At the end of the 1811 passage, with which we began, and which so strikingly identifies the brazen wheels of the goddess as the source of both divine tragedy and a music that anaesthetizes and devastates, Schelling reminds us of the helplessness of essence: there is no midwife to aid the primal essence in its "terrifying loneliness," no one there to help (43). Schelling finds corroboration for the truth of his drastic description of this primordial Age of Chaos in the following happenstance—and with this he closes the section (the third of four in the 1811 printing). The figure of the "spinning wheel of birth," which is the very madness that "wildly lacerates itself," makes it seem as though the cutting of the mother through episiotomy or of the newborn's cord at birth were indistinguishable from emasculation. "Even now," says Schelling, that wheel grinding away on its axis "is what is innermost in all things" *(das innerste aller Dinge)* (43). The innermost essence of things "can be mastered and, as it were, be compensated for, by the light of a higher intellect," which, however, is but one product of "the proper force of nature and all its production" (43). The only thing that remains mysterious—and it remains mysterious throughout Schelling's philosophy, from beginning to end—is how anything like absolute intellect and pure reason could ever have been spun off by such a brazen wheel, spinning with ironclad necessity.

The problem of "The Past," which is the title of the first (and the last) volume of *The Ages of the World*, is that the past is being thought of as an eon that is utterly remote and elevated. The past is, paradoxically, the preworldly time of the world. "That divine Chaos," Schelling calls it (38).[18] Chaos is godly in the sense that it is the ground of divine essence as such—the turf on which ironclad necessity and a nonvoluntaristic freedom struggle. Our passage begins with an allusion to "divine madness" in Plato's *Phaedrus*. Yet whereas Plato is thinking of poetic and mantic inspiration, Schelling is thinking of manic divinity itself—manic, if not maniac. For on its way to glory the absolute suffers every sort of monstrous birth—if only in its head. It could account itself king of infinite space were it not that it has bad dreams—"heavy dreams, welling up from the past" (41). *Angst* is its entire sensibility as it goes to confront "all the terrors of its own essence" (41). It suffers scission after scission, like an onion that feels its outer layers being peeled away and can only fear for its nonexistent center. Essence "trembles for its very existence," as the severed layers, one by one, suggest the truth of the vacuous center.

There is nothing cheering or cheerful in the Bacchic tumult that nature undergoes. The inebriation of those creatures that are caught in the final toils and coils of scission and unification produces not visions of sugarplums but delirium tremens. Like Io, stung by the gadfly, or Pentheus, dazzled and dazed by the god, spirit suffers delusions. Dionysos, left out of the panoply of Olympians in 1802–3, returns with a vengeance to claim his or her rights. (His or her? Pentheus is unsure: he sees Aphrodite smiling out of the eyes of the stranger, and when he goes to spy on the revels of the women in the mountains, he goes in drag, hoping he is one of them.) The great cats, the felines, pull the chariot of Dionysos, which is the first chariot we see in the passage, though it will not be the last.

Traffic thickens. We soon see another chariot. The tumult of nature is also called a *Begeisterung*, which Schelling would want us to understand inspirationally as a kind of enthusiasm that produces spirit. Yet in the context of "The Past," it is more like the classical Walpurgisnacht of Goethe's *Faust II,* the saturnalia of all hundred-armed Giants and craggy Cyclopes. The ancient peoples, intimating the secret heart of nature in Chaos, celebrate Bacchic orgies. These are not suburban adventures in desperado sex but lamentations of the destruction of the old order. The word *Wogegen* now falls in the passage, difficult to translate and to assess. Does it mean that the centripetal force about to be described *opposes* the turmoil? What sense would that make? For it is the closure of essence in its own bad dreams that causes the turmoil in the first place. Chaos is of the essence. For the wheel that is spinning on its own axis is itself called *wahnsinnig,* repeating once again the "divine madness" *(Wahnsinn)* of the opening line and the "drivenness" of the things in "madness" *(Wahnsinn)* of a later line. "It is the wheel of incipient . . ." Schelling begins to write. He first writes *Natur* (nature), then, remembering the lesson of the *rerum natura* in Lucretius and Empedocles, and perhaps also Jacob Böhme, *Geburt* (birth). (In his *Introduction to the Philosophy of Revelation,* Schelling tells us that he has learned this expression, *das Rad der Natur oder der Geburt,* from Böhme—that "truly theogonic nature," who is so important to Schelling from 1809 onward.)[19] These scissions of nature or birth are parturings, cuttings of the cord, the sort of thing that fathers seldom suffer, or suffer only once. The intimating peoples, sensing the frightful forces that drive them about, invent a form of pomp and circumstance that imitates the cycle of births—and, presumably, deaths: they spin in rhythmic dance to the point of entrancement. Or, alternatively, they call for a procession, the shattering or agitating procession "of the mother of all things."

Like Dionysos, the mother too rides in a chariot or wagon drawn by the great cats. The wheels of the chariot turn as the cycles of birth and death in incipient nature—for death is part of the "mix." The wheels themselves are *ehern,* perhaps ironclad, or hooped in bronze, inasmuch as the German translations of Homeric Greek often translate copper and iron indiscriminately, as some sort of unspecified ore or metal. Whatever the metal, it produces a rough sort of music, partly anesthetizing, partly lacerating—*zerreissend,* which is exactly what those great cats of hers would do. The essence of this overwhelming music is the *rhythm* of that clangor, the raw sound of metal on cobblestone or marble pavement, a rhythm that is obeyed by the throwing arm of the Corybants. One would certainly prefer another sort of image and another form of cult, less drastic, but, as Schelling says, there is no one there to help.

Klang und Ton alike appear in the struggle between spirituality and corporeality. Modulation of tone supplies all the differences—the spokes of the wheel joining circumference to hub—in the incipient world of nature. Modulation is sensibility and judgment, and these would be of enormous help to the trembling essence in its present position. Intuition, imagination, and breadth would also help. For melody and harmony alone can supply the constancy and synthetic power that the cycles of nature need to survive the reign of Chaos. Harmony would also provide the flesh tones, melody the architecture and the sculpted bodily frame, the two of them together guaranteeing coexistence and succession. With succession we are back at the hearty affects of rhythm, though the striving and languor of harmony are not far. *Tonkunst,* the art of rhythms and tones, is alone adequate to essence in the time of Chaos. One might prefer a pure Word, or pure Reason, but Kant does not always get what he wants. When it comes to music, Kant's nettlesome neighbors, the prisoners of Königsberg who raise their raucous voices in hymns of praise, prevail. We recall Kant's lament:

> Over and above all this, music has a certain lack of urbanity about it. For owing chiefly to the character of its instruments, it scatters its influence abroad to an uncalled-for extent (through the neighborhood), and thus, as it were, becomes obtrusive and deprives others, outside the musical

circle, of their freedom. This is a thing that the arts that address themselves to the eye do not do, for if one is not disposed to give admittance
to their impressions, one has only to look the other way. The case [of
music] is almost on a par with the practice of regaling oneself with a
perfume that exhales its odors far and wide. The man who pulls his perfumed handkerchief from his pocket gives a treat to all around whether
they like it or not, and compels them, if they want to breathe at all, to be
parties to the enjoyment, and so the habit has gone out of fashion.[20]

Alas, if only the singing of hymns in prisons would go out of fashion,
so that a man could open the windows of his house and not be molested!
Kant to the contrary notwithstanding, however, *Tonkunst* alone supplies
an image—not through programmatic music but in *absolute* music—of
the motions of primeval, incipient nature. *Tonkunst* alone elaborates an
intuition of that cycle of births in which death is part of the mix.

The mother of all things could, of course, be the Great Goddess,
angry with her wretched children and collecting her tribute of severed
members, as though by way of dismal compensation. Turn in your
badges, boys, you're through. Indeed, that is Schelling's image in the
1811 printing of *The Ages of the World*, an image not only the editors of his
works would like to suppress—or repress. It is the moment when the
self-absorbed father, spurning all creatures and swallowing his children,
is forced to remember who she is. That is trauma enough for anyone.
Yet the mother could also be Niobe, mourning those wretched children,
her pride and contumely finally purged in the snowmelt of tears. "Niobe"
is the most rhythmic of sculptures, in which the most musical figure is
Death.

However, if only in order not to end this way, speaking so brazenly of
death, we should invoke the melismatic image with which the passage
closes. (Melisma is a sequence of higher tones, taking their departure
from, and returning to, the *Grundton*, or tonic.) Should night be descending, one may hear these melismas of birth and death in the second movement of Brahms's First Piano Concerto, which strikes the grounding
tone deep in the double bass, allowing the piano to meander through a
series of melismatic tones on high—Brahms always allows his musical
ideas as much time as they want, telling them *You* can *always get what you
want*—until, finally, they cascade downward to their source in the
ground, whereupon they cease. Or, should it be in the brilliant light
of midmorning, one may hear them in the final thirty measures of
Bach's extraordinary Fantasy in G major (*Phantasie und Fuge G-dur;*

Bach-Werke-Verzeichnis 572), perhaps the wildest melismatic venture of Occidental music. Although Bach's *Grundton* is always shifting—as though proclaiming the "the law of *Phantasie*" in absolute mythology, and as though creating the churning ground of essence as such—the melismas bubble with life, are insane with life. *Phantasie*, we remember, fancies Venus Aphrodite above all: the goddess who commands not mutilation but laughter and languor.

NOTES

An expanded version of this paper appears as chapter 6 of D. F. Krell, *The Tragic Absolute: German Idealism and the Languishing of God* (Bloomington: Indiana University Press, 2005).

1. G. W. F. Hegel, *Phänomenologie des Geistes*, ed. Johannes Hoffmeister, 6th ed. (Hamburg: F. Meiner Verlag, 1952), 504. For Schelling's 1811 printing of *The Ages of the World*, see F. W. J. Schelling, *Die Weltalter Fragmente: In den Urfassungen von 1811 und 1813*, ed. Manfred Schröter. This volume, difficult to locate today, is a Nachlaßband to the Münchner Jubiläumsdruck published in Munich by the Biederstein Verlag und Leibniz Verlag, 1946. I will cite my own translations of this text by page number in the body of my text, adding the German text only for passages that are crucial to the argument.

2. "Nicht umsonst haben die Alten von einem göttlichen Wahnsinn gesprochen. [, den sie dem Dichter und jedem andern zuschreiben, in dem eine Kraft sich zeigt, die mehr wirkt als sie begreift. So] {Denn so} sehen auch wir noch die sichtbare [schon beruhigte] Natur, {welche nur das äußerlich gewordne Bild der innern ist,} in dem Verhältniß, als sie dem Geist sich annähert, gleichsam immer taumelnder werden. Denn es befinden sich zwar alle Dinge der Natur in einem besinnungslosen Zustande; jene Geschöpfe aber, die der letzten Zeit des Kampfes zwischen Scheidung und Einung, Bewußtseyn und Bewußtlosigkeit, angehören sehen wir in einem der Trunkenheit ähnlichen Zustand und {gleichsam} [wie] von [zerreißendem] Wahnsinn getrieben dahinwandeln. Nicht umsonst wird der Wagen des Dionysos von Löwen, Panthern, Tigern gezogen; denn es war dieser wilde Taumel von Begeisterung, in welchem die Natur {über dem} [vom] innern Anblick des Wesens geräth, den der uralte Naturdienst ahndender Völker in den trunkenen Festen bacchischer Orgien gefeyert [gleichsam den Untergang d. alten reinen Naturd. zu beklagen]. Wogegen [der schreckliche Druck der zusammenziehenden Kraft,] jenes wie wahnsinnig in sich selbst laufende Rad der anfänglichen {Natur} [Geburt], und die {mächtigen} [darinn wirkenden] furchtbaren Kräfte des Umtriebs in anderem schrecklichem Gepränge uralter götterdienstlicher Gebräuche durch besinnungslose, rasende Tänze, durch den erschütternden

Zug der Mutter aller Dinge auf dem Wagen mit ehernen Rädern, begleitet von dem Getöse einer rauhen, theils betäubenden theils zerreißenden Musik abge- bildet wurde."

3. F. W. J. Schelling, *Abhandlung über das Wesen der menschlichen Freiheit und die damit zusammenhängenden Gegenstände*, ed. Karl Schelling for the *Sämmtliche Werke* (Stuttgart: J. G. Cotta, 1856–61), 7:401. See also the edition by Horst Fuhrmans (Stuttgart: Reclam Verlag, 1964), 121.

4. "Denn weil Klang und Ton allein in eben jenem Kampf zwischen Geistigkeit und Körperlichkeit zu entstehen scheinen: so kann die Tonkunst allein ein Bild jener uranfänglichen Natur und ihrer Bewegung seyn, wie denn auch ihr ganzes Wesen im Umlauf besteht, da sie von einem Grundton ausgehend, durch noch so viele Ausschweifungen zuletzt immer in den An- fang zurückkehrt."

5. The lectures on aesthetics appear as F. W. J. Schelling, *Philosophie der Kunst*, in *Sämmtliche Werke*, ed. Karl Schelling (Stuttgart: J. G. Cotta, 1861). I will cite the text by page number only in the body of my text.

6. F. W. J. Schelling, *Philosophie der Mythologie*, in *Sämmtliche Werke*, ed. Karl Schelling (Stuttgart: J. G. Cotta, 1861), 2:1–674. For the passages on the Great Goddess, see 351–62.

7. F. W. J. Schelling, *System des transzendentalen Idealismus*, Philosophische Bibliothek Band 254 (Hamburg: Felix Meiner, 1957). Schelling's fascination with Greek mythology—and even with a "new mythology" for his own time— in the lectures on art is completely continuous with the 1800 *System*. See *Sämmtliche Werke* 3:619, 629.

8. Schelling refers to the Christ in a phrase that will become vital for Heidegger's *Contributions to Philosophy:* the source of the title of one of the most mysterious sections of the *Beiträge* is clearly Schelling, who refers to the Christ as "the last god" *(der letzte Gott)*. See Martin Heidegger, *Beiträge zur Philosophie (Vom Ereignis)*, Gesamtausgabe vol. 65, from the years 1936–1938 (Frankfurt am Main: V. Klostermann, 1989).

9. The sentence is difficult to unravel: *Da es nun überhaupt Werk der plastischen Kunst ist, jene höchste Einheit darzustellen, so erscheint das absolute Leben, von dem sie die Abbilder zeigt, an und für sich schon, und verglichen mit der Erscheinung, als Tod.*

10. Friedrich Hölderlin, *Sämtliche Werke und Briefe in drei Bänden*, ed. Jochen Schmidt (Frankfurt am Main: Deutscher Klassiker Verlag, 1994), 2:917.

11. I owe this insight to the late Professor Dr. Carlo Petzold of the Univer- sity of Tübingen. In a personal communication, Professor Petzold referred me to the article on "Niobe" in the *Realenzyklopädie*, 17/1:698.

12. Recall, for example, the figures represented in Jane Ellen Harrison's *Prolegomena to the Study of Greek Religion* (Cleveland: Meridian Books, 1966), esp. chaps. 2 and 5, but also throughout.

13. See "Niobe mit ihren Kindern," *Propyläen* 2, no. 1 (1799): 48–91. In the reproductions by J. G. Cotta in Stuttgart and the Wissenschaftliche Buchgesellschaft in Darmstadt, both in 1965, see 410–53. I am grateful to Dr. Lydia Goehr of Columbia University for this reference to Meyer and Goethe's *Propyläen*. Because there is no evidence that Schelling traveled to Italy, I suspect that Meyer is his source for the Niobe group.

14. For the Greek text of Aristotle's *Poetics*, see *Aristotelis De arte poetica liber*, ed. Rudolf Kassel, Oxford Classical Text (Oxford: Oxford University Press, 1965); I have also used English translations by Richard Janko, in *Poetics* (Indianapolis: Hackett, 1987), and by Ingram Bywater, in *The Basic Works of Aristotle*, ed. Richard McKeon (New York: Random House, 1966), 1455–87, along with the French translation by Michel Magnien, *Poétique* (Paris: Livre de Poche, n.d.).

15. Hölderlin, *Sämtliche Werke*, 2:850, 913–14.

16. Lucretius, *De rerum natura*, trans. W. H. D. Rouse, rev. M. F. Smith, Loeb Classical Library (Cambridge, Mass.: Harvard University Press, 1992), II, 598–643.

17. "Also sie selbst ist stumm, als die dem Gotte stille, ganz hingegeben ist, indeß, den heiligen Wahnsinn zu erhöhen, oder die letzte Angst vor dem Polytheismus in dieser Agonie des Bewußtseyns zu übertäuben, das Getöse einer wilden, zerreißenden Musik sie umstürmt, erregt durch donnernde Pauken, gellende Becken, rauh klingende Hörner und die stachelnden Töne der phrygischen Pfeife, dieselben Mittel, deren man auch jetzt sich bedient, den Krieger, der in den grausamen Todeskampf geht, in einen besinnungslosen Zustand zu versetzen."

18. We are once again back in *Die Weltalter Fragmente*, cited by page number in the text.

19. F. W. J. Schelling, *Einleitung in die Philosophie der Offenbarung; oder Begründung der positiven Philosophie* (the Berlin lectures of winter semester 1842–43), in *Sämmtliche Werke*, ed. Karl Schelling, 2/3:123.

20. See this selection from the Analytic of the Sublime of the *Critique of Judgment* in *German Essays on Music*, ed. Jost Hermand and Michael Gilbert, The German Library (New York: Continuum, 1994), 24–25.

4

The Will as World and Music

Arthur Schopenhauer's Philosophy of Music

LUDGER LÜTKEHAUS

Translated by Gerhard Richter

I begin—musically, of course—with a prelude in order then to permit the fugue *(Fuge)*—or, more correctly, the un-fugue or nonsense *(Unfug)*—to follow.

The imposition of this prelude is not insignificant. According to one commentator, the composition in question confronts us with what is "probably the most radical musical piece" in history.[1] "Musical piece" is a tricky designation, however, because, in order to appreciate it, one must liberate oneself from the prejudice that music is audible. We are dealing after all with composed silence—not the relative silence that, as a literally soundless base, is constitutive of all music, the origin from which it sounds, to which it returns with every pause, and, in which, as an "after," it ends—but rather an absolute and total silence. The piece is John Cage's *4'33''*. First performed on August 29, 1952, in Woodstock—which, seventeen years later, would become the site of organized noise and of a happy-go-lucky acoustic megacommune—the piece consists of three individual sets titled, respectively, "Tacit," "Tacit," and "Tacit." Having been generated in aleatory operations according to the *I Ching*, their lengths of 33'', 2'40'', and 1'20'' generate the name *4'33''*. At the beginning of each set, the pianist closes the cover over the keys, opening it once again at the end. *Something* happens, but *nothing* can be heard, except a possible rattling and, in the words of Georg Büchner's *Lenz,* the "voice that one customarily names silence." In spite of these strict numerical requirements, Cage does allow the pianist—and the audience— some room to maneuver: the individual sets can be performed more quickly or more slowly, and the *silentium* can be accelerated or retarded. We hear that the piece not only has a point but is a point.

Yet the theme and the form that here become one are predicated on a nothingness whose musical instantiation is indebted to the inspiration Cage found in Zen Buddhism, which is not unfamiliar with the paradox of abstract "white painting."[2] Schopenhauer, the Euro-Buddhist, concludes his main work in an extraordinary fashion by opening onto a barely audible philosophical *analogon:* a laconic conclusion, set off by a dash that, wishing to perform a true and final cadence, holds its breath and quiets its thoughts before the "real world with all its suns and milky ways" collapses, stating "—Nothing."[3]

Could we not therefore say that Schopenhauer's philosophy, especially his philosophy of music, came into its own with Cage's *4'33''*? In a sense we could. As Lydia Goehr, whose essay "Schopenhauer and the Musicians" inquires into the sounds of silence and the limits of philosophizing about music, points out—without discussing Cage's *4'33''*— three modes of relative silence are at issue: the meaningful silence of musical language as non-discursive and non-conceptual; the silence that occurs when the philosophy that speaks about music reaches its limit; and the silent presence of Schopenhauer in the history of reception.[4] This notion of speaking about a speechless musical language is a paradox to which we will briefly return. On the whole, however, Schopenhauer's philosophy of music took paths very different from those that would result in Cage's *4'33''*. As a result, critics of his philosophy enjoy the indisputable advantage of frolicking without constraint in the realm of the audible.

The historical fate of Schopenhauer's reception, as is well known, has been characterized by extreme variability. Prior to the revolution in March 1848, for instance, his work experienced such limited success as to drive his books into the publishing world's equivalent of nothingness: shredding and recycling. Following the revolution, however, he ascended to the status of *the* philosopher, a position he enjoyed until Nietzsche ungratefully broke his teacher's neck. Yet what is crucial for my topic is an appreciation of Schopenhauer's contradictory reception by certain professions and vocations. Professional philosophers and professors of philosophy, whom Schopenhauer despised and even taunted as "scribblers of nonsense" and corrupt proponents of that which is supposed to nourish—the alma mater—returned the taunting. One hand sullies the other—*manus manem* non *lavat*. In contrast, artists, especially musicians, held Schopenhauer in the highest esteem. But their esteem for him was not without self-interest, since their gesture effectively thanked Schopenhauer for the great esteem in which he held music.

Two elements played a decisive role in artists' reception of his work: first, the *ontological* distinction of music in relation to Schopenhauer's larger ensemble of the arts as well as in regard to his "thing in itself," the Will; and second, the *aesthetic* distinction of music as an autonomous, "self-contained," even "all-containing" art form that is free of the compulsions of mimesis. But it is precisely these ontological and aesthetic distinctions that involve Schopenhauer in conflicts arising from a tension between the authenticity of music that he champions and an intended "reconciliation" of the dialectical poles of music's immediate proximity to the Will and its aesthetic redemption. Aware of the conflict, Schopenhauer attempts a resolution that costs him, if not an obligatory self-contradiction, then at least a few argumentative predicaments that, with symptomatic compromises, ironically follow the dialectical logic he so despised and its—*horribile dictu!*—"synthesis." These compromises once again relativize music's ontological and aesthetic privilege by sacrificing what is musically true to what is musically beautiful in a gesture of forced reconciliation. My general thesis, then, is that Schopenhauer's philosophy of music, essentially a metaphysics of music descending from a metaphysics of the Will whose logic leads, as it should, toward the emancipation of dissonance from harmony, is revoked in the sign of an enharmonic confusion that renders the Will that is in need of redemption capable of reconciliation.

Schopenhauer's metaphysics rests on a rigorous differentiation between the Will as the Schopenhauerian "thing in itself" and the "representation" with which he, on the one hand, energizes and irrationalizes Kant's distinction between a "thing in itself" and an "appearance" *(Erscheinung)* while, on the other hand, subjectivizing it. The third book of volume one of *The World as Will and Representation*, dedicated to the "Platonic Idea: The Object of Art," turns to those forms of the "world as representation" with which a departure from the suffering world of the Will begins. Paragraph 52, the last of the book, along with chapter 39 of the second volume, "On the Metaphysics of Music," which is emphasized architectonically through its placement in final position, lays out Schopenhauer's philosophy of music.[5]

Music lovers of any provenance certainly may feel flattered: here, music is said to be singular and incomparable in the ensemble of the arts, indeed, the "most powerful," the royal one among the arts, an "exceedingly magnificent art." With an inmost and penetrating language that is immediately comprehensible, idiomatic, and clear, yet general, it touches human beings at their core because it touches "the heart of things," the "innermost essence of the world and of our self." In short, it is the aesthetic superlative.

But the status of music as an aesthetic superlative is based upon its ontological distinction, an uncontested proximity to the actual, to essence, to the thing in itself, to Will. Music is an "immediate image [*Abbild*] of the Will itself" in the deep movement of emotion. It has always been serious about the imperative—anti-phenomenological from Schopenhauer's perspective—that drives us "to the things themselves" *(zu den Sachen selbst)*. While the other arts provide mere images of images, shadows of shadows—according to the logic of Plato's complaint against the artistic reproducers of what is secondary and even tertiary—music rises from the reproductive society of mimetic aesthetics, which, in a society based on the word as use-value, performs nothing but recycling.

In the context of Schopenhauer's philosophy, then, music assumes a position in relation to the Will that otherwise is assumed by the world as the objectivation of ideas: *the Will as world and music*. Music partially undoes the philosophical transition from thinking about the world as Will to thinking about the world as representation while, at the same time, continuing, according to the architecture of the system, to belong principally to the world as well.[6] In this way music bypasses both ideas and the world. As a parallel phenomenon of equal standing, music scandalously could exist, if push came to shove, without the world. It is, according to Schopenhauer's often more emphatic handwritten papers, "almost the other pole of the world, a second world" (*HN* 1:322).[7] Music is the metaphysical counterpart to everything physical. Schopenhauer's philosophy of music therefore is essentially a metaphysics of music to be understood as an honorary title not merely in the sense of an objective genitive, but also in the sense of a subjective genitive: a metaphysics that both is and enacts music. "Music as such," Schopenhauer writes, "is the melody to which the world is the text," even as this melody does not require a text. If one could explain music, one could explain the world and thus do precisely what philosophical metaphysics usually undertakes. Thus in his handwritten papers Schopenhauer parodies a Leibnizian arithmetic of music that contents itself with mere counting. Schopenhauer's almost biblical formulation evinces the accumulated heritage of Wilhelm Heinrich Wackenroder: "You have heard that Leibniz said: *Musica est exercitium Arithmetices animi se numerare nescientis* [Music is an (unconscious) exercise in arithmetic in which the mind does not know that it is counting]. That was its consecration of the first degree. But I say unto you: *Musica est Philosophia animi se philosophari nescientis* [Music is an unconscious exercise in philosophy in which the mind does not know that it is philosophizing]. And that is its consecration of the second degree" (*HN* 1:217; author's translations). To perform music is to perform metaphysics, but—in a move essential for rejecting any suspicion of allegorization or rationalization—without having to speak in any way explicitly. Music is, after all, not to be understood in the pejorative sense of a resoundingly boastful metaphysics.

To be sure, the music that stands in immediate proximity to the Will is, in its relation to this very Will, an "image" *(Abbild)* of a "pre-image" *(Vorbild)*, a "representation" of something "represented"—regardless of the fact that in relation to the world this music is and remains "imageless" *(bilderlos)*. As such, music's primary dignity, its ontological privilege, its aesthetic autonomy, all appear to have been surrendered, so that music itself seems to become caught in the undertow of retroactivity and belatedness, of the aesthetics of reproduction and mimesis. But the Will is the prototype of music, since, as a thing in itself, it surpasses all representation, whereas music is a paradox, a representation of the non-representable, an image of what has no image. It is therefore possible to form analogies even in the philosophy of music—something that Schopenhauer, as we will see, does liberally—although nothing can be demonstrated or proven directly. Schopenhauer, therefore, as Goehr observes, is able to write about what is immediate in music only in a mediated fashion, a paradox that remains consistent only if what is at stake is the conceptualization of something transconceptual.[8]

In the terminology of the sirens' song of linguistics: though music is a "sign" and has a "referent," it does not stand in the denotative relation of "signifier" to "signified." Rather, it consists of a de facto autonomy and autarky that speaks its unmistakable "ownmost" language. As such, music always is what the plastic arts only first achieve as they become abstract in the course of the twentieth century: not a form that *signifies* the world, but a world in its own right. Schopenhauer never tires of celebrating music's "self-reliance" and "self-sufficiency" in the eloquent words of his language: "Look at the musician, how he triumphantly performs his art, which casts its self-sufficiency upon him. . . . Here no relation, without end, to an other turns everything into want . . . one has everything, one has reached the goal." And, again, "this art is self-sufficient," "self-sufficient and rich for all eternity" (*HN* 1:210).

A case study can be found in Schopenhauer's harsh judgment of two musical genres in a way that underscores the primacy of music. He regards opera as a mixed genre, a compromise formation of a lower rank, because it amalgamates the autonomous language of music with the "significant" language of words, which is alien to music. Melody is everything, while the lyrics are accessories at best. For Schopenhauer, "words are and remain an addition that is alien to music, of lesser importance. . . . With regard to this superiority of music . . . it may perhaps appear more fitting that the text be composed for the music rather than the music be composed for a text. He continues: "Strictly speaking, opera could be called an unmusical invention for the dilection of unmusical minds for whom music first must be blackened by a medium alien to it." If one finds in this context Schopenhauer's apparently contradictory preferences not only for Mozart but also for Rossini amusing— comparable perhaps to Nietzsche's conversion to Bizet—then one overlooks the fact that Schopenhauer held Rossini in such high esteem not least of all because with him one could just as well make do without the lyrics and concentrate on an absolute, instrumental music. In that case music would speak "purely its *own* language." An interesting experiment indeed, deserving of just as much attention as the popular orchestral renditions of pieces composed for chamber music: opera without words.

In the case of Wagner, the daughters of the Rhine would then intone their sounds and syllables only as recessive forms of significance, reducing denotation to detonation: a Wagnerian Dada. Schopenhauer's estimation of Wagner, who attempted to court his favor by sending him, "out of admiration and gratitude" (*HN* 5:436), an inscribed copy of *The Ring of the Nibelung*, does not seem as mercilessly sarcastic as that of Mark Twain, who wrote that "Wagner's music is better than it sounds." But one ought to read the notes that Schopenhauer wrote in the margins of his inscribed copy. Beside a Wagnerian stage direction that reads: "The curtain quickly falls," one finds Schopenhauer's comment: "Because it's high time." Thereupon follows music's categorical imperative: "Ears! Ears! . . . He has no ears, that deaf musician!" (*HN* 5:436–37).[9] Schopenhauer's delightful malice cannot easily be improved upon when he suggests that Wagner stick to writing and leave music alone, thereby implying that Wagner's music is even worse *when* it sounds.

The second musical genre that Schopenhauer judges harshly is so-called depicting music *(malende Musik)*, also known as sound-painting *(Tonmalerei)*. It may not be an exaggeration to say that in his critique of sound-painting, Schopenhauer incorporates Lessing's genre-based differentiations regarding the limits of painting and music. If in poetic painting a temporal collision occurs between the "coexistence" in space that is characteristic of the plastic arts and the "consecutive" qualities that are characteristic of literary "speech," then in musical painting an absolute, autonomous music is seen to fold back upon the "significant," referential language of the other arts, that is, upon the mimetic aesthetics of reproduction. Haydn's *Seasons*, as well as, in part, his *Creation*, and even the pastoral Beethoven, not to mention the noble art of "bataille pieces," all have strayed into this "reproductive" and thus "reprehensible music," whereas Mozart and Rossini, as far as Schopenhauer knew, never failed in this way.

Beethoven's symphonic work, by contrast, is magnificent because the heart of the Will of the world finds expression in the force fields of antagonism that emerge in the struggle between destruction and order as well as in the expression of all human emotions. In a metaphor characteristic of what is believed to be Schopenhauer's *exclusively* reactionary stance, he speaks of the instrumental concert, the sonata, and, above all, the symphony as the sites in which music celebrates "its saturnalia," its liberation from every cause alien to it. In short, absolute instrumental music is the counterplay of the instrumental, a musical critique of instrumental reason. Even Theodor W. Adorno, who, unlike Max Horkheimer, was not an admirer of Schopenhauer, did not fail to notice the central point: "the conceptless, abstract moment," which "Schopenhauer recommended to irrationalist philosophy, makes [music] unreceptive to the *ratio* of the ability to be sold."[10]

Yet it is precisely the ontological and aesthetic distinction of music from among the ensemble of the arts as an immediate image of the Will that leads to unresolved, and possibly irresolvable, conflicts. These conflicts stem from the tension between, on the one hand, the authenticity of music that Schopenhauer endorses and, on the other hand, the moment of reconciliation that he ascribes to it. If music is said to be the image of a Will that, in Schopenhauer's metaphysics, is deeply unsettled, at odds with itself, never content, tortured by and torturing of all that is alive, that is, the very image of suffering itself—then how can it be a decidedly "beautiful," "exceedingly magnificent" art? If music is *immediately* directed toward the Will—which, for Schopenhauer, unlike for adherents of historicism, does not mean immediately toward God but rather immediately toward the devil—then how can it participate in what could be called the bonus of mediatedness, that acquisition of a distance, an aesthetic version of the psychoanalytical acquisition of an illness, which nourishes the other, ontologically and aesthetically degraded arts while representing the condition of possibility for aesthetic redemption?[11] In short, how can the image of the Will par excellence not stand in the service of the will of the Will?

Readers who had studied only Schopenhauer's philosophy of music hardly would feel emboldened to suspect that it was written by an author who entered the illuminated pathological history of philosophical thought as a pessimistic and even nihilistic metaphysician of the Will. Reading Schopenhauer's philosophy of music in isolation from his larger philosophical corpus, we may well hear a dark tone or two but certainly not an abiding complaint about a world of the Will that is suffering to such a degree that only a philosophical Atlas would be capable of bearing it on his shoulders. On the contrary, music grants "inner joy," and, in fact, everything that the aimless and restless Will, this eternal Flying Dutchman, this Ahasverus, perpetually desires but must never be granted lest it cancel itself out: "complete satisfaction" and "reconciliation." Schopenhauer not only introduces an immediate image of the Will into music, which, like all the arts, is otherwise will-less and without interest, but he also complies with the primary goal of the Will: the Will to satisfaction.[12] Already between the "deepest sounds of harmony" and "high melody" a significant teleological context is established, the connection that is said to determine all objectivations of the Will, ranging from inorganic nature to the rational life of human beings. The correspondences that Schopenhauer observes between bass, tenor, alto, and soprano as categories that are respectively analogous to the realms of minerals, plants, animals, and humans revert once again to a mimetic aesthetics, in a musico-philosophical regression.[13] "Quick melodies," without the kinds of major aberrations that may afflict a

Büchnerian Woyzeck, are "happy." "Quick dancing music" is even said to bring us "happiness" without much delay, albeit only in a "common" version. Even in places such as the *allegro maestoso* that are suffused with more respectability, we may, following "extensive aberrations" that the "more noble pursuit" of loftier aims brings with it, look forward to the "eventual reaching" and "satisfaction of all wishes." And whenever we enjoy the righteousness of a major key, we achieve an instant liberation from all painful, fearful, and embarrassing feelings.

There certainly is in music, in addition to the "inner joy" and even "jubilation" of all the world's Ninth Symphonies—which, we could say, made music a fitting object of festivals and which, as it were, elevated it to the level of a political constitution—also sadness, mourning, and pain, and not simply "this or that pain, but pain *itself*." This is music's general—and, in relation to the emotions, rather than to Ideas—Platonic language as the expression of our innermost being, which, in turn, speaks the language of the innermost "heart of things."[14] Satisfaction is opposed by its painful absence, its delay, the ritardando of happiness, the deferral of desire and its a posteriori, not to mention *post coitum* state, the insatiability of restless new wishes as well as the "empty longing" that corresponds to the boredom of the life of the Will.

Yet, above all, we listen according to that double language of sounds or language of sets that Schopenhauer sees as the immediate expression of the Will; next to each major key we listen for a minor key as an "unmistakable sign of pain," next to each allegro for an adagio that, in tandem with the minor key, becomes a "most disturbing complaint." There is even "dancing music in a minor key": the ontological *valse triste* of a double life. Schopenhauer is fully aware, based on his own musical experiences, that the heart of the most sensitive listener is most profoundly moved by the minor key of an adagio. This susceptibility holds true even if the listener is not fond of the newer products of the musical culture industry that pitches a perpetual adagio as a "music for dreaming" or for meditation, a literal "minor-keyification" and "adagiotization" of the soul, which finally can synthesize its psycho-kitschy "letting go" with its "letting dangle" in the musical "health spas" of this world. For Schopenhauer, "the transition from one key to a different one, because it cancels the connection to what came before," may even resemble death, "inasmuch as within it the individual" comes to an end. And all strife within the self-disintegrating Will becomes not only visible in the world and among humans, but also audible in the dissonances so essential to music, the "natural image of what strives against our *Will*." A completely pure harmonic system of sounds is "impossible." At best one may "hide" the constitutive dissonances. But why would one wish to "hide" anything in an art that is distinguished ontologically and aesthetically by its immediacy to the "heart of things"?

In this point Schopenhauer's metaphysics of music reaches its most advanced position—a position nearly equal to the achievement attained in the unresolved dissonance that Stravinsky's *poetique musicale* will explicitly announce as an "emancipation from dissonance"—after Nietzsche's early musical anthropology with its metaphor of the human being as "the becoming-human of dissonance" became more polemical.[15] But there follows that sleight of hand with which Schopenhauer, the most passionate of anti-Hegelians, introduces into his metaphysics of music a dialectical synthesis or "reconciliation" that, despite occasional aberrations, he ultimately allows to triumph. Even more clearly than in the first volume of *The World as Will and Representation,* his philosophy of music in the second volume is decisively marked by this view.

All musical movement, as an expression of the emotion that constitutes an articulation of the Will, necessarily must return—despite all painful dissonance and its relative right, and despite all the power inherent in the *separation* (this too, is Hegelian)—to a base sound, a final "consonance," toward that "harmonic level" that Schopenhauer regards as the expression of an ultimate satisfaction of the Will. The dialectical play of "separation" and "reconciliation" finally must achieve its goal of "reconciliation." The jubilatory major key even "delivers" its self-negation to us by means of a terminological confusion in which the "reconciling" satisfaction of the Will is inextricably intertwined with its "delivering" or redemptive turn. Music, like philosophy in Schopenhauer's metaphor, may "begin in a minor key," but it does not end with it. The most symptomatic and perhaps most moving example of this requirement is Mozart's *Maurerische Trauermusik,* a piece that disturbingly expresses mourning in the obligatory announcement of immortality only then to conclude with its final tact in a major key. In this way, the Will bound for the major key confirms, even in the most incomparable music, that it is a Will to life and survival. For Schopenhauer music becomes "perfect" only "in perfect harmony." With harmony—and *only* with it—does music become a *panakeion,* or general cure, for "all our sufferings," a victorious counterforce. Such are indeed outpourings from the heart of a harmony-addicted musical friar: Saint Arthur and the omnipotent power of music.

With regard to ontological distinctions, we may say that because of its close proximity to the unholy, self-destructive, suffering, and suffering-causing Will, music can exist only as this Will's adequate, authentic, and true expression if it makes the dissonances audible and, if one wishes to surrender fully to the ascetic rigor of new music, to the extent that it keeps these dissonances unresolved. But where music proclaims "reconciliation" following a "separation" within "perfect harmony," it decomposes into an aesthetico-metaphysically deepened enharmonic confusion. Schopenhauer's metaphysics of music then becomes, as in the fourth book of *The World as Will and Representation,* what is sacred, just as, toward the end of his life, in his *Aphorisms for the Wisdom of Life,* "eudemonology" becomes the site on which "the positive" is said to erupt into philosophy.[16] Schopenhauer is therefore already on his way toward that aesthetic theodicy, toward a celebration of the transfigurative character of music as an affirmative art that the young Nietzsche, who attended Schopenhauer's and Wagner's school, later proclaims as the new gospel.

But just as Nietzsche remains an apostle of art against his better—or, more accurately, his worse, that is, realistic—judgment, Schopenhauer too knows just how far the reconciliation that he administers actually can reach. A great disenchanter, Schopenhauer ultimately remains faithful to his philosophy of music, and "music flatters its way into our heart in a manner that creates for the Will the illusion that it could completely satisfy it" through its reconciliation as an image of the Will's satisfaction. So keen is Schopenhauer's awareness of the illusory nature of this reconciliation that only a couple of pages later, precisely at the close of the third book, he feels compelled to add an apology that he knows is only a kind of appeasement:

> Perhaps someone could take offense at the fact that music, which so often has such an uplifting effect on us that we think it speaks of worlds other and better than ours, only flatters, according to the current metaphysics of our world, our Will to life by representing Will's essence, depicting its success, and by finally expressing its satisfaction and enjoyment. In order to calm such concerns, we may turn to the following passage from Veda: Etanand sroup, *quod forma gaudii est, tov pram* Atma *ex hoc dicunt, quod quocunque loco gaudium est, particula e gaudio eius est.* . . . And

> the highest Atman is called pleasurable, which is a form of enjoyment, because wherever there is a form of fancy, it is a small part of his fancy.

Whatever the Will may be, whatever reality may be, what matters is that the Will desires its amusement, its *gaudium*. With this, the Will already has become the *Atman,* a God.

In Schopenhauer's handwritten notes from the first phase in the development of his system, we already find the wholly disillusioned view that connects the apotheosis of music with a full awareness of its otherworldliness in relation to the all-too-real worldliness of misery itself. Music is said to be "self-sufficient and rich for all eternity" like no other art because "it is also the farthest removed from us," and "from the position of our misery no bridge reaches across to it, and our pain, as well as our doing and striving, remains eternally alien to it: it comes and goes like a dream, while we remain in our misery" (*HN* 1:210). Somewhat more moderately, Schopenhauer relativizes, in the first volume of *The World as Will and Representation,* the paradise regained in music: "That which is unspeakably inward in music, that through which it travels by us as a familiar and yet eternally distant paradise, wholly comprehensible and yet so inexplicable, rests on the fact that music reproduces all movements of our innermost essence, but without reality and far removed from its pain." With this, however, music is reincorporated into the world as representation and into the ensemble of the other arts, from which, thanks to the ontological and aesthetic privilege of being directed immediately toward the Will, it had departed. Music's singular position between Will and representation is cancelled in the name of the rigid architecture of the system. Yet, together with the other arts, music now participates once again in the gaining of distance, a distance that Schopenhauer interprets as an initial turn of the Will toward that to which he subsequently gives the name "redemption" rather than reconciliation.

Even art, however, and even music, although celebrated as all-powerful and self-sufficient, "redeems" not for good "but only for moments." Music remains instead a redemption *à* and *pour la minute.* To put it in a Nietzschean register, the redemption through semblance *(Schein)* remains the semblance of a redemption. Only at the end of the fourth book, after Schopenhauer and the Will have made their way to resignation and an unheard-of conclusion, could one imagine a composition such as Cage's *4′33″.* But would such a composition really be of use for anything more than a punch line?

For now, we find ourselves on a different level of redemption, a level on which it continues to be difficult to wish of others—those others who listen to music and read essays—what Nietzsche, with some smugness, wished of good Christians: that "they should look more redeemed." But even on this level of redemption, music remains competent, albeit, in Schopenhauer, more in the form of a splendid metaphor: "Whereas in reality and its horrors our Will itself is what is so aroused and so tortured, we are now no longer dealing with sounds and their mathematical relations; now we ourselves are the tautened, pinched, and trembling string."

NOTES

1. *Big Nothing: Die jenseitigen Ebenbilder des Menschen*, ed. Johannes Bilstein and Matthias Winzen (Cologne: König, 2001), 56.

2. Cf. Ludger Lütkehaus, *Nichts: Abschied vom Sein, Ende der Angst*, 3rd ed. (Frankfurt am Main: Zweitausendeins, 2003), 623–24.

3. Arthur Schopenhauer, *Die Welt als Wille und Vorstellung*, vol. 1 of *Werke in fünf Bänden*, ed. Ludger Lütkehaus (Zurich: Haffmans, 1988), 528. Henceforth quotations of Schopenhauer will refer to this edition.

4. Lydia Goehr, "Schopenhauer and the Musicians: An Inquiry into the Sounds of Silence and the Limits of Philosophizing about Music," in *Schopenhauer, Philosophy, and the Arts*, ed. Dale Jacquette (Cambridge: Cambridge University Press, 1996), 200–228.

5. In addition, see paragraphs 218–22 in vol. 2 of Schopenhauer's "Parerga und Paralipomena." In what follows, quotations refer to these paragraphs and chapters, without individual citations.

6. Regarding the precarious place of music in Schopenhauer's "theory of two worlds," cf. Günter Schnitzler, "Die Musik in Schopenhauers Philosophie," in *Musik und Zahl: Interdisziplinäre Beiträge zum Grenzbereich zwischen Musik und Mathematik*, ed. Günter Schnitzler (Bonn: Orpheus Verlag für Systematische Musikwissenschaft, 1976), 48–49.

7. Schopenhauer's literary estate and papers are cited in the text by *HN* followed by volume and page number. These references refer to Arthur Schopenhauer, *Der handschriftliche Nachlaß*, ed. Arthur Hübscher (Frankfurt am Main: Kramer, 1966–75).

8. Goehr, "Schopenhauer and the Musicians," 205–10.

9. Cf. Hübscher's comments on Schopenhauer's glosses in vol. 5 of the *Handschriftliche Nachlaß*. For a biographical perspective, see also Raymund Weyers, "Musik in Schopenhauers Leben," in his "Arthur Schopenhauers Philosophie der Musik" (doctoral diss., University of Cologne, 1976), 33–48.

10. Quoted in Detlev Claussen, *Theodor W. Adorno: Ein letztes Genie* (Frankfurt am Main: Fischer, 2003), 165.

11. This tension is correctly emphasized by Paul Guyer, "Pleasure and Knowledge in Schopenhauer's Aesthetics," in *Schopenhauer, Philosophy, and the Arts*, ed. Dale Jacquette (Cambridge: Cambridge University Press, 1996), 110, 114–17, and 127–29.

12. Cf. Lawrence Ferrara, "Schopenhauer on Music as the Embodiment of the Will," in *Schopenhauer, Philosophy, and the Arts*, ed. Dale Jacquette (Cambridge: Cambridge University Press, 1996), 187–90.

13. For a critical perspective on this issue, see Schnitzler, "Die Musik in Schopenhauers Philosophie," 149.

14. On the "generic forms" of the Will's movements in music, cf. Günter Zöller, "Schopenhauer," *Musik in der deutschen Philosophie: Eine Einführung*, ed. Stefan Lorenz and Oliver Fürbeth (Stuttgart: Metzler, 2003), 105.

15. Friedrich Nietzsche, *Die Geburt der Tragödie*, vol. 1 of *Sämtliche Werke: Kritische Studienausgabe in 15 Bänden*, ed. Giorgio Colli and Mazzino Montinari (Berlin: de Gruyter, 1988), 155.

16. Cf. Lütkehaus, *Nichts*, 221–22 and 627–30.

5

The *Ring* as Deconstruction of Modernity

Reading Wagner with Benjamin

SAMUEL WEBER

Translated by Eric Jarosinski

The title of this essay was initially borrowed from the provisional title of the conference for which it was written.[1] Although I do not often use the word "deconstruction," this borrowed phrase made itself at home in my text like an uninvited guest. Wagner, who was certainly thinking of anything but deconstruction when he composed the tetralogy, did, however, write a work that stands in the greatest tension to the tradition to which he himself is bound—that of the autonomous subject, which also marks Western modernity in general. The *Ring* stages the crisis of this subjectivity, responds to it, and gestures toward alternatives that, although not completely formulated, still remain groundbreaking today. The aim of the following observations, which will have to remain fragmentary, is to explore certain ramifications of these alternatives.

Deconstruction and Modernity

At the outset of these reflections stand two questions. First: To what degree can the *Ring* be considered a deconstruction of "modernity" in terms of musical theater? And, second: Assuming this is the case, what are the consequences?

In order for these questions to unfold, the terms they bring into play require clarification. For the meaning of concepts such as "modernity" or "deconstruction" is anything but self-evident. It will therefore be helpful at the outset to indicate how they are being used here.

Let us begin with "deconstruction." In the provisional working title of the Stuttgart symposium, the initial syllable, "de-," was enclosed in parentheses. This styling was probably meant primarily to suggest that "de-construction" and "construction" need not be mutually exclusive; it went further in showing how something can at once be constructed and deconstructed. In this sense a deconstruction of modernity does not necessarily mean abolishing or destroying modernity. The distinction of deconstruction from mere destruction is part of the history of the concept, which begins not with Derrida, who popularized the word in French during the late 1960s, but with Heidegger (and long before).[2] In the opening pages of *Sein und Zeit (Being and Time),* Heidegger describes his task in the work as an attempt to "dismantle" *(destruieren)* the inherited ontology—not in order to destroy it, but rather that "this hardened tradition . . . be loosened up" and that "the concealments which it has brought about . . . be dissolved."[3] On this point, Heidegger writes: "But this destruction is just as far from having the *negative* sense of shaking off the ontological tradition. We must, on the contrary, stake out the positive possibilities of that tradition, and this always means keeping it within its *limits*. . . . On its negative side, the destruction does not relate itself toward the past; its criticism is aimed at 'today' and at the prevalent way of treating the history of ontology. . . . But to bury the past in nullity is not the purpose of this destruction; its aim is *positive;* its negative function remains unexpressed and indirect."[4]

No matter how Derrida distances himself from Heidegger on various important points, this description also applies to deconstruction. As with Heidegger, by re-marking consecrated or conventional boundaries, Derrida releases possibilities from the "hidebound tradition" in which they are otherwise largely trapped. In other words, propositions and artifacts that claim to constitute a comprehensive system are reinscribed with respect to their enabling limits, thus making way for something else to emerge.

For our purposes these brief and highly schematic definitions should suffice to shield deconstruction from the crudest misunderstandings, such as its equation with nihilism. Things become more difficult, however, as soon as one attempts to define the second term involved: modernity. Here no sharp delineation is possible. It is not that the designation "modernity" is entirely vague; but the direction in which its various meanings point cannot be as clearly determined as can the distinction between deconstruction, on the one hand, and destruction, on the other. If the word "deconstruction" signified nothing but "destruction," it could never have exercised the fascination to which its widespread acceptance and usage today attest. Why bother to speak of "deconstruction" when "destruction" would do?

Turning to the concept of modernity, we find a markedly different situation. Here there are so many different usages and interpretations that one is forced to choose if one is not to exceed the limits of a lecture or an essay. To simplify matters as much as possible, I will limit my discussion of the term to the dictionary definitions. Dictionary definitions have two great advantages: they are relatively concise, and their authors need not worry much about conceptual consistency. They simply reflect the way a word is generally used at a given point in time, or rather, the way most people *think* that a word is used. A glance at the practical application of words is sometimes more productive than the dogged attempt to cull a meaning from them. The following are two definitions of the German term *modern* taken from a current (German) dictionary.

> **modern** (adj. adjective) 1. in accordance with fashion, current taste, up to date <the dress is no longer *modern;* all the rooms are *modernly* furnished> 1.1. contemporary <*modern* art; a *modern* person open to the problems of the present>

So far, so good. Yet the second definition contains a surprise:

> **mo-dern** (v. verb, verb 400) to molder, rot <the wet leaves *moldered* on the ground; *moldering* wood>

Naturally, this is a coincidence, simply a case of homonyms. For the adjective mo*dern,* of course, has nothing to do with the German verb *mo*dern, at least not lexically or etymologically. Yet can we be sure that this nonrelationship is absent from the thing itself? Can we exclude the possibility that there might exist a curious—or as Heidegger might have said, a *questionable*—connection between the process of moldering and the nature of the modern?

I am not the first to arrive at this speculation. It haunts the writings of one of the most influential thinkers of modernity, Walter Benjamin. He always insisted on thinking of modernity in relation not only to the archaic but also to processes of decay. The text in which Benjamin most fully fleshes out this view of modernity is his failed habilitation thesis, *Ursprung des deutschen Trauerspiels* (The origin of the German mourning play).[5] The context he examines in the work is seventeenth-century Germany, yet his analysis of this period is undertaken from a perspective that implicitly anticipates all subsequent developments. In the German *Trauerspiel* of the baroque period, Benjamin does not merely view an individual genre during a particular period of German history; rather, in addition and foremost, he examines the very origin of modernity itself. And because for Benjamin origin is not a single occurrence but rather a discontinuous process changing in each iteration, he identifies a particular historical phenomenon, the baroque *Trauerspiel,* as the origin of modernity. According to Benjamin, this modernity is distinguished by two main characteristics: it presents itself on the one hand as a nightmare, on the other as a staging *(Inszenierung).* It is precisely these two characteristics that also mark the notion of myth at the root of Wagner's tetralogy.

To more closely examine whether more than a merely pessimistic notion of modernity links Benjamin's *Trauerspiel* and Wagner's *Bühnenfestspiel* (theatrical festival), the following analysis will proceed in three steps. First, Benjamin's theory of modernity will be briefly outlined on the basis of his treatment of the German *Trauerspiel.* Second, the perspective this opens on modernity will be used as a lens through which to read various passages from the tetralogy as well as Wagner's aesthetic writings. Third, these readings will be used to recast the question of the deconstruction of modernity as a question of theater.

First let us consider Benjamin's notion of modernity. This is somewhat difficult to outline, because nowhere is it systematically explicated; yet *Ursprung des deutschen Trauerspiels* contains some important clues that can be referenced here.

According to Benjamin, modernity consists essentially in two moments. The first is a traumatic shock, which not coincidentally coincides with the *origin* of the German *Trauerspiel.* Benjamin links this shock to the Reformation and to Luther in particular. He describes the relation between Reformation and *Trauerspiel* as follows:

The great German dramatists of the baroque were Lutherans. Whereas in the decades of the Counter-Reformation, Catholicism had penetrated secular life with all the power of its discipline, the relationship of Lutheranism to the everyday had always been antinomic. The rigorous morality of its teachings in respect of civic conduct stood in sharp contrast to its renunciation of "good works." By denying the latter any special miraculous spiritual effect, making the soul dependent on grace through faith, . . . it did, it is true, instill into the people a strict sense of obedience to duty, but in its great men, it produced melancholy. Even in Luther himself, the last two decades of whose life are filled with an increasing heaviness of soul, there are signs of a reaction against the storming of good works. . . . Human actions were deprived of all value. Something new arose: an empty world.[6]

The modern emerges from this violent "reaction" as a countermovement that Benjamin in his work on the baroque associates with the Counter Reformation, whereas a decade later he will identify its return in the nineteenth century with the post-Napoleonic "restoration." The possibility of such a return, however, is already anticipated in his initial determination of the origin, in his "epistemo-critical" prologue to the book on the mourning play. The originary phenomenon, he writes there, consists precisely in a movement of return, one that can never complete itself and therefore never repeats itself *identically*. Like the origin itself, modernity determines its course through a certain striving: "On the one hand, it needs to be recognized as a process of restoration and reestablishment but, on the other hand, and precisely because of this, as something imperfect and incomplete" (45). Accordingly, it alone is the perpetually incomplete "restoration" that is "originary." In the age of the baroque, this origin reacts to the emptying of the world by the Reformation, namely, as the Counter Reformation. This reaction is directed primarily at the "storming of works," which Benjamin relates to Luther's emphasis on faith as the sole path to grace. In the seventeenth century this resistance to the storming of works takes the form of the Counter Reformation, which, however, is not limited to one of the two Christian denominations instead pervading both.[7] It reacts to the radically antinomian questioning of all established authority by Luther, in an attempt to bolster all institutions shaken by it. Viewed as such, this movement, which would later shape all modernity, can be understood as fundamentally reactionary and restorative.

Yet Benjamin's interest in a speculative construction of a philosophy of history does not lie solely in the interpretation of the Counter Reformation as a decisive movement of modernity but rather in the manner in which this countermovement is represented in the seventeenth century. Not until the *Trauerspiel* is seen in this way does its significance become clear: "There was no answer to this except perhaps in the morality of ordinary people—'honesty in the small things,' 'upright living'—which developed at this time. . . . For those who looked deeper saw the scene of their existence as a rubbish heap of partial, inauthentic actions. . . . Mourning is the state of mind in which feeling revives the empty world in the form of a mask, and derives an enigmatic satisfaction in contemplating it" (139).

Mourning as Benjamin describes it here is not primarily an emotional state or a psychological bearing but rather a theatrical practice. Mourned is not only the horrific destruction that the Thirty Years' War left behind but also the near abandonment of the hope that meaning could be found in such destruction. What is mourned are the "good works" that no longer pave the way to salvation. Yet the vacuum this creates is not only experienced negatively: it also becomes the site of new possibilities. If the world exists only in order to fall, it can still be "revived in the form of a mask." Such a masked *revival* relates to Christian *resurrection* as the "natural history" of the *Trauerspiel* does to the eschatological story of salvation. The Lutheran "storming of works" divests that narrative of its claim to be a tale of salvation. For Benjamin, Paul Klee's *Angelus Novus* will come to encapsulate the reaction of history to this storm. What remains implicit in his various accounts of this angel does, however, become manifest in his discussion of the German baroque, namely, that the reaction to the storming of the work can only be *theatrical*.[8]

Why must this response necessarily be theatrical? Because theater has always questioned, implicitly but practically, the status of *works*. It deals with *pieces* or *plays (Stücke, pieces)*, but never with works. Constitutive of the play is that it must be *performed*. Theatrical performances can never be completely separated from their spatial and temporal localizations: They are tied to a stage and hence can never lay claim to the kind of permanence aspired to by (and often attributed to) the "work" of *art*. To the extent that the notion of a durable work is unavailable, the medium of theater offers a more temporal, more transient alternative.

An irredeemable world in which only faith, not works, counts requires a theater to "revive" it—on the condition, however, that this revival be staged "in the form of a mask." Its horizon remains limited to the
profane stage, whose harsh lighting excludes any and all transfiguration.
No resurrection takes place on its boards, apart from that of ghosts and
spirits. As the living dead, these specters get along quite well with a certain moldering *(Vermodern)*. For, cut off from any transcendent consolation, the strict immanence of the modern world takes the form of perpetual disintegration. Or as Benjamin writes in regard to the German
Trauerspiel: "From the vantage point of death, life is the production of
corpses" (218). Production of the corpse is the decay of the (human) body:
From the moment in which the Christian story of salvation is no longer
reliably relayed and embodied in the church and its sacraments—since
the Reformation, that is—the history of the living is increasingly seen
"from the vantage point of death."

It is this vantage point, however, that brings the theater to the fore.
How does it relate to death? It masks it and represents it as allegory,
that is, in the form of things that are cut off from their "natural" significance and can therefore mean everything and nothing. The German
Trauerspiel responds to a world emptied of (eschatological and soterio-
logical) significance by staging it as allegorical theater. As Benjamin
writes, this represents something akin to "natural history," whereby the
"natural" in this history is directly tied to its transience. It appears "as
the tale of woe of a world" that no longer dares to hope for redemption
through good works and therefore has to settle for "masked revival" on
the stage.

Only such theater offers even the most slender hope of slowing, if
not reversing, the fate of the empty world. Only through the incessant
production of spectacle—disconnected from any claim to truth—can
the incessant production of corpses be attenuated, if not eliminated.
Only a theater that interrupts its own forward progress—its plot—can
provide an at least temporary distraction from that temporal movement
leading ultimately to death.[9] Death, to which a clear meaning can no
longer be ascribed, is lodged in a perpetually repeatable, if not eternal,
process of signification that reveals itself to be the last refuge of infinity.

An empty world, storming works, theatrical-allegorical revival of the
world in plays that are no longer works—these are, according to Benjamin, the most salient traits not only of the baroque *Trauerspiel* but of the
modernity it ushers in.

Yet there is still one last move to be recounted, which is of special significance for the *Ring*. The decay of the world affects not only the creation but inevitably also the creator as well, and this includes his various proxies, whether in church or state. Caught up in this natural history of death and decay is the figure of the *sovereign*. Following Carl Schmitt but also modifying and radicalizing his thought, Benjamin argues that the figure of the ruler ceases to function effectively in the German baroque insofar as it itself is caught up in the exceptional circumstances it is supposed to avert (or in Schmitt, to "declare"). In sixteenth-century Germany there emerges an irreconcilable "antithesis between the power of the ruler and his capacity to rule" (70). As a consequence, the sovereign is transformed into first a tyrant and then a martyr, of which Hamlet is only the most famous example (Herod is the preferred baroque figure). Called to action, he hesitates, condemned to indecision by the uncertainty of the circumstances and above all of its consequences.

With the demise of the sovereign, the dramatic hero loses significance and is replaced by another, very different figure. This figure, less dramatic but far more theatrical, is charged less with saving the world than with reviving it as a "mask." This is the "plotter" or "intriguer." As a consummate manipulator, the plotter no longer seeks to seize power; he has no interests of his "own," for he understands that in an empty, decaying world individual interests can be asserted only conditionally. Instead of forging his own plans, he takes pleasure—a hellish, satanic, Saturnine pleasure—in the possibility of serving his lord and master unto death, the death of the master, that is. It is a master-slave dialectic, if you will, but without the sublating movement from servile self-awareness to freedom. What the ruler cannot accomplish on his own, because it means his demise, is carried out for him by his agent, the intriguer. However, every step forward only brings the end that much nearer. Wotan's relationship to Loge exemplifies this tendency. Loge does what Wotan wishes, while leading him only that much more certainly toward his demise. Wotan, who seeks to create a lasting work ("Valhalla") to safeguard his domain, succeeds but at the same time burdens himself with debts that threaten the very survival of the clan he seeks to perpetuate. These are debts therefore that he cannot or will not pay. Only in *Siegfried III* (scene 1) does he finally pose the question that clearly shows him to be the heir of the baroque *Trauerspiel:* "How to hold back a rolling wheel?"

No answer is to be found in the *Ring*, if it is not the *ring* as such. What, after all, is a *ring?* An artifact that is self-contained. Precisely this containment, however, is threatened by all work that depends on others. As absolute sovereign, Wotan cannot acknowledge such dependency. If he did so, the ring would no longer be a ring—something closed or self-contained—and as such, it could not become an object of appropriation. The attempt to usurp it fails because of the heterogeneity of the labor process, which again entails an irreducible relation to others— which is to say, to relations as such.

In the tetralogy, the ring stages, on the one hand, the desire to create a self-contained work and to fashion oneself as creator; and, on the other, the disastrousness of this desire, insofar as it consists in the denial of the other. As the "proper name" of the tetralogy, however, the *Ring* as *title* also refers to the *Bühnenfestspiel* itself, as *Gesamtkunstwerk* (total artwork). Yet can even the *Gesamtkunstwerk* itself withstand the long-standing storming of works? Perhaps only to the degree that it is broken into (four) *pieces (Stücke)* by its own theatricality?[10]

Self-fashioning in the *Ring*

In light of Benjamin's depiction of modernity, which is decisively shaped by his conception of the Reformation and, above all, of the Counter Reformation, a certain paradox of the tetralogy can indeed be characterized as "modern." At the center of the entire myth—or should one say at its origin?—in its treatment by Wagner at least, is the striving of an individual to maintain and assert himself as a self-identical, sovereign subject against all that is strange and other. This striving for autarchy determines the fate of Wotan from the start, insofar as his desire for self-assertion renders him unable to accept his dependency on and debt to others. In this regard his situation is strongly reminiscent of that of the baroque sovereign, who, as we have seen, is subjected to an irreconcilable "antithesis between the power of the ruler and his capacity to rule," culminating in the "indecisiveness of the tyrant" (70–71). Driven to helplessness by fantasies of omnipotence, Wotan takes precisely this path. His wavering is akin to Benjamin's description of the instability of baroque rulers, who are buffeted to and fro by uncontrollable storms, external and internal, including "the sheer arbitrariness of a constantly shifting emotional storm in which the figures of Lohenstein especially sway about like torn and flapping banners. . . . For their actions are determined not by thought, but by changing physical impulses" (71). This description applies not only to Wotan but also to Alberich, whose "limbs" are torn apart and churned about by a "blazing fire." Along with this dismantling of the body through passion, love cannot be discerned from hate, or, in the words of Alberich himself, "Minne" from "Wuth." The fate of both figures calls into question the subject's desire for self-control and wholeness, especially as it affects their bodily existence. Only such a threat explains the fascination of the rhine gold, whose glittering apparition temporarily at least dims the danger of dismemberment. From the beginning, gold is set in opposition to "the power of love" and "erotic desire"; only forgoing both allows for the possibility of mastering "the magic spell" and of "rounding a ring from the gold" (*Rheingold*, scene 1, 68). But as a glittering phenomenon, gold is the first thing that makes such renunciation possible. This task, which Alberich immediately makes his own, is self-contradictory: His gestures of brutally grabbing and extracting enact precisely the dismemberment they seek to preempt. Alberich wrests the gold from the ridge in order to get a better grip on it. The gripping is, in turn, the condition for shaping the gold in order to make it into a possession. Grabbing—shaping—possessing: the gold is made into a ringlet, a circle, a ring, but above all, into a *work* in precisely the sense that, according to Benjamin, is repeatedly called into question by and ever since the Reformation but also defended and reinstated time and again by the Counter Reformation. Modernity defines itself through the permutations of this conflict.

The *Ring* stages this entire confrontation as both the desire for the self-contained work and the struggle that such desire inevitably entails. The result is a wringing or wrestling *(Ringen)* that ultimately consumes everything resembling a work, including the subject, which sought to survive as a foreman, if not as a superman.

This wrestling for the ring comes to a head in the figure of Wotan. His sovereignty is manifested primarily in the form of his dream of "manhood's honor, boundless might and glory," which in turn assumes the form of a completed work, "Valhalla": "The everlasting work is ended!" (*Rheingold*, scene 2, 70). The work must be understood as "everlasting" in order to numb the fear of time as the medium of the noneternal, of the undoing of the work—in short, of time as a medium of transience. At "work" here is the fear of a finitude that undoes all work because its end is not consummation but consumption. The sole escape,

as in the German baroque *Trauerspiel,* leads from the represented world
to the world of representation, that is, to theater. Salvation is to be
found not in Wotan's "eternal work" but in its "masked revival" as a
self-consciously artificial, artifactual *Gesamtkunstwerk.* This is still a work,
to be sure, but one that seeks to regain its sacred meaning by presenting
itself as a *Bühnenfestspiel.* Securing the sacrality of the stage, however, demands a structure that both situates and protects it. In this way the ties
between Wotan and Valhalla mirror those between Wagner and the
Bayreuth Festspielhaus—as the material and specific location of each
individual performance. Bayreuth attempts to avoid what he took to be
the moribund genre of "opera," a term he never accepted. Rejecting
the aesthetic tradition out of which it came, he sought to create a
"work" that would be capable of producing a redemptive effect rather
than being the stillborn result of a moribund genre.[11] As the site of this
redemptive function, an edifice was to be constructed where no mere
operas took place but instead *Bühnenfestspiele* such as *Der Ring des Nibe-
lungen.* Only such ceremoniously housed performances could reconcile
repetition with permanence. *In the* Gesamtkunstwerk *as* Bühnenfestspiel
the redeeming power of the sacrament was to be revived as a mask.

Yet the *Bühnenfestspiel* can only be attributed this ritual function if it
overcomes the fatal isolation of the individual work through the gather-
ing movement of the *Gesamtkunstwerk.* Collecting presupposes a fixed location, a "mighty fortress" (in the sense of the Lutheran hymn). To offer
an alternative to the isolation of traditional "opera," the *Gesamtkunstwerk*
would have to be housed and authenticated by a fixed, recognizable,
and secure location. Only then could the event plausibly make a claim
to permanence despite its relatively exposed situation. Such exposition
requires not only a special stage but also a space in which the action can
freely unfold without losing itself. This space was to be created through
the construction of the *Festspielhaus:* a building that because of its location high on a "fair hill" could ensure the synoptic or panoramic
overview required since Aristotle to unify the disparate elements of a
fragmented world. Thus one of the characteristics distinguishing the
Festspielhaus from traditional opera houses, Wagner insists, is its pecu-
liarly protective function. The building is to be a "protective, monumental structure" endowing "the ideal work [with] its solid endurance"
and able to "secure the stage," as he declares in his speech at the laying
of the cornerstone of the Bayreuth Festspielhaus. Only then, he tells his

audience, will the work they sought to found that day "not be an illusory castle in the sky" but instead become a lasting reality.[12]

In this way Wagner conceived of the Bayreuth Festspielhaus as a condition enabling the permanence of the work while also being a work unto itself, one he did not hesitate to compare to Beethoven's musical masterpieces. The comparison shows that for Wagner the temporal and spatial condition of a work, of its taking place, is as important as the work itself. The inclusion of place as a constitutive moment of the *Gesamtkunstwerk* fundamentally distinguishes Wagner's approach to theater from the traditional aesthetic of the eternal and timeless *work*, held to be independent of its spatial-temporal localization. By contrast, as *Gesamtkunstwerk* the work can only gather, only fulfill its essence and mission by *taking place* in a location proper to it.

Wagner thereby overturns the aesthetic rejection of place, which extends at least as far back as Aristotle. Because place must be determined in terms of time and space, an occurrence that is essentially dependent on location cannot claim to be everlasting. Every event that *essentially* depends on its *localization,* and especially on a *stage,* is thereby determined by a web of relations that does not allow for a synoptic overview. Every stage stands in relation to a space constituted by a divide. This constitutive split does not just separate the audience from the actors but also divides each of these two bodies in itself. The actors represent something located somewhere else and thereby also refer the audience to something other. In order to gain control of this split, Aristotle, in his discussion of tragedy, seeks to subordinate everything connected with *opsis* to his demand for an all-inclusive, unifying *synopsis.* The setting of a tragedy may be split, but in this perspective it should still grant the viewer the possibility of taking in the whole rather than being taken in by it. This overview is designed to close up the divide. Wagner repeats this Aristotelian gesture in his aesthetic writings whenever he emphasizes the necessity of comprehensibility as a precondition for the optical and acoustic transparency deemed essential to the *Gesamtkunstwerk.* In order to bring about such transparency, the orchestra in Bayreuth was to remain hidden in its pit. In its place—that is, in (the) place of a stage-like apparatus—the semblance of a "mystical gulf" was to emerge as a completely "empty space."[13] In this way the (semblance of a pure) ideality of viewing and listening was to be created. By contrast Wagner reserves his most passionate condemnation for "the scandalous thrusting-forward of this picture so that the spectator can almost touch it."[14] Accordingly, the ideality of the stage set is held to preclude all bodily contact.[15] The body, medium of touch par excellence, is supposed to mark the boundary dividing the ideal interior from the real exterior world. As a tactile surface, the body itself casts doubt on this divide.[16] A type of seeing and listening that Wagner terms "clairvoyance" *(Hellsehen)* should be made possible, and through it the invisible precondition of all sight, luminescence *(Helligkeit)* itself, should become accessible to experience—by listening to music. How can such a notion become concrete? Luminescence becomes perceptible not by the eyes alone, even if it remains the precondition for all seeing, but also by the ear, which makes possible the idealization of visual phenomenality. This is supposed to occur primarily by way of the leitmotif. In it melodies, rhythms, timbres, and instrumentations recur in an altered yet recognizable form. Such a (varying) return of the same remains the conceptual core of the Wagnerian aesthetic.[17] Whether melodic, harmonic, rhythmic, or instrumental, each return involves a varying repetition that evokes the identical effect and therefore assures the comprehensibility that Wagner holds to be a crucial condition for all artistic efficacy.[18] Having an effect means that the recognizable musical motifs provide an answer to Wotan's question: they "hold back a rolling wheel."

However, those who see clearly—or more precisely, hear clearly—face the same dilemma as the one Wotan summarizes in act 2 of the *Walküre:*

> How can I make that other man
> who's no longer me
> and who, of himself, achieves
> what I alone desire?—
> Oh godly distress!
> Oh hideous shame!
> To my loathing I find
> only ever myself
> in all that I encompass!
> That other self for which I yearn,
> that other self I never see;
> for the free man has to fashion himself—
> serfs are all I can shape![19]

The Wagnerian aesthetic remains trapped here in the antinomy of self and other. The self needs the other in order to be the self, but admits this other only as a tautological and specular mirror image.[20] Wotan's conjuring of a "free man" who would have to "fashion himself" serves merely to reiterate this dilemma.

The death of Brünnhilde at the conclusion of *Götterdämmerung* in no way breaks through this narcissistic vicious circle, but only confirms it. The ring she throws away does not end up just anywhere: it returns to its point of departure, thereby seeming to close the circle. The artifact is returned to its original, rightful, and natural owners, the Rhine maidens. The *Gesamtkunstwerk* concludes by closing itself and its audience within a circuit that allows no way out apart from taking one's own life.

Is there really then no escape?

Perhaps an alternative can be found in a completely different type of theatrical practice, one abandoning what Wagner could not: the desire for a work that would endure. Staging here, however, does not mean representing things comprehensibly or shaping representations for the benefit of an ideal transparency but instead means exposing it in its division. To whom? To others for whom there exists no proper name, least of all, *das Volk*, nor even "the audience," "the spectator," or "the listener"; it would be more apt to refer to them as witnesses. In any case, the lack of a proper name points to a heterogeneity that does not allow for an unambiguous designation. One can therefore no longer invoke the "reception" of a "work" in order to designate it definitively. The inseparability of a work from its impact cannot simply be understood as a "quality" of the work but rather must be considered as its "task." In being received—that is, repeated, altered, and translated—the work is at once disfigured and adjusted. It enters into a circulation that never again allows it to return to its origin.

Such circulation characterizes the theatrical medium. Aristotle registered this movement in the concepts of *metabasis* and *peripeteia* without thinking through the consequences of these transformations, twists, and turns. His insight drives Wagner further to introduce the Aristotelian term "wonder." According to Wagner wonder should be permitted "in the poetic work" only insofar as it "renders the nature of things . . . comprehensible."[21] This recalls the way in which Aristotle linked *peripeteia* to *anagnoresis,* to a *recognition* that oriented and channeled the unexpected turn back toward the familiar and comprehensible. Thus, the theater audience should not be left in the dark too long. At the same time, however, even the examples that Aristotle cites from *Oedipus Tyrannos* call into question the signifying effect of such recognition.[22]

A similar tension between theatrical surprise and recognition appears to have played itself out between Brecht and Benjamin in regard to the interpretation of the "lesson" to be imparted by theater. Benjamin viewed "epic theater" not only in the political sense of Brecht but also and even more so in the sense of the writings of Kafka, which though not written for the stage have more exactly arrived at its essence. Benjamin compared this essence to a Tao, quoting Kafka's description of the desire "to hammer a table together with the painstaking craftsmanship and, at the same time, to do nothing—not in such a way that someone could say 'Hammering is nothing to him,' but 'To him, hammering is real hammering and at the same time nothing,' which would have made the hammering even bolder, more determined, more real, and, if you like, more insane ["Er"]. This is the resolute, fanatical mien which students have when they study; it is the strangest mien imaginable. . . . It may be easier to understand this if one thinks of the actors in the Nature Theater. Actors have to catch their cues in a flash. . . . Truly, for them 'hammering is real hammering and at the same time nothing'—provided that this is part of their role."[23]

One has only to compare this hammering to that of Siegfried to become aware of the abyss separating Wagner's motifs from Kafka's gestures. In *Siegfried* the hammering has a purpose: the re-creation of the sword that is to serve anew as the tool for reaching a goal. Here one hammers only to reproduce, to bring together. Yet through the repetitions of the leitmotifs the hammering becomes at once more than a mere representative, signifying act. The music echoes the hammering in that it repeats itself and thereby transforms its identity into a surging that refers to something beyond itself. In this way it catches up with the originary phenomenon that according to Benjamin can never completely succeed in its restorative striving. This lack of closure breaches the logic of representation or the economy of meaning. It calls for a different form of logic or economy upon which Kafka as well as Benjamin focused: that of the paradox according to which something can be itself and something else at the same time—a logic of *ambivalence*, not *oppositionality*.

This logic of ambivalence, however, is what radically distinguishes theatrical staging from mere instantiation. Staging refers here to what Benjamin called the "great, ancient opportunity of theater," which he described as its ability "to expose what is present."[24] Those who are present, whether audience or performers, are exposed primarily in that they are subjected to an other or an elsewhere that can no longer be clearly identified or localized. They are called not only to see or to hear but also to witness that they have been, and can be, simultaneously something other or somewhere else.

Wherever such *exposure* takes place, wringing or wresting is never far away, but without a ring, a circlet, or a work to hold on to. In the ring—but on the ropes.

The *Ring* as a deconstruction of modernity? If deconstruction is defined through the alternative of autonomy/autarchy versus outside control, then certainly not. The *Ring* depicts a demise that starkly exposes the narcissism of a certain modernity. At the same time it attempts to give meaningful shape to this modernity as a creative, work-producing offering and idealization. In order to demonstrate such meaningfulness convincingly, it abstains from exposing the conditions of its own operation. The task of pressing ahead with this exposition thus falls to each respective staging, without which no happenings on the stage—also no *Bühnenfestspiel*—could ever take place.

NOTES

1. A conference organized by the Stuttgart Opera in 1999 to commemorate its millennium staging of the *Ring*. The conference initially bore the title "Deconstruction of Modernity."

2. In a recent interview Derrida reminds us that "Luther spoke of *destructio* in order to characterize the necessity of loosening up hardened theological layers that obstructed the stark originality [*la nudité originelle*] of the evangelical message" (*Le Monde de l'Education*, September 2000, 14). Derrida admits that deconstruction may well refer to something "impossible" but only insofar as this impossibility "is that which is arriving" (or, alternately, which "occurs": "l'impossible comme ce qui arrive"). Regarding his own unique contribution to this history, he writes: "I wanted to emphasize what deconstruction, in its course, has inherited from this memory, but what at the same time distinguishes it from an inheritance it both reaffirms and respects."

3. For a discussion of the admittedly unusual translation of *Sein und Zeit* (*Being and Time*), see Samuel Weber, *Theatricality as Medium* (New York: Fordham University Press, 2005), 375n8.

4. Martin Heidegger, *Being and Time*, trans. John Macquarrie and Edward Robinson (New York: Harper & Row, 1962), 44.

5. The published English edition translates *Trauerspiel* as "Tragic Drama," thereby ignoring Benjamin's frequent insistence on the fact that the baroque *Trauerspiel* is neither tragic nor dramatic. "Mourning play" is thus a far preferable if less idiomatic rendition.

6. Walter Benjamin, *The Origin of German Tragic Drama* (London: Verso, 1998), 138–39. The page references that follow refer to this edition (translation occasionally modified—SW).

7. Here we should recall Max Weber's distinction between radical Lutheranism and its domestication by Calvin: Calvinism was the earliest pillar of the spirit of capitalism. To what degree Benjamin knew Weber's work is an important question in need of further investigation.

8. In his commentary on *Angelus Novus*, Benjamin does not go further in remarking how the angel, whose "face is turned toward the past," also looks in the direction of the *observer*, who thereby becomes both a spectator and part of the "past." The "storm" that "is blowing from paradise" and driving the angel "irresistibly into the future" also gusts above the heads of the spectators. By making the spectator part of the happenings, Benjamin's reading makes the "picture" a *theatrical scene*. The spectators, who here are also readers, belong to a "past" from which the "storm" rises and against which the angel struggles. In the figure of the angel the *resistance* to the storm also appears, which is now called "progress." See Walter Benjamin, "On the Concept of History," in his *Selected Writings*, vol. 4 (Cambridge, Mass: Belknap/Harvard, 2003), 392.

9. That is, to the death of the concept of truth as it is traditionally understood: as *adaequatio intellectus et rei*.

10. Here one could perhaps find a point of convergence with Klaus Zehelein's idea of having the Stuttgart Opera's millennial tetralogy staged by four different directors.

11. "'Opera,' plural of 'opus,' this new variety of 'works' was dubbed; the Italians made a female of it, the French a male, so that the variety seemed to have turned out *generis utriusque*. I believe one could find no more apt criticism of 'Opera,' than to allow this name as legitimate an origin as that of 'Tragedy'; in neither case was it a matter of reason, but a deep-set instinct here expressed a thing of nameless nonsense, there a thing of sense indicibly profound." Richard Wagner, "On the Name 'Musikdrama,'" in *Richard Wagner's Prose Works*, trans. William Ashton Ellis, vol. 5 (New York: Broude Brothers, 1966), 302.

12. Richard Wagner, "The Festival-Playhouse at Bayreuth, With an Account of the Laying of Its Foundation-Stone," in *Richard Wagner's Prose Works*, trans. William Ashton Ellis, vol. 5 (New York: Broude Brothers, 1966), 326. This text includes, among other things, the speech at the laying of the foundation stone of 1872, which is quoted here.

13. Wagner, "Festival-Playhouse," 334.

14. Wagner, "Festival-Playhouse," 335.

15. Such an ideality is close to the evangelical tendency to a spiritualization, internalization, and sublimation of corporeality, while in Catholic rites, such as the Mass, the spiritual is still linked to a certain localization.

16. The ideality of this theatrical space was marked by the clear and insurmountable separation of the two spaces of which it consisted: the spectator area and the stage area. Wagner placed proscenia between them not to create a transition or a third space but rather to reinforce the divide between the two by accentuating the "floating atmosphere of distance" between the spaces. From the spectator "the scene is removed as it were to the unapproachable world of dreams, while the spectral music sounding from the 'mystic gulf' . . . inspires him with that clairvoyance in which the scenic picture melts into the truest effigy of life itself" (335).

17. Adorno analyzed this tendency in his *Versuch über Wagner* (Berlin: Suhrkamp, 1952). That this aesthetic guiding principle does not necessarily *also* fully determine Wagner's musical-theatrical practice can be demonstrated only through individual analyses.

18. As Adorno has shown, this identity-effect is also the basis for its usefulness for the commercial media, which early adapted the leitmotifs for their programs, films, etc.

19. *Wagner's Ring of the Nibelung: A Companion,* trans. Stewart Spencer (London: Thames & Hudson, 1993), 152. This dilemma would also apply to music, as defined by Wagner in *Opera and Drama,* as a "female," understood as a "mirror" of man, who therefore can "see in it his very own image." Richard Wagner, *Dichtungen und Schriften,* ed. Dieter Borchmeyer, vol. 7 (Insel Verlag: Frankfurt am Main, 1983), 230 (my translation—SW).

20. In *Opera and Drama,* Wagner identified the essence of music, melody, with self-awareness: "In its significance art is nothing but the fulfillment of the yearning to recognize oneself in a depicted or loved object—of finding oneself again in the mastered appearances of the external world" (153; translation by SW).

21. Wagner, *Opera and Drama,* 207.

22. I attempt to investigate this tension in my book *Theatricality as Medium* (New York: Fordham University Press, 2005), 103–10 et passim.

23. Walter Benjamin, "Franz Kafka," in his *Selected Writings,* ed. Michael W. Jennings, Howard Eiland, and Gary Smith, trans. Harry Zohn, vol. 2 (Cambridge, Mass.: Harvard/Belknap, 1999), 813–14.

24. Walter Benjamin, "The Author as Producer," in his *Selected Writings,* ed. Michael W. Jennings, Howard Eiland, and Gary Smith, trans. Edmund Jephcott, vol. 2 (Cambridge, Mass.: Harvard/Belknap, 1999), 779.

6

"*Not Mere* Music"

Nietzsche and the Problem of Moral Content in Music

MARGARET MOORE and REBEKAH PRYOR PARÉ

> She told me herself that she had no morality—and I thought she had, like myself, a more severe morality than anybody.
> Friedrich Nietzsche (1882)

Friedrich Nietzsche's personal enmity toward Richard Wagner, apparent in the works *The Case of Wagner* (*Der Fall Wagner*, 1888), *Twilight of the Idols* (*Götzendämmerung*, 1889), and *Nietzsche contra Wagner* (1895), has caused scholars to question whether Nietzsche's criticism of Wagner's music has any legitimate philosophical justification. As a result, critics have dismissed Nietzsche's objections to *Parsifal* (1882) as ad hominem attacks on Wagner and have claimed that Nietzsche's praise of George Bizet's *Carmen* (1875) constitutes little more than anti-Wagnerianism. However, a close examination of Nietzsche's position in the debate on extramusical content as presented in his critique of *Parsifal* sheds light on the aesthetic basis for Nietzsche's objections. His harsh assessment of *Parsifal* and related comments in *The Case of Wagner* and *Ecce Homo* can best be understood in the context of the particular method of musical criticism he employs, a method that views the philosophical realms of ethics and aesthetics as inseparably intertwined. Our aim, therefore, is to demonstrate that Nietzsche's rejection of the life-weakening content in *Parsifal* provides a moral and aesthetic justification for his criticism of the opera.

As a founding father of the New German School, Wagner believed music to be capable of portraying extramusical content, a belief that provides the philosophical basis for his leitmotif technique. Unlike Franz Liszt, who maintained that the status of music could be elevated through a unification of the arts, Wagner believed that the renewal of music depended on its inner connection to poetic substance. Ideally the "artwork of the future" *(Kunstwerk der Zukunft)* would lift instrumental music out of the realm of purely formal elements onto a higher, more expressive plane. The composer who sought to achieve this aim would compose music in such a way that it portrayed a particular poetic idea or a narrative.

In his early fragment "On Music and Words," which likely dates from 1871, Nietzsche argues that music is devoid of any extramusical content. Rather, for him, "music can generate images that will always be mere schemata."[1] Nietzsche clarifies this point when he argues that what "we call *feeling* is . . . already permeated and saturated by conscious and unconscious representations and hence no longer directly the subject of music, much less its generator. Take, for example, the feelings of love, fear, and hope: directly, music cannot do a thing with them because each of these feelings is permeated by and saturated with representations."[2] He then extends his ideas about the representation of content to song and opera, arguing that a "necessary relation between poem and music . . . makes no sense, for the two worlds of tone and image are too remote for each other to enter more than an external relationship. . . . Confronted with the supreme revelations of music, we even feel, willy-nilly, the *crudeness* of all imagery and of every emotion that might be adduced by way of analogy."[3] Nietzsche continues his exploration of this problem with a consideration of the finale of Beethoven's Ninth Symphony. His suggestion is that listeners do not actually hear the sung text of Schiller's "Ode to Joy," because the poem is so "incongruous" that the music overwhelms the text, thereby blinding the listeners to its images and words.[4] He asks,

> What then are we to say of the incredible aesthetic superstition that Beethoven in the fourth movement of the "Ninth" gave a solemn testimony concerning the limits of absolute music and thus unlocked the portals to a new art in which music is said to be able to represent even images and concepts and has thus supposedly been made accessible for "conscious spirit"? What does Beethoven say himself when he introduces this choral ode with a *recitativo?* "O friends, not these sounds, but

let us strike more agreeable and joyous ones!" More agreeable and joyous ones! For that he needed the persuasive tone of the human voice; for that he needed the innocent air of the popular song. Longing for the most soulful total sound of his orchestra, the sublime master reached not for words but for a "more agreeable" sound, not for concepts but for the sound that was most sincerely joyous. And how could he be misunderstood?[5]

That Beethoven's finale should represent the limits of absolute music is not just any "incredible aesthetic superstition" but specifically the superstition underlying the basic premise of Wagner's "artwork of the future." Here Nietzsche practices *avant la lettre* some of his first criticism of Wagner.

Nietzsche, who undoubtedly was familiar with *Opera and Drama* (1851), in which many of Wagner's aesthetic philosophies are articulated, poses significant challenges to these theories. Questioning the notion that music is capable of representing feelings, Nietzsche counters Wagner's assertion that the function of music is to "realize the poetic intention for the feelings" and to enable the listener to recognize truth through the material gathered by the senses.[6]

Most important, however, is Nietzsche's early criticism of opera as a genre, which comes as an even greater surprise. Rejecting Wagner's main thesis that music is the means to a dramatic end, he argues:

> To place music in the service of a series of images and concepts, to use it as a means to an end, for their intensification and clarification—this strange presumption, which is found in the concept of "opera," reminds me of the ridiculous person who tries to raise himself into the air by his own bootstraps: what this fool and opera in accordance with this concept are trying to do are pure impossibilities. This concept of the opera demands of music not so much an abuse as—to say it again—an impossibility! Music never *can* become a means, however one may push, thumbscrew, or torture it: as sound, as a drum roll, in its crudest and simplest stages it still overcomes poetry and reduces it to its reflection. Opera as a genre in accordance with this concept is thus less a perversion of music than it is an erroneous representation in aesthetics.[7]

However, we must remember that this essay was omitted from *The Birth of Tragedy from the Spirit of Music* (*Die Geburt der Tragödie aus dem Geiste der Musik*, 1872), if, indeed, it ever had been intended as a section of this work. Oddly, despite an apparently strong commitment to the claims advanced by proponents of absolute music in "On Music and Words,"

Nietzsche refrains from assuming any overtly anti-Wagnerian stance until these concerns resurface a number of years later.

Believing that music can serve dramatic ends, Wagner "gives his name to the *ruin of music*."[8] The "great style," or high classical tradition, has become a means of deception, and Wagner, a composer of large, traditional forms, must be aligned with Brahms as a corruptor of modern music. Nietzsche later explains in *The Case of Wagner:* "What Wagner has in common with 'the others'—I'll enumerate it: the decline of the power to organize; the misuse of traditional means without the capacity to furnish any *justification*, any for-the-sake-of; the counterfeiting in the imitation of big forms for which nobody today is strong, proud, self-assured, *healthy* enough; excessive liveliness in the smallest parts; excitement at any price; cunning as the expression of *impoverished* life; more and more nerves in place of flesh."[9] Here Nietzsche finally expresses the deep disdain for Wagner and his philosophy that is anticipated by his earlier statements in "On Music and Words." Still contending that music is ancillary to Wagner's drama, Nietzsche now accuses the composer of misusing a traditional art form and of deceiving his audience by misrepresenting himself as the leader of an avant-garde.[10]

Nietzsche's frustration with Wagner's insistence on continuing the tradition of composing with large-scale forms goes straight to the heart of Nietzsche's conception of music's purpose. For him music was not a means to serve dramatic ends. Instead, Nietzsche regarded music as being essentially without content and, therefore, incapable of representing concrete images or feelings that he regarded as overly saturated with conscious and unconscious representations.

When one considers the overall trajectory of Nietzsche's musical and aesthetic development, an interesting pattern emerges in which Nietzsche's philosophy appears to be strongly influenced by the figure of Wagner the composer. When, in "On Music and Words," Nietzsche rejects the notion that music can represent semantic content, he undercuts a fundamental aesthetic premise of Wagner's "artwork of the future." It is as if Nietzsche had removed one of the structural beams from the tower of the *Gesamtkunstwerk* (total artwork), forcing it to crumble. As it crashes down, so does Wagner's dream of unifying and uplifting the German people through culture in the face of failed revolutions and forced political unification. As such Wagner no longer could be viewed as Germany's cultural inspiration, heir to Beethoven's legacy, and composer of the music that would be seen as a culmination of the German

spirit. Without semantic content in music, the "artwork of the future"—
and all hopes and dreams associated with it—must fail for lack of theoretical foundation.

Recognizing this problem, Nietzsche acknowledges that music
can possess life-related content, while he continues at the same time to
maintain that semantic content in music is an impossibility. Following
Schopenhauer's perspective in *The World as Will and Representation* (1819),
Nietzsche characterizes music as a representation of the Will in *The Birth
of Tragedy*. Inherently, then, music, the Dionysian element in tragedy,
contains the driving and striving of the unconscious.[11] This transformation of the understanding of musical content would accord Wagner's
music the status of the highest tragic art form, symbolizing the great rebirth of Dionysian spirit and the invigoration of German culture. By
providing this theoretical underpinning for Wagner's "artwork of the
future," Nietzsche preserves—if only privately—his mentor's status as
the greatest contemporary German artist.[12]

A few years after the publication of *Birth of Tragedy*, however, there
occurred a public and well-known rift in the friendship between Nietzsche and Wagner. The demise of the relationship resulted in part from
Wagner's failure to meet the artistic standards that Nietzsche had established in *The Birth of Tragedy* and in part from Nietzsche's mounting
preoccupation with the origins of morality and the ways in which Christianity poses a threat to humankind.[13] In Nietzsche's later writings,
Wagner increasingly is mentioned in connection with the following
themes: the decadence of modern German society, the popularity and
mass appeal of Bayreuth, and Christian ideals such as redemption. By
the 1886 edition of *The Birth of Tragedy*, Nietzsche reinterprets the book's
accomplishments in the introductory "Attempt at a Self-Criticism," rereading the book as raising "the big question mark concerning the value
of existence" and noting the "careful and hostile silence with which
Christianity is treated throughout the whole book."[14] In his reflections
on the work, he now reinterprets his treatise as a first attempt at a critique of Christianity and of the Christian value system that permeates
contemporary society.

Nietzsche's repudiation of Christian values, a project that he refers
to as the "transvaluation" of all values, can be found in his most extended treatment of morality, the *Genealogy of Morals* (*Zur Genealogie der
Moral*, 1887). When Nietzsche speaks of morality, he refers to the Christian notions of good and evil, redemption, and the virtue of suffering;

however, his understanding of morality is problematic because he claims to reject all morality, while, at the same time, making value judgments. These value judgments must be understood in the broader context of a life-affirming ethics. He labels traditional Christian morality harmful when this very label is in fact an ethical judgment, so that the project of transvaluation becomes one of replacing Christian morals with "Nietzschean values." The rejected values are all of a piece: they are the foundation for his judgment of German society, philosophy, the arts, and specifically music, that is, above all, Wagner and *Parsifal*.

The invective toward Wagner increases markedly following Nietzsche's completion of *Human, All Too Human (Menschliches, Allzumenschliches)* in 1879, as his preoccupation with *Parsifal* becomes apparent. Nietzsche now begins to regard the work as symptomatic of the problems he sees in the arts and in society.[15] In his "Attempt at a Self-Criticism," Nietzsche not only introduces his project of transvaluation but also attacks contemporary German music and regrets having seen such hope where there now is such decadence. Inherent in his musical criticism is a condemnation of Wagner, who becomes a symbol of what is wrong with German society. It is no accident that Nietzsche objects to the moral content of *Parsifal:* he abhors its Christian message and believes that promoting such a creation as *Parsifal* as a German masterpiece is sacrilegious to the very notion of art's purpose, since *Parsifal* represents the ultimate shattering of his hope for a rebirth of German spirit through music.

Given the importance of art in Nietzsche's philosophical system, it would be impossible to divorce it from the realm of nonartistic consequences. Far from an autonomist with regard to aesthetics, Nietzsche argues that art must be life-affirming and represent the Dionysian. Thus the ascetic ideals in *Parsifal* are antithetical to everything he held sacred. While Nietzsche's objections to the opera may be linked to the content of the libretto, he speaks ironically of "Christian music" in his notebook description of the prelude to *Parsifal,* and elsewhere he dismisses it as "decadent music." Consider the following notebook entry, especially the irony with which Nietzsche writes about the prelude: "The overture to *Parsifal,* the greatest blessing to be granted me for a long time. The power and strength of feelings, indescribable, I know of nothing that so profoundly grasped Christianity and brought it to such a level of empathy. Completely subtle and moving . . . the greatest masterpiece of the sublime that I know, the power and strength in grasping a fruitful certainty, an indescribable expression of greatness of pity about it."[16] Here his criticism seems to transcend the libretto: it appears to be a criticism of the musical content itself. Thus a further theoretical question arises: how can Nietzsche reject music on moral grounds when music cannot possess semantic content?

An attempt to answer this question leads to the following roadblocks: First, although he had heard the prelude performed and was familiar with the libretto, we know that Nietzsche never attended a full performance of *Parsifal*. Second, in "On Music and Words," he had advanced the thesis that music is incapable of possessing extramusical content, a position that is inconsistent with a critique of *Parsifal* on the basis of its Christian content, since his criticism would have to be of the libretto alone. If, however, as we argue, Nietzsche's aesthetics does allow for music to possess content, and for that content to be moral, then a Nietzschean critique of *Parsifal* as Christian music becomes conceivable. Nietzsche in effect articulates a deeper criticism of Wagner's musical style that was in part a critique of the values represented by Wagnerian music.

The same thesis that allows Nietzsche to provide a conceptual underpinning for Wagner's "artwork of the future" also leads him to reject certain stylistic features that he once admired in the composer. Thus, in 1888, when attempting to make sense of his praise of Wagner in *The Birth of Tragedy*, Nietzsche rationalizes his former position: "A psychologist might still add that what I heard as a young man listening to Wagnerian music really had nothing to do with Wagner; that when I described Dionysian music I described what *I* had heard—that instinctively I had to transpose and transfigure everything into the new spirit that I carried in me."[17] This explanation not only clarifies his marked change in attitude but also makes evident that Nietzsche is not necessarily rejecting the theory that music embodies the Dionysian. A further step in demonstrating that Nietzsche has a moral justification for criticizing *Parsifal* as music is to show that the Dionysian component in music functions, for Nietzsche, as a life-affirming element. Although he claims that the only values recognized in *The Birth of Tragedy* are aesthetic, he also notes that the work exhibits a noticeably hostile silence toward Christianity.[18] It therefore could be argued that these aesthetic values do, in fact, possess an ethical dimension. And, indeed, all of Nietzsche's further criticisms of music focus on this very characteristic: if it is life-promoting, it is good; if it is life-weakening and thereby decadent, it is an abomination.

Several interrelated themes of Nietzsche's philosophy find their first expression in *The Birth of Tragedy*, among them an alliance of music with the Dionysian and the idea of a primal unity, which resembles the undifferentiated Will that Schopenhauer tells us is directly represented in music. The Dionysian is associated with ecstasy, an overabundance of joy, and the basic human drive to triumph over the horrors of the world and to embrace life in its totality. As we have seen, this "life-affirmation" is the value that Nietzsche esteems most highly, contrasting it with the narrow-minded, ascetic tenets of Christian morality.

This theme is closely related to Nietzsche's idea that music should not assume any concrete content, lest it be robbed of its unique power to communicate the life-affirming universal. In ascribing such power to music, he relies heavily on Schopenhauer's concept of the Will, since the metaphysical representation of the Will, still a kind of representation, imbues music with the capability of possessing content. Nietzsche argues that the content of music is the same as that of all the other arts in the sense that "the phenomenal world, or nature, and music are two different expressions of the same thing," that is, the noumenal Will.[19] He illustrates this thesis in *The Birth of Tragedy* by quoting Schopenhauer as saying, "suitable music played to any scene, action, event, or surrounding seems to disclose to us its most secret meaning."[20] If we are to reconcile this idea with the idea that music is the Dionysian element in tragedy, we see that it is just this Dionysian primal unity that is *repre*sented as the content of music. Nietzsche thus widens the notion of content to include the representation of the Will. Although his expanded definition stops short of performing a fundamental break with his earlier writings, it does constitute a significant extension of his concept of content in music that enables Nietzsche to object to the Christian moral content in Wagner's prelude of *Parsifal*.

The inability of music to possess any specific semantic content, however, still would seem to pose a problem with regard to its drive toward a life-affirming content. And in terms of traditional Christian morality, the notion that music ought to represent moral principles such as "the good" or the overcoming of evil would seem to be entirely too particular to be represented in music. But the question remains as to whether music can assume the attitudes of which Nietzsche either approves or disapproves, attitudes that either affirm life or undermine it. While it may be, strictly speaking, incorrect to refer to these attitudes as "moral," since *On the Genealogy of Morals* shows that when Nietzsche speaks of morality he means traditional Christian values, it nevertheless can be argued that insofar as Nietzsche praises and advocates life-affirming attitudes and the factors that promote them, these attitudes take the place of traditional morality. To complicate matters further, Nietzsche finds fault with anything that reinforces or advocates Christian morality. It is apparent that Nietzsche has a sliding scale of values, so that he does not call for the abolishment of value *simpliciter* but rather sees that the values of late nineteenth-century German society are decadent and in need of supplementation by values that affirm life. These "Nietzschean values" are developed in direct opposition to ascetic values. It is useful, therefore, to think of them as opposites that are alike in kind, insofar as both in fact are values, and therefore—in a sense—both are moral.

It follows that whatever role these Nietzschean values play in music, they do so to the extent that music either affirms life or rejects it. This is exactly the power that Nietzsche attributes to the Dionysian in *The Birth of Tragedy*. Music should represent the Dionysian: it must affirm life. Therefore, one could take *Parsifal* as the foremost example of a music that fails because it rejects these Nietzschean values in order to promote the ascetic. However, we cannot be sure that it actually is the *music* that Nietzsche abhors, for the simple fact that he never heard the opera performed in its entirety. Since Wagner mailed him the libretto only, it would appear that Nietzsche did not have any basis for a specifically musical criticism of *Parsifal* beyond the prelude. Yet given the one-time closeness of their friendship and the amount of time that Nietzsche spent at the Wagner home, we may speculate that Nietzsche had heard parts of the opera as it was being composed. It is, nevertheless, striking that Wagnerian music, the vehicle for his text, is so abhorrent to Nietzsche, since there is much in Wagner's music that he loved, and he was pained to see such great art used for decadent and ultimately nihilistic ends.

Examining *Parsifal* with Nietzschean eyes reveals two immediate problems. First, the opera's representation of a decaying society that is redeemable only through Christian ideals is antithetical to Nietzsche's belief that Christian principles are the direct cause of decadence and degeneration in Western civilization. Second, the dual purpose of the *Bühnenweihfestspiel* to consecrate the stage at Bayreuth and to usher in the great German spirit also poses a quandary for Nietzsche, who, of course, is deeply disappointed by Wagner's incorporation of a Christian ritual as the means by which to honor a great stage—and a great art—and by which to evoke the German spirit. Nietzsche, furthermore, makes the accusation that Wagner, in writing a Christian opera for this purpose, was pandering to the masses, a seducer of the public:

> One pays heavily for being one of Wagner's disciples. What does it do to the spirit? *Does Wagner liberate the spirit?*—He is distinguished by every ambiguity, every double sense, everything quite generally that persuades those who are uncertain without making them aware *of what* they have been persuaded. Thus Wagner is a seducer on a large scale. There is nothing weary, nothing decrepit, nothing fatal and hostile to life in matters of the spirit that his art does not secretly safeguard: it is the blackest obscurantism that he conceals in the ideal's shrouds of light. He flatters every nihilistic (Buddhistic) instinct and disguises it in music; he flatters every Christian, every religious expression of decadence. Open your ears: everything that ever grew on the soil of *impoverished* life, all of the counterfeiting of transcendence and beyond, has found its most sublime advocate in Wagner's art—*not* by means of formulas: Wagner is too shrewd for formulas—but by means of a persuasion of sensuousness which in turn makes the spirit weary and worn-out. Music as Circe.[21]

Nietzsche thus views Wagner as having sacrificed his lofty artistic goals in exchange for mere popularity and acceptance by the lowly bourgeois.

Textual themes in *Parsifal* also present complications for Nietzsche; among these leitmotifs are asceticism, redemption, and decadence. Certain details in the plot demonstrate the ways in which these overarching themes are integrated into the core of the opera. For example, Nietzsche's problem with asceticism in the opera reflects his disdain for a general appreciation of self-denial, a thread that is sewn through the entire work. In his recent study, Anthony Winterbourne comments that in *Parsifal* "the spirituality is contrasted not merely with the secular, but with the specifically sexual: it is this . . . that both attracts and repels us, for the sexuality that Wagner uses as a context starkly contrasts an asceticism that the drama as a whole presumably invites us to sympathize with."[22] Of course, sexuality can be a drive toward life, a means for both procreation and pleasure, aspects to which Nietzsche subscribes. The theme of asceticism, for example, is illustrated in *Parsifal* by Gurnemanz's retelling of the story of Klingsor's self-castration in an effort to acquire the Grail in act I. Klingsor's attempt at atonement for some unnamed sin through castration represents self-denial, a means of suffering and rejection of that which embraces pleasure and affirms life. Redemption as a theme overwhelms the opera, as Parsifal is redeemed and becomes a redeemer. The celibate Order of the Grail even waits throughout the entire opera for a single, unknown redeemer—an innocent fool—providing redemption from sickness (Amfortas's wound) and from the general degeneration of the order and its followers. It is not entirely clear what has led this order into its decadent state. In order to understand the redemption, one must assume, in order to be sympathetic to the opera's basic premise, that the society itself is sick and that everyone is a sinner, and that redemption must come from outside. For example, Amfortas's cure cannot come from within. Not until Parsifal redeems him is he cured. Kundry represents yet another example of a character who is in an unspecified state of sin or perhaps a curse, and it is only Parsifal who provides any hope. Kundry appeals to Parsifal for pity, and this plea for pity becomes repugnant for Nietzsche, because it is a call made by the weak, whereas his entire philosophy calls for the weak to overcome their own weaknesses from within. He therefore mocks Wagner's obsession with redemption: "The problem of redemption is certainly a venerable problem. Here is nothing about which Wagner has thought more deeply than redemption: his opera is the opera of redemption. Somebody or other always wants to be redeemed in his work: sometimes a little male, sometimes a little female—this is *his* problem.—And how richly he varies his leitmotif! What rare, profound dodges! Who if not Wagner would teach us that . . . old corrupted females prefer to be redeemed by chaste youths? (The case of Kundry.)"[23] Nietzsche seems to be tired of this theme, for redemption is, according to his philosophy, superfluous. One does not need to be redeemed if one lives according to Nietzschean life-affirming ideals.[24]

These themes of asceticism, decadence, and redemption operate on all levels of the opera. Since Wagnerian operas function, in part, through the reflection of textual and dramatic meaning in the orchestral music by means of the leitmotif technique, we find musical motives representing suffering, the Grail, love, and the spear, in addition to main characters such as Parsifal and Kundry. Never having heard the opera in its entirety, Nietzsche may not have been aware of the specific leitmotifs and their associations; however, he was familiar with Wagnerian technique and must have known to listen for such motifs. Wagner appropriated the "Dresden Amen" as a representation of the Grail and of redemption, and despite what Nietzsche may have thought about music's inability to represent content, this "Amen" was common cultural currency, and it is likely that he would have recognized it in the prelude of the opera. Nietzsche also heard themes of Christianity, suffering, and pity reflected in the prelude, despite only having read the libretto. Significantly, these motives capture the text's moral themes—as Wagner had well intended—and Nietzsche must have known that they also permeated the body of the opera.

Here we do not intend to anticipate Nietzsche's musical criticism of an opera he never heard. Rather, in analyzing themes of *Parsifal*, we wish to show that Wagner's music contains moral themes that Nietzsche would have measured against his system of values. Still, these moral themes primarily are features of the libretto, and if we are to demonstrate that it is possible for Nietzsche to object to moral content in music without conceding that music is capable of representing any specific semantic content, then we must consider his criticism of Wagnerian musical style, even though this criticism is not specific to *Parsifal*.

There is evidence in some of Nietzsche's later works, most notably *The Case of Wagner*, that will allow us to put an aesthetic of music into relief in Nietzsche's work, an aesthetic that shows how music alone can play a role in promoting Nietzschean values. In his self-criticism of *The Case of Wagner* published in *Ecce Homo*, Nietzsche points out that one can truly understand the book only if one has suffered the fate of music: "that music has been done out of its world—transfiguring, Yes-saying character, so that it is music of decadence and no longer the flute of Dionysus."[25] If this is the fate of music, it must have the ability to express values, or at least to embody them in some way, and it remains to be shown how this might be accomplished. Rather than drawing on the overarching theory presented in *The Birth of Tragedy*, we have chosen to glean Nietzsche's aesthetics from actual instances in *The Case of Wagner*. The work to which he gives his most extended treatment, *Carmen*, comes as a surprise.

Indeed, Nietzsche's infatuation with Bizet's *Carmen* (1875), an opera he had attended some twenty times by 1888, always has seemed puzzling to modern readers.[26] Why Bizet, rather than any of the other great European composers of the eighteenth and nineteenth centuries? We now think of Bizet as being rather superficial compared to Wagner, but surely this is part of Nietzsche's point—after all, he says he is not praising Bizet *merely* out of malice. He elaborates, praising Bizet's lightness and his avoidance of "the lie of the great style."[27] Nietzsche continues: "'What is good is light; whatever is divine moves on tender feet': first principle of my aesthetics. This music is evil, subtly fatalistic: at the same time it remains popular—its subtlety belongs to a race, not to an individual. It is rich. It is precise. It builds, organizes, finishes: thus it constitutes the opposite of the polyp in music, the 'infinite melody.' I become a better human being when this Bizet speaks to me. Also a better musician, a better listener."[28] Nietzsche further claims that music liberates his spirit, makes him a better philosopher, and makes him fertile, and this is his best proof that music is good.[29]

While some of Nietzsche's praise is of the libretto of *Carmen*, much of it is of the music alone, so we get some idea of what "good" music is and what it should do for Nietzsche. "Good" music is the opposite of Wagner's musical style. He argues:

> Wagner begins from a hallucination—not of sounds but of gestures. Then he seeks the sign language of sounds for them. If one admired him, one would watch him at work at this point: how he separates, how he gains small units, how he animates these, severs them, and makes them visible. But this exhausts his strength: the rest is no good. How wretched, how embarrassed, how amateurish is his manner of "development," his attempt to at least interlard what has not grown out of each other. His manners recall those of the *frères* de Goncourt, who are quite generally pertinent to Wagner's style: one feels a kind of compassion for so much distress. That Wagner disguised as a principle his incapacity for giving organic form, that he establishes a "dramatic style" where we merely establish his incapacity for any style whatever, this is in line with a bold habit that accompanied Wagner through his whole life: he posits a principle where he lacks a capacity.[30]

Here Nietzsche criticizes Wagner's approach to composition, his leitmotif technique, expressing disgust for Wagner's attempt to disguise ineptitude with an overly dramatic and showy style. For Nietzsche, Wagner has killed melody by overusing his leitmotif technique and by creating a montage rather than lyrical passages. His critique can be seen in the highly ironic sixth section of *The Case of Wagner*, where Nietzsche speaks through the imagined voice of Wagner's success, turned musicologist: "*Principle:* melody is immoral. *Proof:* Palestrina. *Practical application: Parsifal.* The lack of melody even sanctifies."[31] The criticism of immorality in music that Nietzsche mocks goes back as far as *The Republic*, in which Plato argues that melodic structures can corrupt character and incite lustful feelings and therefore ought to be banned from a just society. Thus, Nietzsche adds sarcastically (still in the voice of the conservative musicologist): "Nothing is more dangerous than a beautiful melody."[32]

Since this voice speaks of traditional morality and sanctity, which Nietzschean values directly oppose, one may infer that what Nietzsche actually values in music is beautiful melodies, much like the flute of Dionysus. In the same ironic tone, Nietzsche allows the moralist to say "never admit that music 'serves recreation'; that it 'exhilarates'; that it 'gives pleasure,'" and so we further conclude the opposite: that music in fact ought to exhilarate and give pleasure—abilities that Nietzsche already has praised in *Carmen*.[33] The musical taste expressed here is in keeping with what we have termed Nietzschean values.

One further point of critique that arises in *The Case of Wagner* is that Wagnerian music has lost the whole for its parts. Nietzsche claims that Wagner is perfect and beautiful, but for only five to fifteen measures at a time, calling him "our greatest *miniaturist* in music who crowds into the smallest space an infinity of sense and sweetness."[34] Referring to Peter Gast, he claims there is "only one musician who is still capable today of creating an overture that is *of one piece:* and nobody knows him."[35] Nietzsche's concern with organic unity harbors echoes of the Dionysian transformed by the Apollonian in *The Birth of Tragedy*. Nietzsche sees Wagnerian music as a sickness of overindulgence in particulars. Even this stylistic critique, "his incapacity for giving organic form," has a moral origin, as Nietzsche claims that it is the decadent style that is an "anarchy of the atoms."[36]

One might raise the objection that Nietzsche has created a theoretical inconsistency: how can it be that all music is life-affirming in nature according to *The Birth of Tragedy*, while the music of Wagner is decadent in its very structure? The best explanation is that the early Nietzsche spoke of what music could and should contribute to tragedy in an abstract sense, and that he hoped Wagner's music would fulfill this potential. By contrast, Nietzsche's later writings make a distinction between affirming and decadent musical styles, a distinction that is not present in *The Birth of Tragedy*. This refinement of his aesthetics is a result of his development as an independent philosopher as well as of his disappointment with German society and with Wagner's *Parsifal* as a cultural production.

However one wishes to read this possible inconsistency, it is clear that Nietzsche's specifically musical criticism of Wagner does exceed his treatment of ascetic themes in the *Parsifal* libretto. It would be an exaggeration to say that these criticisms and stylistic preferences constitute a full-fledged philosophy of music, and one might argue that there is little philosophical substance behind the mere invective directed at Wagner and the decadence of German culture, or that Nietzsche is merely attempting to justify his own musical tastes. However, when one considers the ontological status of music more deeply, its ability to represent, perhaps even embody, the Dionysian and thus the all-important embracing of the totality of life, one sees that music is central to Nietzsche's life-affirming value system and his entire philosophy. For Nietzsche the ethical is the aesthetic, and to understand Nietzsche's musical considerations, one must learn to think according to the logic of this principle. In the works of Wagner, Nietzsche had hoped for no less than the rebirth of the German spirit and the overcoming of decadence and nihilism in Western civilization, all to emerge from this new art form driven by music, the *Gesamtkunstwerk*, even the "artwork of the future." He was sorely disappointed to find that even this art had fallen prey to the decadence and asceticism of a dying culture. With this decay Nietzsche saw, or preferred to see, nothing more than the perversion of what he esteemed most highly: music.

NOTES

The conference paper "Re-Reading Nietzsche's Philosophy of Music," out of which this essay developed, was presented by the authors in collaboration with Randal Swiggum.

1. Friedrich Nietzsche, "On Music and Words," trans. Walter Kaufmann, in *Between Romanticism and Modernism: Four Studies in the Music of the Later Nineteenth Century*, by Carl Dahlhaus (Berkeley: University of California Press, 1980), 109.
2. Nietzsche, "On Music and Words," 111.
3. Nietzsche, "On Music and Words," 112.
4. Nietzsche, "On Music and Words," 113.
5. Nietzsche, "On Music and Words," 113.
6. Quoted in Carl Dahlhaus, "Twofold Truth in Wagner's Aesthetics: Nietzsche's Fragment 'On Music and Words,'" in *Between Romanticism and Modernism*, 21. See also Klaus Kropfinger, "Wagners Musikbegriff und Nietzsches 'Geist der Musik,'" *Nietzsche-Studien* 14 (1985): 1–12, for a more extensive explanation of the difference and the similarities in Wagner's and Nietzsche's understanding of "absolute music."
7. Nietzsche, "On Music and Words," 116.
8. Friedrich Nietzsche, "Der Fall Wagner," in *The Birth of Tragedy and The Case of Wagner*, trans. Walter Kaufmann (New York: Vintage, 1976), 186.
9. Nietzsche, "Der Fall Wagner," 187.

10. Frederick R. Love examines Nietzsche's relationships to other composers in "Nietzsche's Quest for a New Aesthetic of Music: 'Die Allergrösste Symphonie,' 'Großer Stil,' 'Musik des Südens,'" *Nietzsche-Studien* 6 (1977): 154–94.

11. Friedrich Nietzsche, "The Birth of Tragedy," in *Basic Writings of Nietzsche*, trans. Walter Kaufmann (New York: Modern Library, 2000), 33–38.

12. We can see how important it was for Nietzsche to please Wagner by keeping his writings consistent with Wagner's aesthetic projects; for example, the anti-Wagnerian theories in "On Music and Words" were never published, and *The Birth of Tragedy* was dedicated, with a tributary forward, to his "noble champion on this same path." Friedrich Nietzsche, "Forward to Richard Wagner," in *The Birth of Tragedy*, trans. Clifton P. Fadiman (New York: Dover, 1995), iv.

13. While this description of the break in their friendship may seem oversimplified, we acknowledge that their intense relationship was marked with many personal and emotional rifts. Here we choose to focus on aspects of the break that have the most direct relevance for Nietzsche's aesthetic development. It is important to note that Nietzsche and Wagner began to part ways in 1876, the year of the first festival at Bayreuth. The break was final by 1878, when Nietzsche received a manuscript copy of the *Parsifal* libretto. Cf. Walter Kaufmann's introduction to *The Portable Nietzsche* (New York: Penguin, 1982), 11.

14. *Basic Writings of Nietzsche*, 17 and 23.

15. *Genealogy* (1887) was written the year after his "Self-Criticism," and it makes clear Nietzsche's greater preoccupation with morality and Christianity during this period. Some scholars have argued that *Parsifal* was a catalyst in shaping a change of direction in Nietzsche's philosophical position—that Nietzsche's work after 1877 (especially the *Genealogy*) was sharpened and refined contra *Parsifal*. For example, Agnes Heller has suggested provocatively that even the structure of the *Genealogy* is based on the opera, with its "Prelude" and "three acts" addressing the opera's fundamental themes in parallel. *An Ethics of Personality* (Oxford: Blackwell, 1996).

16. Friedrich Nietzsche, *Nachgelassene Fragmente 1885–1887*, vol. 12 of *Sämtliche Werke: Kritische Studienausgabe in 15 Bänden*, ed. Giorgio Colli and Mazzino Montinari (Munich: Deutscher Taschenbuch Verlag, 1999), 5n41.

17. Friedrich Nietzsche, "The Birth of Tragedy," in *Ecce Homo* (1888), in *Basic Writings of Nietzsche*, 730.

18. Nietzsche, "Birth of Tragedy," in *Ecce Homo* (1888), 727.

19. Nietzsche, *The Birth of Tragedy* (1872), in *Basic Writings of Nietzsche*, 101. Nietzsche is quoting Schopenhauer's *Die Welt als Wille und Vorstellung*, ed. Julius Frauenstädt (Leipzig: Brockhaus, 1873), 1:309.

20. Nietzsche, *Birth of Tragedy*, in *Basic Writings of Nietzsche*, 102.

21. Nietzsche, *The Case of Wagner*, postscript, 639.

22. Anthony Winterbourne, preface to *A Pagan Spoiled: Sex and Character in Wagner's* Parsifal (London: Associated University Press, 2003), 10.

23. Nietzsche, "The Case of Wagner," in *Ecce Homo,* 616.

24. However, one might appreciate being delivered from Wagner, as Nietzsche jokingly asserts: "It is a curious matter, still remembered, which revealed this old feeling once more at the very end, quite unexpectedly. It happened at Wagner's funeral: the first German Wagner Association, that of Munich, placed a wreath on his grave, with an inscription that immediately became famous. It read: 'Redemption for the redeemer!' Everybody admired the lofty inspiration that had dictated this inscription; also the taste that distinguished Wagner's admirers. But many (strangely enough!) made the same small correction: 'Redemption *from* the redeemer!'—one heaved a sigh of relief." "Case of Wagner," in *Ecce Homo,* 638.

25. Nietzsche, "Case of Wagner," in *Ecce Homo,* 773.

26. Nietzsche, "Case of Wagner," in *Ecce Homo,* 613. See also Stefan Lorenz Sorgner, "Nietzsche," in *Musik in der deutschen Philosophie: Eine Einführung,* ed. Stefan Lorenz Sorgner and Oliver Fürbeth (Stuttgart: Metzler, 2003), 125.

27. Nietzsche, "Case of Wagner," in *Ecce Homo,* 613.

28. Nietzsche, "Case of Wagner," in *Ecce Homo,* 613.

29. Nietzsche, "Case of Wagner," in *Ecce Homo,* 614.

30. Nietzsche, "Case of Wagner," in *Ecce Homo,* 626–27.

31. Nietzsche, "Case of Wagner," in *Ecce Homo,* 624.

32. Nietzsche, "Case of Wagner," in *Ecce Homo,* 624.

33. Nietzsche, "Case of Wagner," in *Ecce Homo,* 625.

34. Nietzsche, "Case of Wagner," in *Ecce Homo,* 627.

35. Nietzsche, "Case of Wagner," second postscript, in *Ecce Homo,* 643.

36. Nietzsche, "Case of Wagner," in *Ecce Homo,* 626.

7

Bloch's Dream, Music's Traces

GERHARD RICHTER

First, there is the question of music, which, strangely, is never a question of music alone.

> Philippe Lacoue-Labarthe, *Musica Ficta (Figures of Wagner)*

For it is still empty and uncertain what is happening sonically.

> Ernst Bloch, *Spirit of Utopia*

The contentious question of whether music is capable of representing anything in particular or only is the play of sonically moved forms misses the phenomenon. Rather, these things are akin to a dream, whose form, as romanticism well knew, is so close to music.

> Theodor W. Adorno, *Beethoven*

Musical Textures

If, as readers of an overtly "political" writer such as Ernst Bloch, our primary interest lies in the progressive use-value and utopian impulses that animate his far-reaching oeuvre, then at times it may be tempting to forget the basic fact that all his works exist in and as *language*. Indeed, for those of us concerned, for entirely understandable reasons, with the solidly political, the strictly historical, or the specifically theological trajectories of his writings—from the early *Spirit of Utopia* (1918, revised second edition 1923) and thought-images in *Spuren* (*Traces*, 1930), through *Heritage of Our Times* (1933), *The Principle of Hope* (1949), and *Atheism in Christianity* (1968) to the late *Experimentum Mundi* (1975)—questions regarding the linguistic nature of his thoughts may seem, at best, like an afterthought to the allegedly stable content of his work or, at worst, like an embarrassment to the methodological project of systematically excavating detachable truth-contents from his texts. Why linger, one might ask, with local questions of textual interpretation and the problems of form and language when one is eager to proceed in Bloch's texts to what really counts, that is, to matters of politics, history, and religion? Apart from a seemingly inconsequential ambiguity here or there, one might take for granted the general transparency and conceptual availability of his texts, as if these were not conceived at and constrained by the limits of language—in Bloch's case, a highly self-conscious, rhetorically saturated, excessive, and poetically stylized German that often betrays his early affinity with expressionism—and the potential unreliability of meaning that such rhetorical gestures imply. But a careful rereading of Bloch's writings hardly warrants such a conclusion. In fact, Bloch himself teaches us time and again a different way of reading his texts and even supplies us with the necessary tools. In the lengthy section of *Spirit of Utopia* devoted to the philosophy of music, we read: "Only in one way, then, can one speak concretely about form: there, namely, where the formal, constructive, objectivating element is no mediation, but a concrete component itself," that is, "as categories of their so-being [*ihres Soseins*], and generally in all art's temporal or spatially anamnestic problems."[1] For Bloch, then, the specificity of form is always something more than a mere vehicle for the transmission of content presumed to exist independent of its specific and singular manifestation. Such an understanding of textual form is incompatible with the notion that lessons learned from a particular text can be refunctionalized so as to enable one to make sense *tout court* of other texts. Rather, what Bloch terms the *Sosein* of artistic form challenges one to invent interpretative strategies anew with every phenomenal form that one encounters. It is no accident, then, that Emmanuel Levinas, one of his subtler readers, suggests that "Bloch's eminent personal culture—scientific, historical, literary, musical—is at the level of the 'documents' he interprets and which he very obviously takes pleasure in interpreting, as if he were scoring, for an orchestra assembling all the geniuses of the earth, the counterpoint of the Marxist concepts."[2] Put another way, Bloch's concern with the formal specificity and singularity of every document to which he turns his attention shows his readers how to attend to the formal specificity of his own language, whether that language speaks to musical and aesthetic problems or to broader ethico-political concerns.

The importance of attending to formal specificity in the case of music, whose existence depends on the performance of its singular forms—a point illustrated by the fact that music can be cited but never paraphrased—is uncontroversial enough. However, as Edward Said reminds us, the relationship of musical notes to letters and words differs from that of spoken language in that music "is not denotative and does not share a common discursivity with language."[3] As such, music constitutes a special case of textuality that cannot be reduced to the conventionally denotative and referential functions of language. Bloch, who shares this view, even extends it in such a way as to leave *no act* of reading untouched in a gesture that will have enlarged the interpretative consequences of the experience of musical form into a broader realm of textuality. For him, the self-referential, non-denotative qualities of music constitute a particularly striking manifestation of the ways in which all acts of signification point to other acts of signification that exceed their adherence to any particular system of referents. Here the question of textual signification becomes a question of *figures* and of *figuration*.[4]

According to a thought-image in *Spuren*, "Montages of an Evening in February," "Being is full of figures, though not of fully arranged ones, with each and every thing in its fixed place. Rather, an *echo of allegorical meanings* will resound everywhere, an instructive echo sending one back and forth, reflecting ambiguously."[5] If Being is full of figures that are neither stable nor arrestable once and for all, and if their allegorical significations thus perpetually threaten to exceed the reliability of this or that predetermined meaning, then we are invited and challenged to read the world as a text. But neither Bloch's moveable figures nor Jacques Derrida's well-known formulation that "there is nothing outside the text" *(il n'y a pas de hors-texte)* should lead us to the mistaken conclusion that everything *is* a text; rather they suggest that everything must be regarded as a textual problem of interpretation that calls upon us to decipher and make sense of it.[6] Such perpetual deciphering also recalls an incessant act of translation and recontextualization, and Derrida himself later insists that the observation "there is nothing outside the text" is only one of the many formulations given to the realization that "there is nothing outside context."[7] The imperative to read as if our phenomena, whether textual or contextual in the stricter sense, were texts to be deciphered and understood is tied to the relentless wish to account for a potentially limitless number of possible translations, iterations, and shifting contextualizations, even as this multiplicity coalesces into this or that "individual" text. The call to perform this kind of reading may be especially urgent when a phenomenon powerfully suggests that its meaning is self-evident and natural rather than constructed, slippery, historically saturated, and therefore open to change. In this deeply historical and figurative way of reading, the concept of "text" cannot be limited to verbal or written utterances but must be extended to include a vast network of modes of signification, from the printed text of books to every kind of image, from political ideologies to religious doctrines, and from the language of dreams to that of musical sounds. Bloch's thought-image, then, does not deny the importance of historical and po-litical content but rather asserts that such content, even in specula-tive philosophy, always is conditioned by the specific textual figures and tropes in which it is lodged. The content "itself," however, does not remain unaffected by its situatedness in figures and tropes. On the contrary, the ethico-political issues that Bloch's sentences may give us to think should be considered in terms of the figurative specificity of their enactment and, as Bloch teaches us, with an ear to the haunting "echo of allegorical meanings." Therefore, when Bloch, in his late work *Experi-mentum Mundi*, tells us that the "world is a singular and abiding question concerning its meaning, which is yet to be excavated" *(Die Welt ist eine einzige noch unablässige Frage nach ihrem herauszuschaffenden Sinn)*, this sen-tence can be understood as a gloss on all his sentences.[8]

The Politics of Musical Aesthetics

If the political messianism and unorthodox utopianism that once prompted Jürgen Habermas to imagine Bloch as a Marxian Schelling can be thought of as a sustained and perpetually reformulated commit-ment to the hope of what is to come, to the nameless other of what merely is, then this hope attaches both to the openness of futurity as such and to the more specific and, in each case, singular openness of sig-nification itself; that is, an openness to the singular significations that mediate our thinking of futurity in general, not simply the futurity of this or that object or idea, but futurity itself, the futurity of futurity.[9] For Bloch, this thinking of the futurity of futurity is invested with the hope of the "not-yet" *(das Noch-nicht)*—not a naive or childish form of wishful thinking in an administered world of reified relations in which such thinking would be utopian in the worst sense, but with an abiding intui-tion that the nonself-identity of thoughts and actions, their internal self-differentiation, is more than a hermeneutic or administrative problem to be overcome in the name of implementing meanings and systems. The not-yet also signals a nameless otherness that, precisely by being at odds with itself and never coming fully into its own, promises an anticipatory glimpse, the Blochian *Vorschein,* of what still remains to be thought and experienced, of what has not yet been foreclosed. As he puts it in his *Tübinger Einleitung in die Philosophie* (Tübingen introduction to philosophy), "if we are wandering along a street and know that, within forty-five minutes, there will be an inn, that is the vulgar not-yet. Along the street, however, along which we are wandering in this precarious world, the inn, especially the right one, has not yet been built."[10]

Given his sensitivity to matters of presentation, figuration, and interpretation, it is no accident that Bloch's preoccupation with futurity and with the nonprogrammable not-yet in the realm of the aesthetic persists throughout his writings, including the many texts on literature now collected in his *Literary Essays* and related works on aesthetic issues in architecture, the fine arts, fairy tales, the detective novel, landscape painting, and many others.[11] But perhaps nowhere do these variegated epistemological, political, and aesthetic concerns convene more forcefully than in Bloch's sustained engagement with the language of music.[12] In his study of music at the university, in his early friendship with Georg Lukács, and in the modulations and tonalities that, in spite of multiple variegations, still work to sustain a recognizable signature throughout Bloch's oeuvre, the language and sound of music and musicological questions are inscribed deep in the heart of his writings. These include, in addition to the substantial section on the philosophy of music in *Spirit of Utopia,* his musico-philosophical discourses in *The Principle of Hope* (especially chapter 51) and *Experimentum Mundi,* as well as numerous essays devoted to problems of music such as the fugue, the sonata form, the funeral march, and the dialectical structure of musical performance, and to individual composers such as Richard Wagner and Anton Bruckner.[13] For instance, *Experimentum Mundi,* implicitly evoking Walter Benjamin's concept of the aura, culminates in a meditation on what Bloch calls musical language's "intensive aura," which for him is figured most forcefully in Mozart's "Finally the Hour Nears," Brahms's "My Slumber Grows Ever Deeper," Wagner's "Dreams," and Mahler's "Departure" in "Song of the Earth."[14] As his friend Theodor W. Adorno reminds us, the "sphere of music takes up more space in Bloch's thought than in that of almost any other thinker, even Schopenhauer or Nietzsche."[15] But while it is almost impossible for Bloch to speak of anything seriously without also speaking of music, it is likewise impossible for him to speak of music without *also* speaking about something else. As such, Bloch enacts Philippe Lacoue-Labarthe's dictum that "the question of music" is "strangely . . . never a question of music alone."[16] To speak of music meaningfully means to translate it into a medium that it is not—for example, spoken or written language and the realm of concepts—and to find any meaning in it, we must resort to concerns that at first seem alien to music proper. "Only the musical note," we read in *Spirit of Utopia*, "that enigma of sensuousness, is sufficiently unencumbered by the world yet phenomenal enough to the last return," so that "whereas paint still adheres strongly to the object and can therefore also be vacated by the thing's spirit without saying a thing, the clash and resonance of sounding brass will spill over" (*Spirit*, 145; *Geist*, 186). Music, for Bloch, is the prime sphere in which we encounter the general other-directedness of signification, an other-directedness that music shares with other forms of signification but which it stages in music-specific ways, that is, beyond any obvious model of referentiality and prestabilized norms of meaning.[17]

When Bloch's concerns with the not-yet and with the radical futurity of possibility are tied to aesthetic questions, and specifically to questions of music, they should not be understood in terms of a mimeticist model such as that of his early friend Lukács. For Bloch, music is non-mimetic in a double sense. First, it does not simply re-present what already is, a mechanical reproduction or exact copy of a given reality—since such a gesture, for him, hardly would contain any utopian possibility, except perhaps that tentative and elusive possibility that may reside in the philosophical negation of that reproduced reality. Second, music does not simply provide a sound image of what should be, a specific and therefore closed presentation of a future world for the sake of which the present one should be discarded. Rather, music, for Bloch, invites us to think the very possibility of possibility itself. In both senses of music's non-mimesis, Bloch departs from earlier philosophers of music such as Schopenhauer, whose philosophy often depends on repressing the difference between aesthetic and empirical reality, a literalism outlined in Paul de Man's concept of aesthetic ideology in which "what we call ideology is precisely the confusion of linguistic with natural reality, of reference with phenomenalism."[18] We may say that the ideological confusion of a set of presentations with an empirical reality alleged to be external to that set is especially charged in the sphere of music because it is possible to think of music as having no direct reference to the world, that is, as a structure of signification that is less able than other structures to create the powerful illusion of a transparent and stable relation between its utterances and a referential world. While musical composition, performance, and reception are materially conditioned effects of social inscriptions and historical determinations, music simultaneously stands in a non-mimetic and non-transparent relation to these governing inscriptions and determinations. If music therefore is textual without being a language in the conventionally referential sense, if it belongs to textuality without fully sharing the textual status of other textual forms, then the fissures and ruptures it emphasizes through the schism between its significations and the idea of a relation to a referential world deserve to be exploited and radicalized as the very core of music, rather than to be glossed over or perfunctorily subsumed into a mimetic model of reproduction and recreation.[19]

The unexpected conceptual proximity between Bloch and de Man in this regard is highlighted by de Man's reading of the function of music in Rousseau, where de Man suggests that the "successive structure of music is . . . the direct consequence of its non-mimetic character. Music does not imitate, for its referent is the negation of its very substance."[20] He reminds us that, not "being grounded in any substance, the musical sign can never have any assurance of existence," and that "the nature of music as language" leads to a certain difficulty that is embodied in the temporality of music, to which the more synchronic experience of painting is not subjected in the same manner. "On the one hand," de Man argues, "music is condemned to exist always as a moment, as persistently frustrated intent toward meaning; on the other hand, this very frustration prevents it from remaining within the moment. Musical signs are unable to coincide: their dynamics are always oriented toward the future of their repetition, never toward the consonance of their simultaneity." Therefore, he concludes, even "the apparent harmony of the single sound, *à l'unisson*, has to spread itself out into a pattern of successive repetition; considered as a musical sign, the single sound is in fact the melody of its potential repetition," and music itself emerges as "the diachronic version of the pattern of non-coincidence within the moment."[21] If music therefore is, to its very core, predicated upon a temporality in which it cannot coincide with itself and in which it stages, above anything else, what we might call its ability to be repeated—its fundamental iterability—it also assumes the status of an allegory of presentational non-coincidence and of iterability as such. Unlike Schopenhauer, for whom music is privileged because it names the trajectory and force of Will itself, music for Bloch and for de Man cannot but be allegorical, unable to coincide with itself yet offering a perpetual and illuminating commentary on that very inability.[22] Expressed in utopian terms, Bloch suggests that a host of human tensions are intensified in the history and philosophy of music, in which, among other things, "melody's most remarkable attribute—that in each of its notes, the immediately following one is latently audible—lies in human anticipation and thereby in expression, which is here above all a humanized expression."[23] The humanized expression of musical unfolding is a matter of music, along with its listeners, to come to terms with the temporality and iterability that makes music what it is without allowing music to come into its own once and for all. What de Man calls music's non-coincidence with itself and what Bloch imagines as a deferred and deferring musical temporality that creates a form of expression that is always yet to come, promising itself with every performance—these are the qualities that structure music's history, musical history, and the history of the human ear, the qualities that turn on an irreducible series of deferred anticipations.

This history of anticipation and deferral, of non-coincidence and temporal otherness, cannot be thought in isolation from what Bloch imagines as the perpetual labor of producing sense in the world, the "singular and abiding question of its meaning, which is yet to be excavated." Indeed, the knotted relation between a textually conditioned labor of producing sense, literally of making sense, of manufacturing sense as sense itself, and the question of music and musical sense will not leave Bloch, even when he is not thinking about music alone. To grasp more fully Bloch's insistence on this perpetual and uncertain making of sense and the movement of non-coincidence in the temporality of music, we may turn to Jean-Luc Nancy's explication of the sense-producing and undoing gestures of musicality and its significations. As Nancy observes in the thought-image "Music" in his book *The Sense of the World:*

> A signification is proposed, but it must be deciphered or understood . . . in accordance with the execution of its presentation, the way in which its statement is stated. Thus, the musical score (text?) including the words, whenever there are words, is inseparable from what we call, remarkably, its *interpretation:* the sense of this word oscillating then between a hermeneutics of sense and a technique of "rendering" [*rendu*]. The musical interpretation, or *execution,* the putting-into-action, or entelechy, cannot simply be "significant": what it concerns is not or not merely sense in this sense. And reciprocally, the execution cannot

itself be signified without remainder: one cannot *say* what it *made* the "text" *say*. The execution can only be executed: it can *be* only as executed.

As Nancy continues:

> Further, music can only be played, including by those who only listen. The entire body is involved in this play—tensions, distances, heights, movements, rhythmical schemes, grains, and timbres—without which there is no music. The "least" song demonstrates it—and even more, no doubt, it is demonstrated by the existence of the song itself, as a permanent, polymorphic, and *worldwide* execution of musicality. That which is propagated, apportioned, and dispersed with the song, in its innumerable forms, is at the very least—and stubbornly—a playful execution of sense, a being-as-act through cadence, attack, inflection, echo, syncopation.[24]

Music, then, can be thought as the perpetual manufacturing, performance, and displacement of sense: a specific sense and the very idea of sense, sense's "senseness." It cannot simply enact a pre-musical, pre-presentational meaning: its presentation *is* its meaning, and its meaning *is* its performance. If there is nothing but interpretation—in music as in making sense more generally—then music and sense are exposed as those spheres in which what executes music and sense is exposed as execution itself. This being-exposed of sense, through and as music, to what executes it, to the very idea of it as something to be executed, its exccutedness and its necessary executability, cannot, in its generality, be reduced, despite its necessarily idiomatic and singular manifestations, to a local phenomenon. It participates in a global execution of sense, of music as the execution of sense, among other things because, while it must travel through the singularity of a specific form (of a particular melody, movement, set, etc., that is always tied to a local and particular material performance), this traveling of musical sense itself, whenever it is repeated in its singularity, also is one of the most general phenomena imaginable. We could say there are only particular acts of music and *at the same time* there are only global executions of music and its mobilizations of sense. From the perspective of the worldwide execution of singularity that music occasions, it is possible to read Bloch's insistence on the world as "*eine einzige noch unablässige Frage nach ihrem herauszuschaffenden Sinn*" as resonating, and indeed radicalizing and fulfilling itself, in his abiding preoccupation with the overly complex role of music in the making and interpreting of sense. As we shall see, the fact that this role has not yet been decided upon once and for all gestures, for Bloch, toward future possibilities and toward a commitment to a certain non-naive hopefulness.

If the hope that Bloch lodges in the not-yet resonates on the far side of any aesthetic ideology, it likewise should not be discarded because of its apparent otherworldliness. To be sure, Bloch's project is invested in what can be thought and experienced in the form of alterities to Being as Being currently presents itself to us. But this does not mean that this other, or these others, to Being are confined to the purely speculative and inaccessible realm of the otherworldly. Rather—and more recent thinkers who have addressed the issue of the "other" such as Levinas are explicitly indebted to Bloch on this point—"what exceeds Being is allowed to govern our relation to Being," to take up a formulation offered by Robert Bernasconi.[25] To the extent that what exceeds Being can be allowed to govern our relation to Being, that relation is always also a question not only of this or that relation but of relation itself, of the very idea of relation, of our relation to relation as a function of the very idea of a relation and its possibilities. In the case of Bloch, this relation to the relation can be neither fully established nor exhaustively interpreted because what makes Bloch's relation what it is cannot be thought in isolation from the ways in which it is always already a figure of excess of the other (it exceeds Being), of excess of the self (it exceeds itself by not always remaining self-identical), and of differentiation (it does not fully coincide with the precepts and demands for a relation that the world in which it unfolds would stipulate). I wish to argue that two interlaced models of such thinking in Bloch's philosophy of the not-yet bear the names "music" and "dream": the music of dreams, and the dreams of music. More generally, I argue that these complexly mediated terms are central to the aesthetic and ethico-political impetus of his unorthodox utopian reflections.

Musical Dreams, Dreams of Music

Dreams and music, of course, are not innocent or isolated concepts in Bloch's writings. We could even say that these concepts traverse all his texts in a variety of modulations and tonalities. This is not to say that every text Bloch wrote thematizes dreams or music overtly—although many of them do—but rather that no text of his remains unaffected by the peculiar logic and far-reaching claims that Bloch makes on behalf of these concepts. I will concentrate in what follows on his first major work, the expressionistically suffused *Spirit of Utopia*, in conjunction with his aesthetically most accomplished text, the literary-philosophical thought-images collected in *Spuren*, with an eye to how both projects are connected by a rhetorical and conceptual emphasis on dreaming, sleeping, longing for the not-yet, and the attendant music of futurity. It is as though *Spirit of Utopia*, with its dreams of music and its music of dreams, were the dream-text whose leitmotifs would serve as the point of departure for all subsequent texts both within Bloch's own trajectory and to a certain extent within the orbit of his friends and colleagues. As even the early Walter Benjamin relates to Ernst Schoen toward the beginning of the Weimar Republic (1919), anticipating a troubled but mutually fruitful collaboration despite some reservations, *Spirit of Utopia* is "the only book . . . against which" he could "measure" himself.[26] The same sentiment is echoed by Adorno, who, a few years before his death, recalls: "The book, Bloch's first, bearing all his later work within it, seemed to me to be one prolonged rebellion against the renunciation within thought that extends even into its purely formal character. Prior to any philosophical content, I took this motif so much as my own that I do not believe I have ever written anything without commemorating it, either implicitly or explicitly."[27]

If it is surprising that the better part of a book on the intricacies of utopian thought should be devoted—next to more likely candidates such as the phenomenon of deep astonishment or Karl Marx and socialist thought—to a philosophy of music, then it should be no less surprising that this philosophy of music begins not with a systematic exposition and clarification of some key concepts but rather with a dream. This early dream anticipates the many theoretical modulations of dreaming that permeate Bloch's later work, such as the sustained discussion of the distinction between day dreams and night dreams that constitute chapter 14 of *The Principle of Hope*, the essay "Dream of a Thing" in the *Philosophische Aufsätze zur objektiven Phantasie* (Philosophical essays on the objective imagination), and the conversations with Bloch collected in *Tagträume vom aufrechten Gang* (Daydreams of an upright walk).[28] As though it were one of the thought-images from *Spuren*— which were largely composed between 1910 and 1929, thus overlapping with the composition of *Spirit of Utopia*—the short thought-image

"Dream" functions as an enigmatic overture to Bloch's philosophy of music:

Traum
    Wir hören nur uns.
    Denn wir werden allmählich blind für das Draußen. Was wir sonst auch gestalten, führt wieder um uns herum. Es ist nicht genau so ohne weiteres ichhaft, nicht genau so dunstig, schwebend, warm, dunkel und unkörperlich wie das Gefühl, immer nur bei mir, immer nur bewußt zu sein. Es ist Stoff und fremd gebundenes Erlebnis. Aber wir gehen in den Wald und fühlen, wir sind oder könnten sein, was der Wald träumt. Wir gehen zwischen den Pfeilern seiner Stämme, klein, seelenhaft und uns selber unsichtbar, als ihr Ton, als das, was nicht wieder Wald werden könnte oder äußerer Tag und Sichtbarkeit. Wir haben es nicht, das, was dies alles um uns an Moos, sonderbaren Blumen, Wurzeln, Stämmen und Lichtstreifen ist oder bedeutet, weil wir es selbst sind und ihm zu nahe stehen, dem Gespenstischen und noch so Namenlosen des Bewußtseins oder Innerlichwerdens. Aber der Ton brennt aus uns heraus, der *gehörte* Ton, nicht er selbst oder seine Formen. Dieser aber zeigt uns ohne fremde Mittel unsern Weg, unseren geschichtlich inneren Weg, als ein Feuer, in dem nicht die schwingende Luft, sondern wir selber anfangen zu zittern und den Mantel abzuwerfen (*Geist*, 49).

[*Dream*
    We hear only ourselves.
    For we are gradually becoming blind to the outside. Whatever else we still shape leads back around us. It is not exactly as readily self-like, not exactly as hazy, hovering, warm, dark, and incorporeal as the feeling of being always only by myself, always only conscious. It is material, and an other-bound experience. But we walk into the forest and we feel that we are or could be what the forest dreams. We walk between the tree trunks, small, soulful, and imperceptible to ourselves, as their sound, as what could never again become forest or external day and visibility. We do not have it, that is, all that which surrounds us, this moss, these strange flowers, roots, stems and shafts of light is or means—because we ourselves are it, and stand too close to it, this ghostly and yet so nameless quality of consciousness or of becoming-inward. But the sound flares out of us, the *heard* sound, not the sound itself or its forms. Yet it shows us our way without alien means, shows us our historically inner path as a flame in which not the vibrating air but we ourselves begin to tremble, and throw off our coats.] (*Spirit*, 34)

We could say that Bloch dreams to the music of thought-images. His thought-images stage a self that is in retreat from vision ("becoming blind") and thus on the way toward other senses, including the acoustic. The musical note, Bloch tells us, traverses our selves in an event of hearing that at once empties the self and exposes it to its own internal otherness, its self-differentiation, in which the dream can no longer simply be distinguished from the dreamer and in which the very trembling that occurs at the sound of a musical note orchestrates a gesture in which the self ex-poses itself: in the "vibrating air" of the musical note we "throw off our coats." Denuded and exposed, traversed by the otherness of the musical note, one no longer is a fully conscious, self-identical subject but rather has become the venue for a transmutation of the dream and the dreamer as each is translated into and as the other. This "ghostly" musical interpretation renders "nameless" the consciousness that designates the musical self that dreams or is dreamed—its name has not been uttered; its movements are heard and felt but not fully understood. This want of understanding is a perpetual condition for Bloch as he exposes his ear both to the otherness within itself and to the notes that penetrate it. We could even say that an extensive and obsessive meditation on all the permutations of this ontological and hermeneutic lack comprise a leitmotif for his entire philosophy of music.

It is therefore no accident that the section "On the Theory of Music" in *Spirit of Utopia* begins with the observation that listening "is and will remain weak enough. For too many, listening would come more easily if one only knew how one ought to speak about it" (*Spirit*, 94; *Geist*, 124). For Bloch, knowing how to speak about listening is the perpetual problem with which music confronts us. In fact, to the extent that knowing how to listen to music and knowing how to talk about listening to music are inextricably intertwined, the interpretive challenge we face is to translate music into an object of knowledge that remains anchored in discourse as a describable and knowable phenomenon while, at the same time, allowing it to remain an incommensurate form that refuses to yield its secret to the doctrines and efforts of conceptual language. But Bloch's philosophy is not aimed at clearing the stage for easy listening and the joyous certainty of hermeneutic closure by clarifying once and for all how one should talk about listening to music. Indeed, actually knowing how to talk about music would be the death knell of music's interpretation—just as giving up on *attempting* to learn how to

talk about it also would be, since the far-reaching potential of music as
an aesthetic form resides as much in its perpetual invitation to be understood as in its simultaneous refusal to be comprehended in non-musical
terms. We could say, then, that Bloch's entire philosophy of music is
predicated upon a perpetual return to the basic question of how to listen, with music emerging not only as the object of that return but also as
the agency that itself provides a ceaseless commentary on that very return. Precisely because we do not yet know how to talk about listening
to it, music is a name for what remains to be thought and questioned
anew with every attempted reading of that performance. According to
Bloch in *The Principle of Hope*, the consequence of this perpetual deferral
of meaning is that "*nobody has as yet heard Mozart, Beethoven or Bach as they
really are calling, naming, and teaching.*"[29] Speaking philosophically about listening to music, then, always unfolds in the Kantian "as-if" mode so
that we make our points about music *as if* we already knew how to speak
about it.

From the perspective of having to learn how to speak about the musical experience of music as such, Bloch's reflections appear as sustained
attempts that always start over one more time in their effort to speak
about listening to music. These reflections compose and then abruptly
abandon a wide-ranging network of discourses that might serve as the
basis for generating a language for listening to music: from a historical narrative concerning the beginnings of music in antiquity and the
middle ages, via sociological aspects of music's reception and production in the great Italian composers and in Romanticism to sustained
readings of a series of paradigmatic composers such as Bach, Mozart,
Beethoven, Wagner, Bizet, and Brahms, from case studies of specific
works such as *Missa Solemnis, Fidelio,* and *Carmen,* all the way to a formal
encounter with the more technical aspects of music, such as harmony
and rhythm. Music here emerges not merely as one example to be used
in more general philosophical explanations that exist independently of
it, a purely illustrative sensualization of an abstract logic that just as well
could find its instantiation in a very different aesthetic form. Rather,
Bloch urges us to think about the philosophical nature of music and the
musical nature of philosophy in a way that leaves neither realm unaffected and intact. As such, the two emerge as impossible but necessary
translations and perpetual transmutations of each other.

With these considerations, Bloch discovers in music many elements
deserving of philosophical attention that are not to be found in the

Kantian aesthetic paradigm, of which *Spirit of Utopia* is keenly aware. We recall that in paragraph 53 of the *Critique of Judgment,* in which Kant offers a "comparison of the aesthetic value of the beautiful arts among each other," music is accorded the lowest rank because it ultimately is "more pleasure than culture."[30] Kant writes that "music occupies the lowest place among the beautiful arts (just as it occupies perhaps the highest place among those that are estimated according to their agreeableness), because it merely plays with sensations [*bloß mit Empfindungen spielt*]."[31] Unlike other art forms such as poetry and painting, music cannot enter the aesthetically charged interplay in which judgment, pleasure, imagination, and intuition *(Anschaung)* perpetually interact. "Besides," Kant adds,

> there is a certain lack of urbanity in music, in that, primarily because of the character of its instruments, it extends its influence farther (into the neighborhood) than is required, and so as it were imposes itself, thus interfering with the freedom of the others, outside of the musical circle, which the arts that speak to the eyes do not do, since one need only turn one's eyes away if one would not admit their impression. It is almost the same here as in the case of the delight from a widely pervasive smell. Someone who pulls his perfumed handkerchief out of his pockets treats everyone in the vicinity to it against their will, and forces them, if they wish to breathe, to enjoy it at the same time; hence it has also gone out of fashion.[32]

Kant here articulates a devalorization of music with regard to the other arts that is shared by other writers in the eighteenth century who also frequently privilege painting because of its presence and stability, over music, which they regard as more elusive and temporally volatile. For Kant, music cannot be connected to the realm of freedom for the following reasons: first, because it appeals primarily to the emotions and to the production and experience of pleasure alone; and second, because it imposes the opposite of freedom on those who at any given time are unattuned to its performance or who do not wish to be addressed by it. Music, then, for Kant, behaves somewhat like the moment of interpellation in Louis Althusser's subject of ideology, the subject that invariably turns around and feels addressed by the authority of the law when the generic "Hey, you!" is issued. Music, according to this reading, only ever says, "Hey, you there," in a gesture of hailing that contradicts the right of non-response, which is so deeply imbricated with the concept of freedom. Yet, at the same time, the break with freedom that music enacts is also the advent of pleasure—in response to music's appellation, the subject experiences involuntary pleasure rather than being arrested by agents of the state. It is striking that Kant's passage moves synaesthetically from hearing to smelling, from one sense to another, drawing on the second sense to explicate the experience of the first. In so doing, Kant's example rhetorically performs the argument that it makes conceptually. Unlike the eye, which may close itself to block out vision, the ear has no easy defense against the intrusion of an unsolicited musical sound, in the same way in which the language that describes the experience of one sense (hearing or listening) is not immune to the intrusion of the language that describes the experience of another sense (smell and the perfumed handkerchief). The synaesthetic slide from the auditory to the olfactory, from ears to noses, in the meditation on music gestures toward the idea that music cannot be thought alone—there is always something else that wishes to be thought and experienced along with music, such as music's relative promotion of freedom or unfreedom or its relation to other sensorally mediated experiences.

Even though the Bloch of *Spirit of Utopia* proclaims himself to be closer to Kant than to Hegel, from Bloch's musicological perspective, Kant's insistence on music's allegedly narrow appeal to the emotions, its lack of urbanity, and its tendency to impinge upon the freedom of others, all would require qualification. To begin with, Bloch wishes to rectify what one might call a latent "ocularcentrism" that unites Kant with so many other thinkers of the eighteenth century who privileged the epistemo-critical function of the eye over the other senses (most notably hearing) by evoking an ideological tradition that regards vision as "the noblest of the senses" from Plato to Descartes via the Enlightenment and its fear of darkness all the way to Merleau-Ponty, Sartre, and, ultimately, the postmodernists.[33] In a neo-romantic gesture reminiscent of the Jena Romantics and of Novalis's polemic against the lucidity of daylight encrypted in the anti-ocularcentric, anti-Enlightenment tropes of his *Hymns to the Night,* Bloch dethrones vision as the sense that—owing to its capacity to transform the world into a modern *Weltbild,* or world image, as Heidegger later terms it in his reading of Descartes—is capable of standing metonymically for all the other senses, able to subsume the variegated perceptions that they offer under the hegemony of the eye.[34] For Bloch, in musical creation "the sound employed makes every event more acute, penetrating, sensuous. For as listeners we can also still get in close touch, as it were. The ear is, in small part, more deeply embedded in the skin than even the eyes" (*Spirit*, 101; *Geist*, 132). Because of what Bloch sees as the ear's greater degree of embeddedness in the skin, its tactile and corporeal basis, the music that penetrates the ear cannot be thought in isolation from that organ's abiding material inscription. Among other things, the material inscription of the ear complicates the relation between sound and image. As Bloch suggests:

> Therefore we bristle at having to watch a silent film image, not without reason. For here only the monochrome optical impression has been excerpted, and since it is simply given as it is, there arises in accordance with the ear's exclusion the disagreeable impression of a solar eclipse, a mute and sensuously diminished life. But then the ear assumes a peculiar function: *it serves as the representative and place holder of the remaining senses;* from things it removes alive their crackling, their friction, and from people their speech, and so the film's musical accompaniment, however vague or precise it may finally be, thus comes to be felt as the exact complement in its way to photography. (*Spirit*, 101; *Geist*, 132)

Here, the ear, rather than the eye, becomes the metonymic representative of all the other senses. Even when the sound that penetrates the ear is meant to "supplement" the image, that image becomes what it is only by virtue of its putatively superfluous and secondary supplement—sound. To become what it is, the photograph or "light image" *(Lichtbild)* requires the supplement of sound not for the reason that sound "completes" an unfinished whole or pleasantly accompanies an otherwise independent visual unity, but because sound as supplement reveals that the status of that which is supplemented is something that is itself already a form of mediation and supplementation. Indeed, it is a form in which what is supplemented structurally shares the qualities that we believed to be the properties only of the supplement itself. Derrida explains this logic in his reading of the dangerous supplement in Rousseau as follows: "Through this sequence of supplements a necessity is announced: that of an infinite chain, ineluctably multiplying the supplementary mediations that produce the sense of the very thing they defer: the mirage of the thing itself, of immediate presence, or originary perception. Immediacy is derived."[35] As with the image of Rousseau's mother that Derrida addresses, Bloch's trope of the musical supplement of the image emphasizes differential relations, chains of signs and signifiers that are not simply the retroactive imposition of forms of presentation onto a pre-textual reality in which the idea of secondary supplements and self-identical origins can be reliably upheld; instead, this

trope speaks to the undoing and disappearance of a presence that powerfully creates the false impression of naturalness and self-identity, of
independence from any supplements. Bloch refers to this quality as
music's "photographic supplementarity," thereby emphasizing music's
relation to and simultaneous break with the image while also stressing
the exemplarity of music's perpetual flow as a dangerous supplement—
the exemplarity of the supplement of which one would like to arrest an
image, a photographic keepsake to commemorate its movement around
an absence. We could say that, for Bloch, music is a photograph in notes
that captures the inversion of its own status as a mere supplement to
vision by delivering a commentary on its very movements of mediation
and substitution.

In addition to his anti-ocularcentric, supplementarist intervention
with regard to Kant's low estimation of music, Bloch also implicitly addresses the issue of freedom as it is presented in the *Critique of Judgment* by
situating his discussion of music within a transformed framework. While
Kant emphasizes the inscription of music in pleasure and emotion along
with its attendant lack of freedom, Bloch chooses to think of music as the
distant yet deeply resonant experience of what has yet to be experienced,
a conceptual and aesthetico-sensual nostalgia for the future and a com-
memoration of what is still to come, rather than as an instantiation of
freedom that has already been achieved and only needs to be expressed
in notes or as the site where judgment, imagination, and aesthetic pleasure combine to yield the experience of subjective affirmation. Thus,
what chiefly occupies Bloch is not the speculative complication and re-
habilitation of music as aesthetic form vis-à-vis Kant or, by extension,
the repetition of certain elements already present in Nietzsche's and
Schopenhauer's projects. Rather, his thinking resonates in a variety of
tonalities centering around the ultimate unreadability of music, the impossibility of formulating stable programs with which to speak about it,
and its inseparability from (the dream of) its ethico-political promise.
Bloch's project, as Christopher Norris puts it, envisioned "a new kind of
listening" in which "music was the truth to which philosophy aspired but
which could never reach the point of articulate understanding since language itself, and philosophical language in particular, dealt only in concepts or abstract figures of thought."[36] For Bloch, then, the truth that
music is capable of imparting is the internally fissured and non-self-
identical nature of all aesthetic forms, a nameless anticipatory glimpse of
what always is yet to come and only just underway.

Something's Missing

The non-self-identical quality of music that inhibits the pervasive impulse to foreclose what still deserves to be thought, an elusive incompleteness that must not be casually dismissed as merely a deviation from the marching plan of a knowing system, constitutes the internally self-differentiated condition of possibility for what is yet to come. In a remarkable 1964 radio conversation with Adorno on the internal contradictions in utopian longing, Bloch draws our attention to a pertinent sentence in Bertolt Brecht: "'Something's missing [*Etwas fehlt*].' What that is, one does not know. This sentence, which is in *Mahagonny,* is one of the most profound sentences Brecht ever wrote, in two words. What is this 'something'? If it is not allowed to be cast in a picture, then I shall portray it as in the process of being. But one should not be allowed to eliminate it as if it really did not exist so that one could say about it: this is what it's all about."[37] Bloch here implicitly refers to his discussion in *Heritage of Our Times* of the sentence in scene 8 of *Mahagonny,* "But something's missing" *(Aber etwas fehlt),* and that sentence's central function for a kind of thinking that is perpetually to come.[38] In Brecht's work, the character Paul Ackermann repeats this line time and again in response to the other characters' various propositions regarding what constitutes a happy and fulfilled life, from such modest thrills as smoking and swimming to more refined pleasures such as observing water or forgetting. "But something's missing" *(Aber etwas fehlt).*[39] The experience of thought, and of embodied, critical thought as a form of what Husserl calls the phenomenon of our *Lebenswelt,* or "life world," is inseparable from the experience of a fundamental lack or absence. Something is missing, but that something resists revelation even as a distant presence in which it would be absent only for us but present in a potentially legible *elsewhere.* Rather, "something's missing" *(Etwas fehlt)* names the aporetic and unfulfilled condition of human cognition and experience under the very circumstances that make possible an awareness of this lack and, by extension, that open up the possibility of imagining an entirely different life world—a world characterized by an openness born of the condition of being fundamentally at odds with itself—that resembles the Lacanian real as void but is charged with an irrepressible politico-aesthetic impulse. Because something is missing, a supplement is needed to fill the void. But in assuming the form of a supplement to such charged utopian longings, music subjects itself to a state in which something is missing, that is, it becomes a supplement in need of supplementation. After all, if music embodies the aesthetic spirit of utopia, then it also must yield to the demands of cognitive analysis and to an empirically transformative potential. But because music cannot be fully grasped by conceptual means or translated without remainder into norms of reason in the service of an empirical struggle, it too belongs in a sphere in which something is missing. Yet it is precisely this quality of incompleteness that would be required for music to be fully translatable into the cognitive terms that might serve as a supplement to music, so that the supplement in need of supplementation becomes an allegory of the endless chain of supplementations that vex any attempt to mediate between a signifier and its absent referent, between the world of signs and notes and the sphere of what we sometimes call reality.

We could say, therefore, that Bloch's logic of the musical supplement situates music at the site of a struggle between the material world and aesthetic form, reason and imagination, cognition and illusion, understanding and emotion. At the same time, one may question whether the sphere of music actually constitutes an appropriate object upon which to focus such a degree of philosophical energy. Is not the elusive character of music, as it unfolds and disappears into temporality itself, absolutely other to the rigorous logical requirements of conceptual thought? With what authority, then, does a philosophy like Bloch's take so seriously the potential truth-content of music—especially when so many philosophers, of both the Continental and so-called analytic traditions, studiously avoid the slippery topic of musical discourse and when so many practitioners and historicist scholars of music distance themselves from philosophical speculation as though it were a tone-deaf practice contrary to the spirit of music itself? Taking Bloch's philosophy of music seriously requires that we eschew not only the use of philosophical concepts as mere tools for the description—later to be verified or rejected—of self-identical, present empirical phenomena whose more or less transparent nature allows us to evaluate the truth content of a philosophical claim, but also an approach to artworks in general, and musical works in particular, that is the hedonistic non-conceptual equivalent of slipping into a relaxing bath.[40] If the first is an unfortunate example of how to philosophize with a hammer to the sounds of Mozart, the latter reduces Bach's *Well-Tempered Clavier (Wohltemperiertes Klavier)* to a "well-tempered bath" *(Wohltemperiertes Bad)*.

This struggle leaves no philosophy of art unaffected. Indeed, Bloch's evocation of Brecht's multiply determined "something's missing" resonates even in the thought of the Early Romantic critic Friedrich Schlegel, who writes: "In that which we call philosophy of art, there is usually one of two things missing: either the philosophy or the art."[41] Bloch, however, asserts that "here too the ear hears more than the concept can explain. Or, to put it differently, one senses everything and knows exactly where one is, but the light that burns in one's heart goes out when it is brought into the intellect" (*Spirit*, 139; *Geist*, 178). Artworks, and above all music, can exist only as the embodiment of a formalized mode of resistance to the unchecked domination of reason, opening up new and unexpected conceptual spaces to allow for more playful creativity and imagination. Just as longing is predicated upon the experience that something is missing—after all, if nothing were lacking, there would be no point in analyzing the world, in imagining it differently or, finally, in the very act of thinking—so music depends as much on that which it cannot fully reflect as it does on that which it cannot fully yield to rational comprehension. As the Blochian supplement, then, music contains within itself the very tension that exists between nonconceptual aesthetic pleasure and the systematicity of logic and concepts. This musical tension, according to Bloch, also is deeply political.

A full consideration of the textuality of musical experience, including its aesthetic, pleasurable, cognitive, and political resonances, requires us to question the very idea that the "what" of music has been understood. "For it is still empty and uncertain," Bloch reminds us, "what is happening sonically *(was tonhaft geschieht)*. He continues:

> It is hopeless to allocate music to already exact emotions. Not even whether a melody *can* express anger, longing, love at all unequivocally—that is, if it is these emotional contents, already experienced by us anyway, at which music aims, and where it could easily excel a statue—is so easy to identify, once its upheavals begin to edge into one another. . . . If one considers a musical piece in its technical aspect, everything is correct but says nothing, like an algebraic equation; if, on the other hand, one considers it in its poetic aspect, then it says everything and defines nothing—a strange conflict lacking any median or any equilibration accessible to the understanding, in spite of its fermenting content. Here it does no good . . . to keep to the poetic in order to force "music's infinitely blurring essence," as Wagner said, into categories which are not its categories. (*Spirit*, 100–101; *Geist* 131)

Challenging the notion of pre-musical emotional categories that are simply reflected *as themselves* in a musical work of art, Bloch wonders to what extent music not only performs but also invents a certain tonal system of emotional specificity and affective range that the listener, perhaps too hastily, ascribes to an extra-musical world assumed to precede musical inscription. By the same token, music's resistance to assimilation by discourses such as literature can be attributed to an obedience to its own enigmatic laws such that "if I wish to communicate the essence of some musical work, I simply whistle the first theme. If, however, I am asked to narrate the essence of a literary work, then I will not cite the first sentence, but rather report the basic features of the plot or the layout of the whole" (*Spirit*, 104; *Geist*, 135). Music always enacts itself otherwise. If music is the name for an irreducible experience of openness, an aesthetic form that has no common measure with other discourses even while sharing a common textuality, it deserves to be called a "pealing of bells in an invisible tower on high" (*Spirit*, 101; *Geist*, 132). Its sounds penetrate us while leaving their full meaning as occluded as their source, the invisible tower whence they emanate.

The perpetually deferred meaning of music also links Bloch's "invisible tower" to broader questions of musical presentation. As Philippe Lacoue-Labarthe suggests in his commentary on Adorno's reading of Schönberg's opera *Moses und Aron*, music can be understood as an "art (of the) beyond (of) signification, which is to say (of the) beyond (of) representation." Relating music's unfolding in and as the beyond of signification to Adorno's understanding of art as a withdrawal from communication, as well as to Benjamin's concept of "pure language" and Hölderlin's caesura of "pure speech," the "ultimate paradox" for him lies in the gesture by which the echo of "the naked word—the language of signification itself—comes to tell of the impossible beyond of signification, something that Benjamin would not have denied."[42] What music gives us, then, is not simply the transmission of a communicable content and not even the communication of its own incommunicability. Rather, music tells of its own beyondness, the persistent beyondness inscribed deep in the heart of signification itself that it simultaneously takes as its leitmotif. When Bloch therefore speaks of the experience of music as displacing by politicizing, and politicizing by displacing, the very binarism of emotive pleasure and concept-driven reason, his argument always also reverberates in a musical space beyond: as the beyond of signification and as the signification of the beyond.

Revenant Dreams

To the extent that music's performance of the beyond of signification and the signification of the beyond can be heard at all, for Bloch it is best experienced in dreams. If this musical textuality, which Bloch refers to as the uncanny "ghostly realm of music" (*Spirit*, 157; *Geist*, 200), takes the form of Beethoven's "gigantic rhythmic shape, his . . . Luciferan-mystical kingdom," or of Bach's "song of the spiritual soul, shining into itself, to the great, towering organ fugue with its staircases and stories, a single self-illuminating, gigantic crystalline glory, . . . the promises of a messianic homeland beyond every expedition," then none of its instantiations can exist fully in isolation from the dream itself (*Spirit*, 157; *Geist*, 200). As Bloch suggests: "To the latter [the metaphysics of presentiment and utopia], too, even when it stands as near as possible to us, we come near only in dreams. But it is no longer a dream recollecting the past or burrowing into the various baser passions. Rather only that yearning which brings with it what was unfulfilled, what could have absolutely no earthly fulfillment, the waking desire for what alone is right for us, which glimmers in well-correlated sound" (*Spirit*, 156; *Geist*, 199). He concludes:

> But finally, as soon as everything grows silent on this earth, within earthly action—completely dispensing with the text and even the Shakespearean world of dreams, the world of dance, masque, intoxication, and magic—then music assembles the features of the other word, the Word from another larynx and logos, the key to the inmost dream within the object's Head, their own newly meaningful expression, the multiply singular, final expression of the Absolute. Now still a fervent stammering, music, with an increasingly expressive determinacy, will one day possess its own language: it aims at the word which alone can save us, which in every lived moment trembles obscurely as the *omnia ubique*: music and philosophy in their final instance intend purely toward the articulation of this fundamental mystery. (*Spirit*, 158; *Geist*, 201)

For Bloch, the music of the dream and the dream of music are mediated by "that which is not yet; what is lost, presensed; our self-encounter, concealed in the latency of every lived moment; our We-encounter, our utopia calling out to itself through goodness, music, metaphysics, but unrealizable in mundane terms" (*Spirit*, 158; *Geist*, 201). To approach the thinkability of the possible is to encounter it in and as a dream. Bloch does not recommend a kind of wishful thinking in which unrealistic, infantile hopes are given the weight and determining momentum of the concrete. Rather, to the extent that the world deserves to be thought as that which is at odds with itself, as that which is not simply given and self-evident but articulated and historically saturated, the space in which this philosophical refusal to reconcile with the world as it currently presents itself can take place is the dream: the dream of music and the music of the dream.

In a thought-image from *Spuren*, "Some Left-Handed Schemata," Bloch writes: "'Should one,' someone said, 'only dream when one is asleep and not at all when one is awake? . . . With open eyes one feels the air that is just as dreamlike, in which the wind blows and which is perhaps even haunted.'"[43] Not just in bed, and not only when he sleeps, Bloch dreams the possibility of the impossible, a somnambulant state in which dreaming and waking are not mutually exclusive, a state in which the precepts of reason that characterize enlightened thinking also are imbricated with the less rational dimensions of thought that manifest themselves in the aberrant acts of aesthetic disenchantment. The utopian dream of music and the music of the dream that traverse Bloch's project are marked not only by an emphasis on the aesthetic dimension of dreams and thoughts but also by an emphasis on the ethico-political implications of these dreams and their compatibility with the demands of a responsibility to come. For Bloch, the philosophical negativity, the *negativity* with which philosophy opposes the dream, names the site of a utopian vision that will not be placated with escapism or the certainty of enlightened transparency. One awakens from such a dream without betraying its insights or fully repressing the paradoxes that serve as possible objects of reflection and of experience. To be awake and asleep at the same time, in an aesthetically mediated musical space, is the condition of possibility for not resigning oneself once and for all to what announces itself as the limit of the possible. Without this wakeful dream and this dreaming wakefulness—one name for which, as Bloch suggests, may be "music"—philosophy confines itself to the affirmative. As Bloch tells us throughout his book *Thomas Münzer als Theologe der Revolution* (Thomas Münzer as theologian of the revolution), revolutions, even theological ones, often are ignited by those who have the courage to dream, and to hear in and through that dream, what is right: "Whoever opens himself to it, is capable also of dreaming and hearing what is right."[44] Therefore, any philosophy worthy of its name must remain faithful to the dream of the more that permeates his *Tübinger Einleitung in die Philosophie* and that casts "the dream of what is commensurate with the human" as that which "is searching for more."[45] From the perspective of this dream of the more, and even the dreamed "moreness" of the more, it is hardly a surprise that Bloch's original title for *The Principle of Hope* was *Dreams of a Better Life.*[46]

The dream, although conventionally associated with images rather than with sounds—Freud's *Interpretation of Dreams,* for instance, features an extensive index of dream images and their possible meanings but no index of dream *sounds*—can nevertheless be understood as a translation of sorts: one between image and sound. The link between dreaming and music so crucial to Bloch's project is addressed implicitly by Roland Barthes's meditations on music and inscription. In "Listening," Barthes writes:

> In dreams, the sense of hearing is never solicited. The dream is a strictly visual phenomenon, and it is by the sense of sight that what is addressed to the ear will be perceived: a matter, one might say, of acoustic images. Thus, in the Wolf Man's dream the wolves' "ears were cocked like those of dogs when they are alert to something.' The "something" toward which the wolves' ears are cocked is obviously a sound, a noise, a cry. But, beyond this "translation" the dream makes between listening and looking, links of complementarity are formed. If little Hans is afraid of horses, it is not only that he is afraid of being bitten . . . but also [of] the noise these movements [of the horses] occasion. (The German term *Krawall* is translated as "tumult, riot, row"—all words associating visual and acoustic images.)[47]

The dream, then, can be said to create images of all kinds: visual images, sound images, perhaps even thought-images. Yet if the dream translates musical notes and other sounds into acoustic images, we could say that it performs the most radical translation of music, a translation that is at the same time a form of untranslatability: the dream translates music as music, that is, in terms of an otherness (the image or acoustic image) without which the music itself could not first be experienced, even when it is not being "translated." If what music is or does is ultimately more then we can say—"for it is still empty and uncertain what is happening sonically," as Bloch reminds us—then any attempt at speaking and thinking about music is always already to speak of something else, even when we are speaking strictly about music. The translation of music by the dream indicates that music is that which is always en route to an elsewhere, always saying something more, less, and other than itself. It is allegorical, in the Greek sense of *allegorein,* or saying something else. From this perspective music can be understood not simply as an allegory *of* something but, because of its differential and other-directed being, as an allegory of allegory itself. Through a kind of Freudian delayed action or retroactivity *(Nächträglichkeit)* and Derridean supplementarity, the work of translation that the dream performs makes visible the other-directedness of music, the allegory of the allegory that it inherently performs.

Musical Dreams of the Thought-Image

Lest his philosophical compositions be perceived as deaf to their own claims—claims regarding the dream of music and the music of dreams, the aesthetic, the musical, and the dream-like quality of hope and a thinking of what is to come—Bloch enacts the theories of music and dreams set forth in *Spirit of Utopia* in the poetic language of *Spuren.* This collection of thought-images, which Bloch composed in close proximity to the literary-philosophical prose snap-shots that his friends Adorno, Benjamin, Horkheimer, and Kracauer each were devising at the time, gathers and deepens themes and preoccupations that Bloch had put into circulation in *Spirit of Utopia* and in the 1923 collection of essays *Durch die Wüste* (Through the desert).[48] Although revised with the addition of numerous new thought-images for its 1969 republication in his collected works, the 1930 version of *Spuren* poetically condenses—under cryptic and playfully allusive literary titles such as "Sleeping," "The Gift," "Lamp and Closet," and "The Lucky Hand"—most of the philosophical motifs from the early Bloch's intellectual orbit. Schooled on his teacher Georg Simmel's method of micrological reading, Bloch gives us a series of elusive traces to read, *Spuren,* that emerge and retreat, playing with presence and absence, meaning and its departure, and thereby enacting the poetic structure of his philosophical thought while, at the same time, pointing the way, like indexical footprints in the sand, toward a thinking and experiencing that has not yet been achieved, a homeland in which nobody has yet been.

In *Spuren,* we find, among the many images that thematize dreaming and sleeping, two thought-images that are representative of the collection as a whole:

Sleeping

In ourselves we are still empty. Thus we easily fall asleep if there are no external stimuli. Soft pillows, darkness, silence allows us to fall asleep, the body grows dark. If one lies awake at night this is by no means wakefulness but rather a sluggish, consuming crawling around on the spot. It is then that one notices how uncomfortable it is to be with nothing other than oneself.[49]

Small Excursion

Even he who falls asleep grows lonely, though he can certainly be like someone taking a journey. When we are awake, we prefer to sit with the wall behind us, our gaze directed at the establishment. But how astonishing: when falling asleep, most turn toward the wall, even though in so doing they turn their backs to the dark room which is becoming unknown. It is as if the wall suddenly attracted, paralyzing the room, as if sleep discovered something in the wall that otherwise is the exclusive prerogative of a better death. It is as if, in addition to disturbance and strangeness, sleep too enrolled one in death; here, however, the stage appears differently, opening the dialectical semblance of a home. . . . For the pride of departure, in which the happiness and the pride of dying were already at work, is here distinctly filled with a triumph of an arrival. Especially if the ship arrives with music; then, within the Kitsch (not the petit-bourgeois kind) something of the jubilation of the (possible) resurrection of the dead conceals itself.[50]

Sleeping, we give ourselves over to the experience of a certain multiplicity. It is while sleeping and even more while dreaming that we depart from the entrenched illusion structuring most of our waking hours, namely, that we are no more than one. It is when we cannot sleep and dream that we become most acutely aware of the uncanny strictures that enforce a unified sense of self-identity and self-presence, when in fact the self *also* exists as a multitude of voices, sounds, images, and emotions that do not simply and strictly speaking amount to a single coherent self. If it is "uncomfortable to be with nothing other than oneself," as Bloch writes, then this is so because a limiting and essentializing sense of self-identity prevents the self from dreaming and imagining something other than that which now dissimulates itself: defined, self-identical, and therefore, ultimately, empty. It is in the darkness of the dreamed moment—as in those rare moments when one is dreaming and knows that one is dreaming, that is, when one experiences the dissolution of the rational waking self *and at the same time* can give oneself a rational account of this dissolution even as the dissolution continues—in the darkness of this dreamed moment Freud's insistence that the ego is not master of its own house emerges not simply as a threat to the project of an ever-progressive enlightenment but also as the uncontrollable displacement that opens the self up to its own internal contradictions and to the possibility of a world that would or could be *entirely different*. Bloch returns to this idea when he reminds us that "there is not one of us who could not also be someone else."[51]

In the Blochian sense, falling asleep also can be like embarking upon a journey. He is careful not to say simply that being asleep is like being on a journey, but that the experience of falling asleep, of being between sleeping and waking, the moment that can only be anticipated ("I am about to fall asleep") or retroactively verified ("I must have fallen asleep") but, like the moment of death itself, can never be articulated in the moment in which it occurs (one can hardly proclaim to oneself or to another, "In this very moment, here and now, I am making the final transition from waking to sleeping and now I am sleeping"). Indeed, such a sentence can only be uttered in the uncanny temporality of literature itself, the site of the inarticulable, as when Edgar Allen Poe stages the spectral paradox of a recently deceased man reporting to us, "and now—now—*I am dead*."[52] An erratic and unprogrammable caesura occurs, an interruption that marks a liminal space, both inside and outside consciousness, waking and sleeping, within and without the bounds of reason, here and there, departing and arriving in an arrival that is also a departure, in short: the experience of otherness and displacement as such, even if these are general functions and aspects of a self that often conceives of itself as singular.

When Bloch speaks of such an uncanny departure, from one's self and from the very idea of self-identity, as a moment of pride, he emphasizes the role that music plays in this dynamic—"especially when the ship arrives with music." The arriving ship that brings music along, that arrives *to* music and, perhaps, even *as* music, is filled not with the cargo of self-identical propositions and truth claims but with the very hope without which the notion of redemption, the return of the dead, and the restoration of all—what the Greeks called *apokatastasis*—could not even be thought. "Especially when the ship arrives with music": far from a triumphalist certainty in this or that program, Bloch insists on the radical openness with which the music of the dream and the dream of music signal that non-self-identity and self-differentiation within the self and within the self's life world are possible names for a certain utopian long-ing that is at any time radically exposed to the threat of ship wreck. If one of the names for the radically unprogrammable nature of the dream of transformation is music, then music stages the ways in which, as he says in his Tübingen lectures, "all our dreams and anticipations of a possible reality are not thereby relegated to a planning office and its designs—especially not the most important ones, among them the dream that is called freedom, leisure, and finally the terra incognita of freedom."[53] What is to come cannot be planned or programmed in ad-vance, administered by an imaginary office for the implementation of freedom and justice, any more than one can decide what to dream about when one goes to sleep. Yet beyond the unprogrammability of this or that future system of freedom and justice—the very idea of a freedom and justice as always yet to come, as always inscribed, even if only in the traces of a weak hope—is preserved in and as the dream, as the openness and potential of what is at odds with itself, of what hovers between imagination and concept, mysticism and enlightenment.

To imagine, then, a ship always about to arrive to the notes of music is to imagine Bloch as one of its passengers sleepwalking on deck, vigi-lantly somnambulant, waking and dreaming at the same time, analyz-ing relentlessly what is, yet dreaming of an absolute otherness, perhaps even of what one of his readers, Levinas, calls *the wholly other*—the third term that cannot be assimilated or reduced to the binary logic of self and other, remaining a wholly other not simply to any self but to *the very structure* of self and other. The absolute otherness that Bloch imagines in the dream of music and the music of the dream is sealed in what he calls "the darkness of the lived moment." As he tells us, "we do not have an organ for the I or the we, but we keep to ourselves in the blind spot, in the darkness of the lived moment, whose darkness ultimately is *our own darkness*, our being unknown, disguised, or lost, to ourselves" (*Spirit*, 276; *Geist*, 343). The darkness of the lived moment registers the way in which experience remains at odds with itself, which is to say, displaced as the void that prevents the self from ever being fully conscious and awake to itself. In *The Principle of Hope*, Bloch takes up this discussion when he writes that this "blind spot in the soul, this darkness of the lived mo-ment, must nevertheless be thoroughly distinguished from the darkness of forgotten and past events." For, as he explains, if the "darkness of the lived moment . . . stays in its sleeping-chamber," then "together with its content, the lived moment itself remains essentially invisible, and in fact all the more securely, the more energetically attention is directed toward it: at this root, in the lived In-itself, in punctual immediacy, all world is still dark."[54] The lived moment, as the actuality of experience, remains a blind spot not simply because we have failed to awaken properly but because we have mistaken the imbrication of light and darkness, waking and dreaming, for absolute lucidity. To acknowledge that we are partially sleeping when we believe ourselves to be awake, and to recognize that we also are partially awake when we are sleeping, is, for Bloch, the name of a hopeful refusal: the refusal to give up on the dream that imagines modernity differently, the dream that dreams of enlightenment *through* and not in opposition to its own dialectic and that struggles in every moment not to forget that, for all its achieved progress and lucidity, it is always also traversed by the blind specters of barbarism and the night of its own dialectical reversal. Here, in the night of a simultaneous waking and sleeping, in perpetual fluctuation between levels of consciousness, the Blochian dream resides in a nocturnal space defined by transition and transgression "in which nothing that exists, and certainly no material that has been shaped elsewhere, makes the transition to another cosmos, the categories called Mozart, Bach, and Beethoven are at home. *They are the figures of a transgression of boundaries in the spheres of sound.*"[55] The transgression of boundaries of all sorts, for which the perpetual transgression of waking and sleeping, dreaming and awakening are privileged tropes, assumes in the sphere of music the proper names of Bach, Mozart, and Beethoven—though not as empirical composers but as the incommensurate designation of "categories" and principles that for Bloch stage themselves musically as sound figures of transgression as such.

While audible, the meanings of these transgressive sound figures remain deferred. Indeed, their meaning *is* deferral. Thus, Bloch argues, if the "tomorrow lives within the today," if "it is always sought," and if this tomorrow of the promise can take the form of "the trumpet call in *Fidelio,*" we also must recognize that "there are so many and such heterogeneous witnesses and images, but all grouped around that which speaks for itself by still remaining silent."[56] The tomorrow encrypted in Beethoven's opera, therefore, does not promise an achieved meaning in the closed hermeneutic sense of a pre-programmed future, but promises instead to confront its own inability to address fully the futurity of the future. This inability is also its promise. The trumpet signal to which Bloch returns in many passages and contexts, the call of liberty and justice that occurs in *Fidelio* as the governor arrives, therefore belongs to those heterogeneous "witnesses" who, by speaking in many voices rather than with only a single meaning, articulate the ways in which they cannot speak transparently, and who honor what is to come by remaining silent about it.[57] Clustered around an absent center, a void that speaks of its own status as void, they point to the beyondness of signification that is the rightful territory of music and to the excessiveness to which hope attaches.

The dream of music and the music of the dream for Bloch stage the possibility of understanding our being *otherwise*. If his project is to articulate that which cannot be reduced to what merely is and to imagine that which merely is as the irreducible and non-self-identical itself, then the music he hopes one day to hear—that of Bach, Mozart, Beethoven, and others whom no one as yet has really heard—is the sound of a radical openness, mediated by what the Bloch of *Spirit of Utopia* calls "the secret" and "the form of the unconstruable question." Music, we could say, is one of the forms that the unconstruable question assumes: as an irreducible otherness it resists full explication by rational argument and remains a question that must always pose itself one more time.

Anticipatory Hope

If we perceive that Bloch's ear listens to the sounds of an unorthodox Marxism that is not without transformative messianic elements even while it registers an uneasy harmony with certain forms of socialism— as, for instance, when Bloch assumed a professorship at Karl-Marx-Universität Leipzig in the German Democratic Republic upon his return from exile in the United States in 1948—then we are in a position to grasp more fully what Bloch's project, fueled by the difficulty of aporias and paradoxes, may hope to articulate. The hope that Bloch does not wish to relinquish in his meditations on, and dreams of, music— indeed, the dream of music as an allegory of an entire constellation of aporetic aesthetico-political practices—is far removed from the essentializing dogma of certainty and ideological delusions of the availability of full hermeneutic meaning. Bloch's enigmatic sounds, audible in the night of his musical incantations, are closer to what recent proponents of radical democratic practice such as Ernesto Laclau and Chantal Mouffe call the "deconstructive effects in the project for a radical democracy," a "form of politics which is founded not upon dogmatic postulation of any 'essence of the social,' but, on the contrary, on affirmation of the contingency and ambiguity of every 'essence,' and on the constitutive character of social division and antagonism." Here, ultimately, the ground for any political order "exists only as a partial limiting of disorder" and "of a 'meaning' which is constructed only as excess and paradox in the face of meaninglessness."[58] The hope that resides in this recognition cannot be separated, in Bloch's conceptualization, from an incessant and productive return to the difficulties and possibilities of learning how to listen and, by extension, of learning how to read and think.

In the same way that Bloch, in *Spirit of Utopia*, speaks of an artwork's "Vorschein," or anticipatory illumination, one also could speak of a musical "Vorklang" in describing the anticipatory sound of hope. It is in this context that Bloch advances the notion of "Hellhören," a musically mediated, visionary listening experience or clairaudience that cannot be separated from the thinking of futurity itself: "In other words: clairvoyance is long extinguished. Should not however a clairaudience, a new kind of seeing from within, be imminent, which, now that the visible world has become too weak to hold the spirit, will call forth the audible world, the refuge of the light, the primacy of flaring up instead of the former primacy of seeing, whenever the hour of the language of music will have come? For this place is still empty, it only echoes obscurely back in metaphysical contexts. But there will come a time when the sound speaks" (*Spirit*, 163; *Geist*, 297–80).

Once the visionary capabilities associated with the eye, sight, and light—and, by extension, with their Enlightenment heritage—have exhausted themselves as potentially libratory instruments, the auditory possibilities of the ear still hold out promise. Through a kind of "visionary listening"—that also echoes in the German idiom *hellhörig werden*, to sit up and take notice—the ear attunes consciousness to the ways in which the futurity of hope has not yet been fully exhausted in the available ideologies and aesthetico-political programs that structure cognition. Without catachrestically transforming the Enlightenment into a mere "ensoundment," Bloch nevertheless wishes to invest the ear with a transformative capability that would enable the dream of the future— a dream that acknowledges the dialectically charged relation of reason and myth—to unfold also as the future of a dream from which one awakens to face the ethico-political aporias that will not permit us fully to decide whether we are dreaming or awake.

The dream of music, then, names a radical openness to what still remains to be heard and thought. As Bloch suggests: "If sound remains only allusive, unactualized, then it has surely not been put into signs, and its puzzle language does not wish to conceal from us something already resolved supernaturally; music's function is rather the most complete openness and the secret, what is comprehensible-incomprehensible. Symbolic in music is the proper object of humanity *objectively* veiling itself from itself. Sound walks with us and is We" (*Spirit*, 163; *Geist*, 207).

The "vollste Offenheit," or "most complete openness," which Bloch locates in the dream of music, cannot be reduced to a stable meaning that has already secretly been decided elsewhere. Rather, music itself comprises this abiding and enigmatic negotiation of meaning, that, in its inability to come into its own, points to a socially just way of responding to the other and to otherness itself that is still lacking. For Bloch, the human tone sings of nothing else. Standing in the service of this "most complete openness," the dream of music, we could say, is inscribed in what Bloch, in *Atheism in Christianity*, terms "a transcending without transcendence" *(ein Transzendieren ohne Transzendenz)*.[59] To locate music within the Blochian notion of transcending without transcendence is to claim for it the volatile property of a process rather than that of a stable state. As a form of transcending without transcendence, music never is quite itself. Composed of a multitude of differential relations of which those of major and minor, harmonic and dissonant, are only among the most transparent, music always is alone, even if one can speak of it only in conjunction with something else. The transcending without transcendence to which music belongs also works to keep alive a certain structure of transcending, even when the concrete manifestation of that transcendence has no common measure with what, in the history of philosophy, has been associated with transcendence—such as the supersensuous, independence from consciousness, the inexperiencable, the otherworldliness in ontological thought, or the otherworldliness of God. As a transcending without transcendence, Bloch's music is both deeply historical and simultaneously at odds with its own history: it refunctionalizes the gesture of its own abandonment as a non-instrumental instrument placed in the service of a futurity that still deserves our action, hope, composition, performance, and dreaming.

Because music is composed of a process of transcending without ever reaching a final state of transcendence, its work can never be completed and, indeed, can always only have just begun. Its principles of polyphony and dissonance endlessly point to an elsewhere that is yet to come and yet to be thought. In a sense then, to speak of "new" music would be superfluous, since music never can be anything but new. One is correct in thinking of music as a truly *modern* art, in fact, the youngest of the arts, not only because it, unlike architecture or poetry, has no known model in classical antiquity, but also because its signification as that which lies beyond signification is ever new and inexhaustible, regardless of the frequency with which it is performed, heard, or dreamed. In Bloch's own words: "New music no longer has a recapitulation, with a principle key restored, on which victory could be recognized; after all, it is its greatness and its future that it no longer possesses a theme that has been placed at the beginning and that has been decided upon but that it, instead, constitutes music that is only still forming itself and that takes seriously the New and the infinity of the end" *(die mit dem Neu, Unendlich des Endes Ernst macht)*.[60]

For music to be serious about itself *(Ernst machen)*, then, it cannot simply put to notes a pre-thought and pre-administered extra-musical program. The theme of music, its formal dream that also is its leitmotif, is the thinking of the end that has no end, the end whose proper end is endlessness itself, the end that takes its own endlessness, its perpetually unfinished spectral business, seriously as the end that has not ended once and for all and that thus puts an end to the end—"mit dem . . . Unendlich des Endes Ernst macht." What Bloch ultimately gives us to learn, then, is how to hear music that is always only just forming itself ("die sich erst bildet"), a music that takes seriously, *ernst,* its own infinity by breaking with the finitude that also is a condition of its existence—*mit dem. . . . Unendlich des Endes Ernst macht.* With a play, albeit a serious play, *ein ernstes Spiel,* on his own name—"Ernst macht"—Bloch signs the notes and sounds of his musical dream. If, as is apparent in *Heritage Of Our Times,* he is concerned with the problem of how to inherit something properly, seriously, *ernsthaft* (earnestly or like an Ernst), of how to relate ethically *ernsthaft* to an inheritance and a heritage, then the heritage that he himself bequeaths to us—in and as a dream, in fact, his singular dream that nonetheless is shared and dreamed by others—is one that demands, aesthetically, ethically, and politically, that what he, in all earnestness, calls *"das Unsagbare der Musik,"* the "unsayable of music" (*Spirit,* 163; *Geist,* 208), also always will remain the pleasurably sublime yet torturous music of the unsayable. Let's get serious.

NOTES

1. Ernst Bloch, *The Spirit of Utopia*, trans. Anthony A. Nassar (Stanford, Calif.: Stanford University Press, 2000), 115; idem, *Der Geist der Utopie*, 2nd ed., *Werkausgabe*, vol. 3 (Frankfurt am Main: Suhrkamp, 1985), 149. Subsequent references are given in the text, using the abbreviations *Spirit* for the English and *Geist* for the German edition.

Wherever two references to an individual text are given, the first one refers to an English edition, the second one to a German edition. Where only a German source is cited, translations are my own. I have modified existing translations when necessary to increase their fidelity to the original.

2. Emmanuel Levinas, "On Death in the Thought of Ernst Bloch," in *Of God Who Comes to Mind*, trans. Bettina Bergo (Stanford, Calif.: Stanford University Press, 1998), 33–42, here 34.

3. Edward Said, "On the Transgressive Element in Music," in *Musical Elaborations* (New York: Columbia University Press, 1991), 35–72, here 40. Among the many general assessments of the relationship between music and language and considerations of music as a possible form of language, see the essays collected in *Sprache und Musik: Perspektiven einer Beziehung*, ed. Albrecht Riethmüller (Laaber: Laaber Verlag, 1999), as well as *Music and Text: Critical Inquiries*, ed. Steven Paul Scher (Cambridge: Cambridge University Press, 1992), and *Dichtung und Musik: Kaleidoskop ihrer Beziehungen*, ed. Günter Schnitzler (Stuttgart: Klett-Cotta, 1979), in the latter especially the contribution by Carl Dahlhaus, "Musik als Text," 11–28. Cf. Peter Faltin, "Ist Musik eine Sprache?" in *Die Zeichen: Neue Aspekte der musikalischen Ästhetik II*, ed. Hans Werner Henze (Frankfurt am Main: Suhrkamp, 1981), 32–50.

4. From this perspective, more traditional questions of music history and theory too could be expanded and recast as questions of textuality and of discourse in the broadest sense. Among the gestures toward that possible future direction, see, for instance, the historiographic and tropological concerns in Hayden White, "Form, Reference, and Ideology in Musical Discourse," in *Figural Realism: Studies in the Mimesis Effect* (Baltimore: Johns Hopkins University Press, 1999), 147–76.

5. "*Das Dasein ist voller Figuren, doch nicht auch voll eingeräumter, mit allem und jedem an seinem festen Platz. Vielmehr wird überall noch ein* Echo allegorischer Bedeutungen *widerhallen, ein lehrreich hin und herschickendes, vieldeutig reflektierendes.*" Ernst Bloch, *Spuren, Werkausgabe*, vol. 1 (Frankfurt am Main: Suhrkamp, 1985), 167.

6. Jacques Derrida, *Of Grammatology*, trans. Gayatri Chakravorty Spivak (Baltimore: Johns Hopkins University Press, 1976), 158.

7. Jacques Derrida, "Afterword: Toward an Ethic of Discussion," trans. Samuel Weber, in *Limited Inc* (Evanston, Ill.: Northwestern University Press, 1988), 111–54, here 136.

8. Ernst Bloch, *Experimentum Mundi, Werkausgabe*, vol. 15 (Frankfurt am Main: Suhrkamp, 1985), 248.

9. Jürgen Habermas, "Ein marxistischer Schelling," in *Über Ernst Bloch*, ed. Martin Walser et al. (Frankfurt am Main: Suhrkamp, 1968), 61–81.

10. Ernst Bloch, *Tübinger Einleitung in die Philosophie, Werkausgabe*, vol. 13 (Frankfurt am Main; Suhrkamp, 1985), 224.

11. A useful overview of the range of Bloch's aesthetic concerns can be found in his essay collection, selected from the vast *Werkausgabe* of his collected works, titled *Ästhetik des Vorscheins*, ed. Gerd Ueding (Frankfurt am Main: Suhrkamp, 1974). Many of the most significant essays in this collection are available in English translation as *The Utopian Function of Art and Literature: Selected Essays*, trans. Jack Zipes and Frank Mecklenburg (Cambridge, Mass.: MIT Press, 1988).

12. For studies relevant to the multifaceted relationship between Bloch's philosophy of music and his politico-utopian concerns, cf. especially Anna Czajka-Cunico, "'Wann lebt man eigentlich?' Die Suche nach der 'zweiten' Wahrheit und die ästhetische Erfahrung (Musik und Poesie) in Ernst Blochs *Geist der Utopie*," *Bloch-Almanach* 19 (2000): 103–57; Roger Behrens, "Hören im Dunkel des gelebten Augenblicks: Zur Musikphilosophie Ernst Blochs," *Bloch-Almanach* 17 (1998):101–17; Christopher Norris, "Utopian Deconstruction: Ernst Bloch, Paul de Man and the Politics of Music," *Paragraph* 11 (1988): 24–57; Wolfgang Matz, *Musica Humana: Versuch über Ernst Blochs Philosophie der Musik* (Frankfurt am Main: Lang, 1988); Albrecht Riethmüller, "Der Fortschritt in der Musik, gesehen von Bloch, Lukács und Adorno," *Bayrische Akademie der Schönen Künste Jahrbuch* 4 (1990): 75–95; Robert Lilienfeld, "Music and Society in the 20th Century: Georg Lukács, Ernst Bloch, and Theodor W. Adorno," *International Journal of Politics, Culture, and Society* 1 (1987): 120–46. Frieder Reininghaus, "Musik wird Morgenrot: Ernst Bloch und die Musik," *Sozialistische Zeitschrift für Kunst und Gesellschaft* 3–4 (1977): 78–90; Heinz Paetzold, "Utopische Musiklehre," in *Neomarxistische Ästhetik 1: Bloch und Benjamin* (Düsseldorf: Schwann, 1974), 113–24; and Gianni Vattimo, "Sprache, Utopie, Musik," *Philosophische Perspektiven* 4 (1972): 151–70.

13. A substantial selection of Bloch's writings on the philosophy of music was edited by his wife and appeared as *Zur Philosophie der Musik*, selected and edited by Karola Bloch (Frankfurt am Main: Suhrkamp, 1974). A partial English translation was published as *Essays on the Philosophy of Music*, trans. Peter Palmer (Cambridge: Cambridge University Press, 1985).

14. Bloch, *Experimentum Mundi*, 205.

15. Theodor W. Adorno, "Ernst Bloch's *Spuren*," in *Notes to Literature*, trans. Shierry Weber Nicholson, vol. 1 (New York: Columbia University Press, 1991), 200–215, here 207; idem, "Blochs Spuren," in *Noten zur Literatur*, vol. 11 of *Gesammelte Schriften* (Frankfurt am Main: 1997), 233–50, here 240.

16. Philippe Lacoue-Labarthe, *Musica Ficta (Figures of Wagner)*, trans. Felicia McCarren (Stanford, Calif.: Stanford University Press, 1994), xvi.

17. I borrow the term "other-directedness" from Samuel Weber's discussion of textuality as "a figure that designates the *other-directedness of structures of signification*," which "entails an approach to the other as articulation and to articulation as other." "Catching Up with the Past," in *Mass Mediauras: Form, Technics, Media* (Stanford, Calif.: Stanford University Press, 1996), 168–208, here 201.

18. Paul de Man, "The Resistance to Theory," in *The Resistance to Theory* (Minneapolis: University of Minnesota Press, 1986), 3–20, here 11. These concerns are enlarged and deepened in the essays collected in his *Aesthetic Ideology*, ed. Andrzej Warminski (Minneapolis: University of Minnesota Press, 1996).

19. For a general discussion of the status of music as a special kind of "text" and of resulting questions of composition and experimentation in posttraditional musical practices, see Claus-Steffen Mahnkopf, "Der Strukturbegriff der musikalischen Dekonstruktion," *Musik und Ästhetik* 21 (2002): 49–68.

20. Paul de Man, "The Rhetoric of Blindness: Jacques Derrida's Reading of Rousseau," in *Blindness and Insight: Essays in the Rhetoric of Contemporary Criticism*, 2nd ed. (Minneapolis: University of Minnesota Press, 1983), 102–41, here 130.

21. De Man, "Rhetoric of Blindness," 128–29.

22. Christopher Norris makes this point in his remarkable reading of Bloch and de Man, "Utopian Deconstruction," 52.

23. Ernst Bloch, *The Principle of Hope*, trans. Neville Plaice, Stephen Plaice, and Paul Knight, vol. 3 (Cambridge, Mass.: MIT Press, 1986), 1062; idem, *Das Prinzip Hoffnung*, vol. 3, in *Werkausgabe*, vol. 5 (Frankfurt am Main: Suhrkamp, 1985), 1248.

24. Jean-Luc Nancy, "Music, " in *The Sense of the World*, trans. Jeffrey S. Librett (Minneapolis: University of Minnesota Press, 1997), 84–87, here 86.

25. Robert Bernasconi, "A Love That Is Stronger Than Death: Sacrifice in the Thought of Levinas, Heidegger, and Bloch," *Angelaki: Journal of the Theoretical Humanities* 7, no. 2 (August 2002), 9–16, here 15.

26. Walter Benjamin, *Correspondence, 1910–1940*, trans. Manfred Jacobson and Evelyn M. Jacobson (Chicago: University of Chicago Press, 1994), 148; idem, *Gesammelte Briefe*, vol. 2 (Frankfurt am Main: Suhrkamp, 1996), 46.

27. Theodor W. Adorno, "The Handle, the Pot, and Early Experience," in *Notes to Literature*, trans. Shierry Weber Nicholson, vol. 2 (New York: Columbia University Press, 1992), 211–19, here 212; idem, "Henkel, Krug und frühe Erfahrung," in *Noten zur Literatur*, vol. 11 of *Gesammelte Schriften* (Frankfurt am Main: Suhrkamp, 1997), 556–66, here 557.

28. Ernst Bloch, "Grundsätzliche Unterscheidung der Tagträume von den Nachtträumen," in *Das Prinzip Hoffnung*, 86–128; idem, "Traum von einer Sache," in *Philosophische Aufsätze zur objektiven Phantasie* (Frankfurt am Main: Suhrkamp, 1985), 163–69; and idem, *Tagträume vom aufrechten Gang: Sechs*

Interviews mit Ernst Bloch, ed. Arno Münster (Frankfurt am Main: Suhr-kamp, 1977).

29. Bloch, *Principle,* 1069; idem, *Prinzip,* 1257.

30. Immanuel Kant, *Critique of the Power of Judgment,* trans. Paul Guyer and Eric Matthews (Cambridge: Cambridge University Press, 2000), 205; idem, *Kritik der Urteilskraft,* ed. Wilhelm Weischedel, *Theorie-Werkausgabe,* vol. 10 (Frankfurt am Main: Suhrkamp, 1991), 267.

31. Kant, *Judgment,* 206; idem, *Urteilskraft,* 269.

32. Kant, *Judgment,* 207; idem, *Urteilskraft,* 269–70.

33. "Ocularcentrism" and "anti-ocularcentrism" are the terms that Martin Jay suggests for the debate concerning the hegemony of "the noblest of the senses" in his philosophical history of vision, *Downcast Eyes: The Denigration of Vision in Twentieth-Century French Thought* (Berkeley: University of California Press, 1993).

34. Martin Heidegger, "Die Zeit des Weltbildes," in *Holzwege* (Frank-furt am Main: Klostermann, 1980), 73–110. For a discussion of the role that music plays in the philosophies of German Early (or Jena) Romantics such as Friedrich Schlegel and Novalis, see Barbara Naumann, *Musikalisches Ideen-Instrument: Das Musikalische in Poetik und Sprachtheorie der Frühromantik* (Stuttgart: Metzler, 1990).

35. Derrida, *Of Grammatology,* 157.

36. Norris, "Utopian Deconstruction," 27.

37. Ernst Bloch, "Something's Missing: A Discussion between Ernst Bloch and Theodor W. Adorno on the Contradictions of Utopian Longing," in *The Utopian Function of Art and Literature: Selected Essays,* trans. Jack Zipes and Frank Mecklenburg (Cambridge, Mass.: MIT Press, 1988), 1–17, here 15; idem, "Etwas fehlt . . . Über die Widersprüche der utopischen Sehnsucht: Ein Rundfunkgespräch mit Theodor W. Adorno," in *Tendenz-Latenz-Utopie, Werkausgabe,* supplementary volume (Frankfurt am Main; Suhrkamp, 1985), 350–68, here 366.

38. Ernst Bloch, *Heritage of Our Times,* trans. Neville and Stephen Plaice (Berkeley: University of California Press, 1990), 232; idem, *Erbschaft dieser Zeit, Werkausgabe,* vol. 4 (Frankfurt am Main: Suhrkamp, 1985), 254.

39. Bertolt Brecht, *Aufstieg und Fall der Stadt Mahagonny, Stücke in einem Band* (Frankfurt am Main: Suhrkamp, 1987), 203–26, here 210–11 (scene 8).

40. I owe this image of wanting to experience music as slipping into a hot bathtub to my conversations about music with Jost Hermand, who reiterates it with eloquent ambivalence. Compare further his *Nach der Postmoderne: Ästhetik heute* (Cologne: Böhlau, 2004), 27. As an antidote to such hedonistic aberrations, see his *Konkretes Hören: Zum Inhalt der Instrumentalmusik* (Berlin: Argument, 1981), 142–50.

41. Friedrich Schlegel, "Kritische Fragmente," in *Schriften zur Literatur,* ed. Wolfdietrich Rasch (Munich: Deutscher Taschenbuch Verlag, 1985), 7–24, here 8.

42. Lacoue-Labarthe, *Musica Ficta,* 144–45.

43. Bloch, *Spuren,* 142.

44. Ernst Bloch, *Thomas Münzer als Theologe der Revolution, Werkausgabe,* vol. 2 (Frankfurt am Main: Suhrkamp, 1985), 198.

45. Bloch, *Tübinger Einleitung,* 100.

46. This according to his wife and posthumous editor, Karola Bloch, in the introduction to the edition of her husband's letters. "Zu dieser Ausgabe," in *Ernst Bloch: Briefe 1903–1975,* vol. 1 (Frankfurt am Main: Suhrkamp, 1985), 7–12, here 11.

47. Roland Barthes, "Listening," in *The Responsibility of Forms: Critical Essays on Music, Art, and Representation* (Berkeley: University of California Press, 1991), 245–60, here 257.

48. Incisive commentaries on Bloch's *Spuren* can be found in the essays by his friends and fellow writers of the thought-image, Kracauer and Adorno. See Kracauer's 1931 essay "Spuren," in *Ernst Blochs Wirkung: Ein Arbeitsbuch zum 90. Geburtstag* (Frankfurt am Main: Suhrkamp, 1975), 44–45; and the essay by Adorno, "Große Blochmusik," reprinted as "Blochs Spuren," in *Noten zur Literatur.*

For more recent suggestive studies of a variety of issues arising from Bloch's thought-images collected in *Spuren,* cf. Anna Czajka, "Poetik des Augenblicks. Zu Ernst Blochs *Spuren,*" *Bloch-Jahrbuch* (1994): 36–49; Ekkehard Roeppert, "Erzählformen in Blochs *Spuren,*" *Bloch-Almanach* 11 (1991): 137–48; Klaus L. Berghahn, "A View through the Red Window: Ernst Bloch's Spuren," in *Modernity and the Text: Revisions of German Modernism,* ed. Andreas Huyssen and David Bathrick (New York: Columbia University Press, 1989), 200–215; Martin Zerlang, "Ernst Bloch als Erzähler: Über Allegorie, Melancholie und Utopie in den *Spuren, Text und Kritik,* special issue on Ernst Bloch (1985): 61–75; and Rainer Hoffmann, *Montage im Hohlraum: Zu Ernst Blochs Spuren* (Bonn: Bouvier, 1977).

Finally, for a consideration of Bloch's narrative strategies, see Liliane Weissberg, "Philosophy and the Fairy Tale: Ernst Bloch as Narrator," *New German Critique* 55 (1992): 21–44, on *Spuren* especially 34–38.

49. Ernst Bloch, "From *Spuren* by Ernst Bloch," trans. Jamie Owen Daniel, in *Not Yet: Reconsidering Ernst Bloch,* ed. Jamie Owen Daniel and Tom Moylan (London: Verso, 1997), 215–23, here 215; idem, *Spuren,* 11.

50. Bloch, *Spuren,* 130–31.

51. Bloch, *Principle,* 930; idem, *Prinzip,* 1093.

52. Edgar Allan Poe, "The Facts in the Case of M. Valdemar," in vol. 5 of *The Complete Works* (New York: AMS, 1965), 154–66, here 163.

53. Bloch, *Tübinger Einleitung*, 98.

54. Bloch, *Principle*, 1062; idem, *Prinzip*, 1248.

55. Bloch, *Principle*, 1088; idem, *Prinzip*, 1279.

56. Bloch, *Principle*, 1375; idem, *Prinzip*, 1627.

57. For extended discussions of the trumpet signal in *Fidelio* and its relation to the messianic tradition that links trumpet signals to expressions of hope, such as the biblical scenes of trumpet-playing angels, the playing of trumpets that opens graves and that causes the walls of Jericho to fall, cf. Francesca Vidal, "Bloch," in *Musik in der deutschen Philosophie: Eine Einführung*, ed. Stefan Lorenz Sorgner and Oliver Fürbeth (Stuttgart: Metzler, 2003), 135–54, here 144–48, as well as the discussion by Bloch's friend Hans Mayer, "Der geschichtliche Augenblick des *Fidelio*," in *Abend der Vernunft: Reden und Vorträge, 1985–1990* (Frankfurt am Main: Suhrkamp, 1990), 33–45.

58. Ernesto Laclau and Chantal Mouffe, *Hegemony and Socialist Strategy: Toward a Radical Democratic Politics* (London: Verso, 1985), 193.

59. Ernst Bloch, *Atheism in Christianity: The Religion of the Exodus and the Kingdom*, trans. J. T. Swann (New York: Herder & Herder, 1972), motto, n.p.; idem, *Atheismus im Christentum: Zur Religion des Exodus und des Reichs, Werkausgabe*, vol. 14 (Frankfurt am Main: Suhrkamp, 1985), motto, n.p.

60. Bloch, *Principle*, 1094; idem, *Prinzip*, 1286.

8

Dissonance and Aesthetic Totality

Adorno Reads Schönberg

BEATRICE HANSSEN

Music, the Divine Fragment

For all his renown as a post-Hegelian thinker who pushed Hegel's philosophy to its negative limits and for all his prominence as a dialectical
materialist, devoted to the operations of the negative dialectic, Theodor
W. Adorno, in much of his mature philosophy, held fast to the theological figure of the Absolute; at the same time, he acknowledged the impossible return of the divine in the postsecular present. Like the work of his
friend Walter Benjamin, many of Adorno's writings bear witness to and,
indeed, seem intent on detecting the presence of the divine name, whose
aura can be discerned fleetingly amid the all too secular, for, in modernity, the loss of meaning has made all metaphysics equally meaningless.

Not just in his grand philosophical treatises—*Negative Dialectics* and
the unfinished *Aesthetic Theory*—but also in the many essays Adorno devoted to the philosophy of music in his capacity as music critic and theorist, the same overarching question returns: whether the presentation of
the Absolute is still possible today and whether the lingering presence of
the divine can still be perceived. However, in the scholarship dedicated

to Adorno's philosophy of music, his Hegelian pronouncements about music have found far greater resonance than Adorno's own quasi-metaphysical musings about music's affinities to the divine. The recent reissuing of the *Philosophie der neuen Musik* (in a new English translation), arguably Adorno's most Hegelian treatise on music, once again seems to bear this out. Devoted mainly to Vienna's Second School (Schönberg, Berg, Zemlinsky, Webern), the *Philosophy of New Music* unambiguously states that music is the development of truth in its antinomies or contradictions. Rejecting empirical forms of art history, Hegel's lectures on aesthetics had argued for a genuine philosophy of art, which would recognize art—together with philosophy and religion—as one of the privileged ways in which truth could be manifested. Marked by *Schein* (appearance, in its distinction from mere semblance), art represents the mode in which the Idea could come to a sensuous appearance. Indebted to this Hegelian perspective, Adorno's philosophy of music unambiguously presents music as the disclosure of knowledge, as a form of knowing *(Erkenntnis)* that, rather than rivaling the work of philosophy, engages in an "elective affinity" with philosophy, as the book's polyvalent genitive construction, *Philosophy of New Music,* implies; in presenting a philosophy about music the book hopes to disclose the philosophy particular to music. Adorno's study does not just "philosophize" about music but offers the very unfolding of music's own nonconceptual philosophy.

Applying this Hegelian vantage point to the modernist present, Adorno understands the Second Viennese School to be a critique of the metaphysical tradition in classical music. Its truly revolutionizing music announces itself as the negation of the metaphysical category of illusion, or *Schein* (*Schein* in this instance is not to be confused with the necessary aesthetic *Schein* that constitutes every work of art, as Hegel had stressed in the lectures on aesthetics). The radical atonal music pioneered by Arnold Schönberg and realized most fully by Alban Berg—Adorno's own musical master—takes on the so-called second nature of tonality and melody, dismantling their deceptively natural appearance as a form of historically generated *Schein* (illusion). The new music rises up in rebellion against the reified "lexical items" that consciousness has imposed on musical language, a process of reification analogous to the rule of concepts in nonmusical language.[1] In the process, music's truth seems restored: music, in essence, is an imageless, nonimagistic art—an insight at the center of Schopenhauer's *World as Will and Representation,* in which music emerges as the nonrepresentational art par excellence. However, as Adorno's *Philosophy of New Music* goes on to argue, the truth of music's imageless essence has been corrupted in and throughout the history of Western music. The trajectory of Western music leads from the sacrality of polyphonous music—or the nonsolipsistic collectivity of the religious community—to its decline during the era of bourgeois, individualistic art. The few exceptions include Beethoven's magisterial symphonies, especially the Ninth, whose return to a choral collectivity consecrates the community. On the whole, however, bourgeois music distinguishes itself by its dissimulation, which anticipates the celebration of kitsch that is to mark the musical entertainment industry of the twentieth century. In kitsch and cheap, trivial entertainment music, as well as in jazz—at least according to Adorno's problematic assessment—the hegemony of the culture industry emerges to the point where the faculty of hearing and the art of listening have been corrupted.[2]

Next to these texts and essays, exemplifying the quasi-Hegelian unfolding of music's inner truth, one encounters other writings that pronounce a more mystical, even esoteric truth. Music here is thought to participate in the realm of the sacred or the divine Absolute. To that extent, Adorno also questions Hegel's taxonomy of the arts, which culminates in the rule of the Word   poetry and prose (philosophy)—and in Hegel's totalizing pronouncement that philosophy may have overcome art, including music. Taking on the age-old question of the elective affinities between language and music, a question that had preoccupied Rousseau, Schopenhauer, and Nietzsche, Adorno invokes a topos dear to Benjamin's early aesthetic theory, namely, that of the nonintentionality of the truth and of the Name. These terms, signaling a critique of phenomenology, define Benjamin's thoughts on Early Romanticism, the task of the translator, and the origin of the mourning play, or *Trauerspiel*. In an enigmatic short essay, called "Music and Language: A Fragment," Adorno contends the following: "The language of music is quite different from the language of intentionality. It contains a theological dimension. What it has to say is simultaneously revealed and concealed. Its Idea is the divine Name which has been given shape. It is demythologized prayer, rid of efficacious magic. It is the human attempt, doomed as ever, to name the Name, not to communicate meanings."[3]

Although a modicum of intentionality still structures music, to prevent it from becoming a mere "kaleidoscope" of disparate "sensory stimuli" (Baudelaire), it is the writer Kafka, who, using the language of the parable, has most adequately revealed music's inner truth. To cite

Adorno: "[Kafka] treated the meanings of spoken, intentional language as if they were those of music, parables broken off in mid-phrase" (*QUF*, 3).

The seeming paradox that ensues can perhaps best be formulated as follows: while music is a form of knowledge *(Erkenntnis)*, with "rules of musical grammar and syntax" (*QUF*, 6), at other moments music is said to defy the discursive or conceptual logic of language, consecrated in philosophy, amounting to nothing less than the fragment of the sacred, or a sacred fragment (to borrow the title Adorno uses to qualify Schön-berg's opera *Moses und Aron*). In this manner, music lives up to the critical task Adorno formulates in his *Negative Dialectics*, namely, to what extent it might be possible, philosophically speaking, to think the other of conceptual language, and, more paradoxically still, to think alterity "outside" concepts. In "Music and Language: A Fragment," this insight returns: "Music as a whole incorporates intentions not by diluting them into a still higher, more abstract intention, but by setting out to proclaim the non-intentioned at the moment when all intentions converge and are fused together. Thus music is almost the opposite of a meaningful totality, even when it seems to create one in contrast to mere sensuous existence. This is the source of the temptation it feels to abstain from all meaning from a sense of its own power, to act, in short, as if it were the direct expression of the Name" (*QUF*, 5).

In this distinctly Benjaminian and decidedly metaphysical meditation on the relation of music to language, Adorno suggests that music, despite its articulation into discrete sounds, remains closed off to a discursive investigation, which is centered in the meaning-seeking intentionality of the subject. Music as the voicing of the divine Name indirectly figures in Benjamin's more gnomic essay, "The Task of the Translator," whose opening lines aver that "no poem is intended for the reader, no picture for the beholder, no symphony for the listener."[4] Unlike Hegel, who encapsulates all human art—the only genuine form of art—in the reflexive model of a self-conscious and self-producing subject, coming to itself in and through art, Benjamin (and in his wake Adorno) thus seek to rescue poetry, visual art, and aural art from the grip of intentionality. Considering the artwork as an end in itself rather than ascribing to it a world-historical use-value, Benjamin goes so far as to question music's seeming raison d'être: the reception of its echoes in the ear of the listener.

In a post-Hegelian climate, defined by the absence of totality and by the impossibility of ever attaining a total or totalizing meaning, music is left behind as a divine fragment, a retained splinter or shard of the divine name, of the Absolute. Moreover, in the absence of religious cults that define modernity, music—the highest form of art—will remain one of the last cultic rituals. Only perhaps in the distant future can the soldering, the reconstitution and reconnection of these fragments be attained, that is, with the arrival of *tikkun*—the mystical Jewish anticipation of the making whole again of creation through the reconnection of its disparate fragments.[5]

For Adorno these observations about the nonintentional, non-psychological, and nonimagistic formal structure of music also generate limitations on the way music is to be approached or interpreted. For although interpreting language means understanding or decoding it based on the largely intentional linguistic structure of language, interpreting music, by contrast, is possible only through *making* music. Interpretation here is the nonmediate or immediate "mimetic" praxis of music. Seen against the context of a mundane, banal, often violent modernity, music's anti-iconic and nonvisual rupturing of modernity takes the form of a caesura. As the incursion of the expressionless *(das Ausdruckslose)*—another Benjaminian term—music provides a fleeting glimpse of the divine or the Absolute, making its presence felt.[6] "Intentional language wants to mediate the Absolute, and the Absolute escapes language for every specific intention leaves each one behind because each is limited. Music finds the Absolute immediately, but at the moment of discovery it becomes obscured, just as too powerful a light dazzles the eyes, preventing them from seeing things which are perfectly visible" *(QUF,* 4).[7]

Music thus overcomes language's instrumental relation to intentionality, spelling the death of the intentional subject and its quest for an enveloping meaning. Ripping apart the glaring phenomenal veil, music opens onto a transcendent, theological *confinium* in a movement that, whether willed or not, recalls the momentary uncovering of the divine sanctum at the center of Hegel's sublime.

In many ways Adorno's fragmentary essay answers one of the main questions in the unfinished *Aesthetic Theory:* if Adorno there asks how the de-artification *(Entkunstung)* of art, and with it the attack on art's ethical task through the violence of the culture industry, is to be stopped, then the answer seems to point to the creation of a new cult: the cultic, sacred art of music. True to what one could call the "skeptical utopianism" of Adorno's philosophical system, however, the philosopher can only cherish such hope in the full realization that the actualization of this new "total" art might forever remain impossible in the (bad) immanence of the present. In trying to circumscribe how a nonmediate or immediate translation of music into hope is possible, Adorno proves faithful to a Benjaminian adage. The only thing remaining is to determine how one can keep the hope for the hopeless awake.

Adorno, Composer-Musician

It is uncertain whether the young Adorno already cherished the faint hope of the *tikkun,* of the reconstitution of an original whole in and through music, a wish he was to treasure at a later age in his more metaphysically inclined writings. At least no such mystical intimations seem to inform his more sober writings on music from the 1920s; such a wish certainly is missing from the correspondence Adorno conducted with the man he was to call his musical master, Alban Berg. Traveling from his native Frankfurt to Vienna, traditionally known as the music capital of Europe, Adorno hoped to learn the profession of musical composer, if not from Arnold Schönberg, then from one of his most gifted students, Berg, who would become renowned through the operas *Wozzeck* and *Lulu.* Having met Berg at the 1924 Frankfurter Tonkünstlerfest, Adorno was elated to receive an invitation to study with Berg in the Austrian capital. And so as a twenty-two-year-old, having already completed his dissertation on Husserl, he set off for Vienna in March 1925. In the five to six months he would spend there, he studied piano with Eduard Steuermann, dedicating himself mostly to Beethoven, while he refined his insights in composition and harmony under the guidance of Berg. In December 1925 Adorno and Benjamin together even attended the Berlin performance of Berg's opera *Wozzeck.*[8] That the sojourn in Vienna amounted to a childhood wish come true emerges from Adorno's later recollection of the auratic experience he had as he made his way to Berg's home in a Viennese suburb. Much like Nietzsche, who first heard the dissonance of Siegfried emanate from Wagner's home in Triebschen before laying his eyes on the master, so Adorno first heard the dissonant accords of Berg playing the piano as he approached his house.

While honing and refining his musical talents, Adorno also continued to work as a music critic, publishing, for example, the highly appreciative 1925 essay on Schönberg, "Schönberg: Serenade, op. 24 (I)."[9] Vehemently rejecting the negative valuation to which Schönberg's allegedly anarchic music had been subjected in the more conservative press, Adorno calls attention to the composer's antipsychological irony and to the limit of forms enacted in opus 24, the first explicit use of the twelve-tone technique. However, the relation between Schönberg and Adorno would rapidly take a different turn after Adorno wrote a review of Berg's *Wozzeck* in 1926. Even before the review was written, one finds Berg pleading with Adorno. A letter admonishes Adorno to be as understandable as possible: "I have one request: please don't write difficultly" "To write difficultly" was a code term meaning "to write incomprehensibly," a potential disaster, as Berg stresses, since the review was to be read by musicians who were not philosophers.[10] As for Schönberg—"the harsh one," as Adorno liked to call him—he absolutely abhorred Adorno's *Wozzeck* essay for the way in which it defined Berg's relation to the master and for its impenetrable philosophical language. Having learned this from Berg, Adorno crafted yet another epithet for Schönberg: "the terrorist."[11] Interestingly, quite a few of Adorno's compositions from the Vienna period survive, bearing the marks of his experimentation with the formal innovations of the new music. Welcoming its deconstruction of tonal music—melody, harmony, classical instrumentation—Adorno recognized in it the negative dialectical movement of a nonmetaphysical truth coming to the fore. Berg, for his part, warmly applauded Adorno's musical talent and, indeed, Adorno's Two Pieces for String Quartet, op. 2, premiered in Vienna in December 1926, where it was performed by the famous Kolisch Quartett.[12]

However, if, according to the later *Quasi una Fantasia,* to interpret music means to make music—not to decode or transliterate it into the discursive language of concepts—then it is also true that the greater part of Adorno's intellectual career seems to violate that very principle. Posterity shows that Adorno was to make his name not as a composer but as a philosopher, music critic, and theorist; his actual sojourn in the realm of musical composition proved all too short. For that very reason, it is interesting to read in his early correspondence that he encountered extreme difficulties in his early academic phase, as he first tried to secure support for a habilitation. Early on, Adorno confided to Berg that he preferred Vienna or Prague over Frankfurt, and that it by no means was clear that he would choose an academic or professorial life. By that time, however, Berg knew better. Already in 1926, he warned Adorno that he would have to make a decision, would have to choose between Kant or Beethoven.[13] Adorno, as we now know, was to choose neither Kant nor Beethoven, but rather Beethoven with Hegel, thus dedicating himself to what he, in another context, was to call "thinking with one's ears."

The eventual return to Frankfurt thus meant the return to the study of philosophy and, more specifically, to a critique of Heidegger's existentialism, which Adorno was to take on vicariously, in the figure of the Danish philosopher Søren Kierkegaard, to whom he dedicated his habilitation under the direction of Paul Tillich. The critical concern with music, however, persisted, a critical task that Adorno had embraced in the early 1920s as the editor of the music periodical *Anbruch;* to this journal, he would contribute reviews dedicated to Bartók, Mahler, Schönberg, Berg, Webern, Eisler, and Krenek. However, in the early 1930s, on the eve of the National Socialist dictatorship and in the wake of the impact Benjamin's Marxism would have on Adorno, Adorno's music theory would take a decidedly sociological turn. This was the period when Adorno composed his critiques of mass music, popular music, and kitsch. At the center of Adorno's critical rejection of entertainment music is jazz, which becomes the exemplar of all that is wrong with contemporary popular music. Jazz supposedly displays the banal, powerless reflexes of a regressive subject, thus documenting the power and hold of the culture industry over the aesthetic domain. Choosing Freud's psychoanalytic discourse to engage in a racially charged analysis that accuses African American music of a regressive fixation on and return to the autoerotic libidinal stage, Adorno's problematic critique thus reproduces, in mediated fashion, the German idealist, especially Hegelian, castigation of African culture.

Schönberg's Dissonances

The uneasy personal relation between Adorno and Schönberg sometimes surfaces in the uneven writings that Adorno dedicated to the composer. That the strong personal dislike between philosopher and composer was mutual is evident from Schönberg's personal reminiscences, such as the ominous "I really never could stand him." Schönberg strongly objected to what he regarded as Adorno's sweeping denunciations of composers such as Stravinsky, noting "one can simply not write like that about Stravinsky."[14] To Schönberg, who considered the twenty-two-year-old Adorno somewhat of an overbearing young man, it must have come as little surprise that the mature Adorno, while in exile in California, would end up becoming the personal music adviser to Thomas Mann, then at work on *Doctor Faustus*. Both the novel and the later *History of a Novel* relied on Adorno's letters and observations about Schönberg's twelve-tone music. In what can only be considered an extraordinary plot twist, Thomas Mann projected the Christian Faust myth, with its idolatry of the devil, onto the Jewish composer of twelve-tone music. This strange association seems peculiar—even historically inaccurate and insensitive—insofar as atonal music, twelve-tone music, and the Second Vienna School as a whole were subjected to vociferous attacks of anti-Semitism in Vienna and Berlin. The non-Jewish Alban Berg, for example, was attacked for making so-called Jewish music or for what the Nazis were to call "degenerate music." It is therefore strange to see Thomas Mann unwittingly fall victim to the distrust that, since medieval times, had linked musica ficta—or unacceptable chromatic modulations—to the mythical figure of the devil. Driven by superstition, the church placed a ban on so-called dissonant, devilish chords, or tritones, the *diabolus in musica* (the devil in music).[15]

However, rather than concentrate on Adorno and Schönberg's difficult personal relationship, the present essay seeks to shed light on the aesthetico-political presuppositions that underpin Adorno's interpretation of Schönberg's work. Not infrequently, Schönberg's twelve-tone music—sometimes also his expressionistic paintings—formed a negative force field in Adorno's postwar writings. Despite the words of praise that Adorno reserved for Schönberg's early compositions, such as the *Gurrelieder* or the Second String Quartet, op. 10, his later compositions more often than not became negative exemplars of the vicious circle in which avant-garde art, culture, and aesthetics were caught. Schönberg's music was seen to corroborate the plight of the avant-garde, namely, the increasing impossibility of creating nonreified culture and art, or of engaging in an aesthetic practice even though the ethical demand or the imperative to do so continued unabated. These dire conditions only became more pronounced in the wake of World War II and the Holocaust, resulting in Adorno's well-known interdiction, or negative imperative, that in the wake of Auschwitz it would be barbaric to create poetry again. So broadly was this interdiction conceived, as his *Aesthetic*

Theory and other writings document, that it in fact applied to all artistic or aesthetic production *tout court*. Moreover, as one might argue, the interdiction also became the internal negative limit of postwar philosophy, enacted in Adorno's own *Negative Dialectics*. Only Beckett, to whom Adorno was to dedicate his unfinished *Aesthetic Theory*, was able to shoulder the formidable task of creating art that did not simply trivialize the loss of meaning in the wake of the Holocaust, namely, in *Endgame*, through the nothingness of the absurd.[16] Schönberg, by contrast, often emerged as Beckett's negative counterimage, indeed, as the diabolical Leverkühn of Mann's *Doctor Faustus*, who, mired in myth, superstition, and formalistic magical rituals, had betrayed the critical labor— the work of critique—of avant-garde art. Schönberg's pre- and post–World War II compositions allegedly symbolize the negativity of an aesthetic avant-garde art that gradually had relinquished its philosophical ability to address the problem of "order" from the perspective of the thing itself. It had exchanged art's dialectical form for an aestheticized, stylish formalism that gives in to the longing for orderliness in seriality or serialization. Having relinquished the explosive, revolutionizing impetus of his pre–World War I phase, Schönberg emerged as the belated classicist epigone *malgré lui*. Schönberg's so-called belated classicism stamped the unfinished biblical opera *Moses und Aron*, to which Adorno was to dedicate a central essay of his *Quasi una Fantasia*. In Adorno's reading, Schönberg shows himself eager to preserve sacred music—the oratorio—in the absence of cultic art; eager to preserve the claim to aesthetic totality in the absence of classicist music; eager to give voice to the divine Absolute despite the injunction against graven images that forbid such idolatry. Begun in the 1930s in Berlin, yet never completed, *Moses und Aron* exists as a fragment, whose two completed acts—including the interlude, the "dance of the golden calf"—capture the battle between the idolatrous representational realm of visual superstition and the force of Jewish law. The abject idolatry signaled by the singing voice of Aron, sung by a tenor, was to be counterbalanced by the declamatory speaking voice, the *Sprechstimme*, of Moses, sworn to the ten commandments and to the Jewish injunction against graven images. In this dialectic, the potential cantabile allure of all song was to be suspended. The title of Schönberg's opera, *Moses und Aron*, with its twelve letters, arguably can be seen to invoke the twelve-tone system, the twelve notes of the chromatic scale; as is well known from Schönberg's biography, the composer deleted the thirteenth letter of the original title, *Moses und Aaron* (the correct German spelling of this name), in an attempt to avoid the mythical number thirteen. Schönberg, who suffered from a phobia of the number thirteen, was born on September 13, 1874, and died on July 13, 1951.[17]

One of the masterpieces produced by Schönberg's twelve-tone system, *Moses und Aron* exemplifies the crisis of representation in twentieth-century art, as well as the battle between the imagistic, iconographic faculty of the imagination and the nonrepresentational force of music (aesthetic representation in the sense of the term *Darstellung*). At the same time, the opera thematically addresses the other meaning of representation, namely, political and theological representation, in the sense of *Vertretung*, "speaking in the stead of, for another." This masterful yet interrupted opera captures the fated dialectic between law, sovereignty, power, and demagoguery. In its opening scene, the listener is taken to the deep crisis in representation with which Moses, according to Deuteronomy, is confronted as he is called upon to speak for or in the stead of God. Stumbling, stuttering as he is summoned by the disembodied voice of God emerging from the thornbush, Moses replies that his tongue is clumsy. Having given voice to his failure to exercise the art of rhetoric, or to speak well, Moses consents to Aron becoming his mouthpiece, or vessel. Upon his descent from Mount Sinai, however, Moses finds Aron and the people steeped in shameless, lecherous idolatry, which culminates in the orgiastic dance around the golden calf. Not only does Moses make the golden calf disappear—for in "representation" the Almighty has no place—but he also shatters the tables when Aron calls them but an image, a part or fragment of divine thought.[18] Indirectly, however, Aron gives voice to the deeper political truth that animates the people at this stage: demagoguery through images. For Schönberg, writing in the thirties, this insight did not just capture the plight of the Hebrews, but also came to symbolize the political demagoguery and lawless state of National Socialism. Aron throws these sneering words at Moses: "Never did your word reach the people uninterrupted; images lead and control this people, which you have liberated."[19] Given the political context within which Schönberg composed the oratorio in Berlin, these words also evoke Nazi idolatry, National Socialism's political usurpation of the iconic and of political demagoguery. Sworn till the end to the force of the Word, not the idol, Moses nonetheless persists in his role of declamatory speaking voice until his voice eventually falters, turning from articulated sound into anguished

shriek: "O word, O word that I lack." Breaking off at this point, except
for the existing fragmentary third act, Schönberg's opera thus comes to
a complete halt as it ends in silence. In the process the opera turns into
the fragment of a fragment and thus dialectically seems to live up to the
irrepresentability of the power that escapes all representation.

In identifying with Moses, Schönberg thus becomes like Moses,
unable to capture sublime truth in the vessel of musical language. The
burden of that insight constitutes the first moment in the essay Adorno
wrote in 1963, four years after the first showing of the opera in Berlin.
Dedicated to Gershom Scholem, Adorno's "Sacred Fragment: Schönberg's 'Moses und Aron'" avers that Schönberg might have recognized
the blasphemous nature of having to become God's mouthpiece: "He
must have grasped the fact that its absolute metaphysical content would
prevent it from becoming an aesthetic totality. But by the same token he
refused to accept anything less" (*QUF*, 226).[20] This representational
condition simultaneously signals the deep tragic side of the biblical
opera, that is, the unsolvable contradiction between the finite and the
infinite. As such, the opera merely inherits the idealistic theory of the
tragic of Hegel's philosophy and Hölderlin's poetry. In his *Annotations to
Sophocles,* Hölderlin presents the caesura as the necessary metric interruption that *ex negativo* allows the incommensurable might of the divine
to break through in tragedy. For Hegel this incommensurability of representational form and the content of the Absolute constitute the divine sublime, rendered magnanimously in Hölderlin's fragmentary and
paratactic late poetry. Reaching the threshold of self-awareness and self-
reflection, Adorno implies, Schönberg seems to realize the impossibility
of reaching an aesthetic whole because the work has an absolute metaphysical content: "Important works of art are the ones that aim for an
extreme; they are destroyed in the process and their broken outlines survive as the ciphers of a supreme, unnameable truth" (*QUF*, 226). The
clash between the aesthetic quest for form and the magnitude of the divine constitutes the inner formal logic of Schönberg's biblical opera,
which necessarily gives rise to its fragmentary state. However, as Adorno
goes on to argue, this formal condition is compounded by another historical condition: *the impossibility of sacred art today.* An abyss emerges between the transsubjective, transcendent aim of sacred art, as ordained
by the Torah, and the free aesthetic *Gesetztheit* of the work of art, in other
words, between the transsubjective sacred and the individualism of a
bourgeois aesthetic. It was not just Beethoven's *Missa Solemnis* or

Bruckner's work that had failed to reach the "promised land" of sacred music; Schönberg's opera all the more explicitly attests that one cannot simply wish for the return of cultic music. If from a Hegelian perspective sacred cultic music is to be *substantiell,* that is, is to be carried in *Gehalt* (content) and *Form* (form) by society, then the secular world that marks modernity hardly tolerates sacred art. By rejecting the mere citation of past music, Schönberg shows that he still believes in the *autonomous "Gestalt" of the aesthetic "Gebilde"* (construct). Nonetheless, Schönberg's work inevitably raises the Kantian question: how is cultic music possible in the absence of a cult? (*QUF,* 229).

To argue that Schönberg was unable to rise to the formidable task of composing cultic music, Adorno lays bare the imagistic and idealist baggage bogging down the opera, miring it in myth. To be sure, Adorno acknowledges that Schönberg's composition was part of his rediscovery of his Jewish roots: following the rise to power of National Socialism, Schönberg reconverted to Judaism, leaving behind the Protestantism of his Vienna years. *Moses und Aron* thus presented an antidote to the emerging political horrors, a process that came to a halt when Hitler rose to power, leaving Schönberg unable to continue the score. Brushing aside these historico-political concerns, Adorno instead charges Schönberg with lapsing into the very realm of imagistic idolatry he had sought to criticize. Thus, Adorno notes, music by its very nature shares the iconoclastic tenor of Judaism in that it is essentially imageless; tarrying with its own essence, Western music historically had become entangled in the *Bildwesen* (imagistic essence) of all European art, falling into the traps of musica ficta, *stile rappresentative,* or expressive music. In Europe expressive music learned to imitate. Though Schönberg opposes the ornamental nature of pictorial music, much as did the architect Adolf Loos ("Ornament ist Verbrechen [ornaments are criminal]"), he inadvertently resorts to the imagistic when he presses the "expressive moment" on the dramatis personae; as a result, the opera itself lapses into musica ficta: "The pictorial essence of music, at which the idea of image-less music recoiled, is now pressed upon the individual figures, as if, through their demise, the image-less emerged. As if, for this process itself remains a fiction"(*QUF,* 234). Conceived according to the anticlassicist philosophy of twelve-tone music, the opera unwittingly embraces the classicist urge for the kind of totality that allegedly persists in opera. Citing the critic Heinrich Jalowetz, Adorno contends: "[Schönberg's] relation to Vienna classicism was such that he held on to the spirit of totality

and that he turned also against its *Erschleichung* [totality's devious re-
turn], as if his compositions wanted to produce the language of music as
such." Despite its fragmentary nature, the opera—so Adorno's verdict—
exudes the longing for idealist totality: "Self-contained and free-floating,
[classical music] tended towards the Absolute, like the philosophical
systems of a bygone age. And in these the theological legacy becomes
fused with the task, inherited from the past, of creating that absolute
just once more, but this time in freedom and within man himself. . . .
Every music that aims at totality as a simile of the absolute has its
theological dimension, even if it is unaware of it and even if it becomes
anti-theological by virtue of presenting itself as creation" (*QUF*, 233–34).
Paradoxically, this logic of totality undermines the radical logic of
Schönberg's dissonant twelve-tone model. Thus, the taming of dissonance, which for Adorno is integral to the twelve-tone technique, becomes the formal principle of the opera. Totality rules the detail, thus
further enhancing the effect of the static.

Despite the seemingly positive name Adorno gives to Schönberg's
opera—"sacred fragment"—and the effusive last lines with which
Adorno ends his interpretation, the bulk of his essay is meant to identify
three cardinal errors that mar the work. First, the metaphysical fallacy
that it might be possible in music to represent the Absolute without lapsing into an imagistic representation, thus violating the Jewish interdiction against graven images; second, the aesthetic error that twelve-tone
music escapes the claims to totality of the classicist musical composition;
third, the political fallacy that the opera eludes the specter of aestheticized politics of the kind symbolized by Wagner's operatic work. Fundamentally, Schönberg's metaphysical error, that it might be possible to
capture the Absolute in and through opera—according to Adorno, the
most sensuous of musical genres—translates into an aesthetico-political
error, signaled by the mythical return of Wagner's specter in *Moses und
Aron*. To make matters worse, the same structure is at play in Schönberg's 1947 work, *A Survivor from Warsaw*, which Adorno, in one of his
more shocking pronouncements, accuses of trivializing the Holocaust.
Schönberg's opera bears within itself the threat of aestheticizing politics;
in the realm of music this means the production of *imagistic music*—a
seeming oxymoron that signals the decline of the Western musical tradition, culminating in Wagner's operatic work. It should be noted here
that the Second Viennese School never made a secret of its reverence
for Wagner's technical or formal innovations, just as little as did Mahler,

who revered Wagner's chromatic liberation of music. Rejecting such a purely formal, apolitical assessment of Wagner, Adorno seeks to expose the mythical ramifications of the "endless melody" and monumentalism that characterized Wagner's operatic work (*QUF*, 244). Politics and aesthetics engage in an ineluctable dialectic: rather than achieving the politicization of aesthetics through twelve-tone music, Schönberg's *Moses and Aron* replicates the aestheticization of music at the core of the Wagnerian cult. Through its inability to create genuine sacred or cultic music, on the other side of imagistic *Schein, Moses und Aron* emerges as less than a sacred fragment. Transforming Hegel's verdict that modernity is marked by the end of art, Adorno sees in Schönberg's biblical opera the end of all truly cultic art. Yet, ironically, the very movement of Hegel's philosophy returns in Adorno's own philosophy of music: for, in the end, Adorno's philosophical critique overcomes and crushes the possible dissonances of the artwork, unable to give expression to the nonconceptual philosophy that is music.

The quasi-Hegelian overcoming that animates Adorno's reading of *Moses und Aron* returns more vehemently in Adorno's comments about *The Survivor from Warsaw*. Indeed, it is perplexing to see how for Adorno *The Survivor of Warsaw* ultimately demonstrates the palpable postwar aestheticization of the Holocaust. Here, too, however, Adorno's deeply negative critique exposes more about the basic philosophical and conceptual tenets of his own aesthetic theory than about Schönberg's artwork. Adorno's aesthetic critique presupposes the following: first, the critique of totality as an aesthetic category; second, the irredeemable and irrecuperable loss of meaning in the wake of the Holocaust; third, the horrific dialectic or horror of the dialectic according to which such loss of meaning turns into the very production of meaning, at the expense of the victims and their suffering. These insights, as noted earlier, underpin Adorno's verdict that it is impossible to write poetry after Auschwitz. By implication this verdict also strikes at the core of the philosophical production of meaning out of nothingness and destruction. In *Negative Dialectics* and other writings, Adorno takes on postwar existentialism, which transforms meaninglessness into a constitutive, life-enabling category, thus making the condition of becoming human dependent on senseless inhumanity.[21] Opposing the reification of the horror, Adorno concludes that the horror needs to be left standing rather than be sublated through poetry or existential philosophy. Though pressured by Hans Magnus Enzensberger and other postwar poets, Adorno at first refused to soften the verdict. Only in later writings did he acknowledge that the victims and their suffering deserved the same right to expression as did the henchmen.[22] In many ways, it seems to me, Paul Celan's postwar poem "Death Fugue" manages to give voice to the suffering of the victims without endorsing the merely poetic production of meaning. In the confluence of music and poetry, this death fugue movingly avoids the abyss of sublimating such production of meaning as it seeks to reclaim Bach's polyphonic fugal art from the barbarous Nazi industry, which turned classical music into a torture instrument. In the fugal poem, the victims' voices collectively and polyphonically rise up against the violence—a seemingly victorious moment that, in the end, becomes only a faint echo as the poem comes to a halt in the horrific extinction of the choral voices.

If Adorno eventually softens the verdict that all art after Auschwitz is intrinsically barbaric, it also seems true that his fundamental insights into the aporetic nature of all postwar art remain unchanged. Since the foundation of art itself has been shattered, art can no longer entertain an unbroken relationship to the aesthetic realm. The very idea of art after the Holocaust remains illusory or nonsensical, as corroborated by individual artworks. Yet in Adorno's revised understanding of art after the Holocaust, this aesthetic failure is coupled with a historico-political duty: precisely because the world has survived its own total demise, it needs art—and this is decisive—as its unconscious form of history writing. The authentic artwork will be a work in which the trembling of an incomparable historic horror resonates, a work that seismographically registers the trembling of aftershocks caused by this historical earthquake.[23] While Adorno recognizes the necessity of a commemorative, collective recollective art—much as Celan does through his phrase "der Daten eingedenk bleiben" (remembrance of the dates)—he warns against the dynamic of political recuperation that animated postwar German consumption of a new meaning-producing Holocaust art, as it strove to come to terms with the past. The genocide thus represented is transformed into mere culture, into cultural property, allowing its consumers to continue to play a part in the culture that had given rise to the genocide in the first place.[24] Recognizing that the suffering should not be forgotten, Adorno now revises his insight: the suffering at once demands art's continuation and simultaneously prohibits art's production. Experimental artworks, which explicitly reflect on the incommensurability of their form, might be able to do justice to this double task. Less likely to succeed, by contrast, are artworks that labor under the illusion of "immediacy" as they directly lend voice to the suffering. This, precisely, proves to be the case with Schönberg's *Survivor from Warsaw*. Much as in *Moses und Aron*, in which Schönberg violates the anti-idolatry verdict, so *The Survivor from Warsaw* is unable to render the suffering of the victims of the Holocaust nonimagistically. Uncompromising in his assessment, Adorno takes issue with the way in which an artwork is manufactured out of the sufferers, who in the process are thrown as fodder to the same world that had killed them. Schönberg engages in the production of pleasure as he artistically reproduces abject suffering and horrific deaths; the festive aesthetic stylization of the choral prayer at the end ennobles the unthinkable fate, giving it meaning: "Something of the horror has been taken away." [25] In true postwar art, by contrast, the horror is left undisguised, not aestheticized: the dissonances of the horrific are not to be tamed by the harmonious resolution of consonant production of meaning. Adorno's interpretation of *The Survivor from Warsaw* thus becomes the fulfillment of the fated logic he recognizes in *Moses und Aron*, Schönberg's work from the middle period. Schönberg's dissonant twelve-tone music creates a new version of totalizing harmony: despite Schönberg's intent to produce a "pure, unalloyed" music, or music "an sich," removed from classicist theories of harmony and the violence of key and tonic, it relapses into a reconceptualized and aestheticized music—for Adorno a "second conformism" or "second formalism." [26] In essence, Schönberg in the final analysis failed to lay the foundations for a new music that returns the sacred cult to the present or recognizes its philosophical task. As such, in the end, his music fails to provide "hope for the hopeless."

Having pursued thus far how philosophy understands music, we must also ask, conversely, what music exposes about the limitations of philosophy. If the previous analysis retraced the daunting ethico-political task that Adorno formulated for Schönberg's music, then, in a moment of reversal, one must ask what limitations the art of music— Schönberg's music—exposes in the work of philosophy. In these concluding observations, I would like to formulate, be it in a preliminary manner, some of the ways in which Schönberg's music might confront Adorno's philosophy with critical challenges. Adorno's writings expose the aporetic relation, the moment of fissure in the relation between music and philosophy, putting pressure on their "elective affinity." If music, on the one hand, is like philosophy, or knowledge-producing, and if indeed it unfolds truth in the movement of its dialectical contradictions, it remains, on the other hand, nonetheless radically unlike philosophy or philosophical language. Music remains marked by a radical alterity that escapes conceptual, discursive language, including the language of Adorno's negative dialectic, which seeks to approach the limit of the concept by thinking the nonconcept. Within the logic of Adorno's own philosophy (which does not always escape identity thinking, or even analogical thinking), music itself comes to represent the very movement of the negative dialectic. Music emerges as the wished-for-object insofar as it is negative dialectic's wish to think outside the violence or power of the concept, to think at the limit of conceptual language, and to reach its outside in a pure moment of mimesis that is no longer derivative or mechanically reproductive. To be sure, Adorno seems aware that the unrelenting logic of his negative dialectic is accompanied by the danger that it might produce its very opposite, so that the limit inadvertently might also turn into a limitation. Two elements in Adorno's philosophy point to his model's potential limitations. First, Adorno's category of negativity or nothingness risks becoming the producer of meaning, turning into a constitutive category of *Negative Dialectics*. This unwanted by-product of the negative dialectic remains despite Adorno's attempt to extract a positive, philosophically productive mode of negativity (vaguely reminiscent of Nietzsche's distinction between active and passive nihilism) from the gray, undifferentiated mass of nothingness that has defined modernity's nihilistic inclination. Once again Adorno invokes Beckett's exemplary philosophy of absurd nothingness, arguing that its category of the negative needs to be separated from the nihil of Nietzschean and Wagnerian nihilism, no less than from the obliterating nothingness of National Socialism and the Holocaust. Only Beckett's aesthetic of the absurd seems able to inaugurate a new beginning, which—despite Adorno's deep-seated distrust of Kierkegaard—here takes a Kierkegaardian redemptive figure as its model: Beckett's theater of the absurd is the radical leap out of the negating force of negativity. Second, as suggested earlier, Adorno's dialogical encounter with Schönberg, as the encounter between philosophy and music, still exposes a Hegelian trap: the desire of philosophical discourse to overcome music, through which the act of aesthetic judging might become judgmental. Does not Adorno's interpretation of Schönberg's music then amount to the sounding of a second end or ending of art? Rather than bring these questions to a formal conclusion, however, I wish to leave these observations or challenges here in all their disquieting dissonance.

NOTES

This essay is based on research I conducted at the Arnold Schönberg Zentrum, Vienna, and at Schönberg's house in Moedling, Austria, during the summer of 2003. The research was funded in part by a Presidential Travel Grant from the University of Georgia.

1. Theodor W. Adorno, "Music and Language: A Fragment," in *Quasi una Fantasia,* trans. Rodney Livingstone (London: Verso, 1992), 2.

2. Theodor W. Adorno, "Philosophie der neuen Musik," in his *Gesammelte Schriften,* vol. 12 (Frankfurt am Main: Suhrkamp, 1997).

3. Adorno, *Quasi una Fantasia,* 2. This work will be cited henceforth in the text as *QUF* with relevant page number(s).

4. Walter Benjamin, "The Task of the Translator," in *Illuminations,* trans. Harry Zohn (New York: Schocken, 1968), 69–82, here 69.

5. On the concept of *tikkun,* see the work of Gershom Scholem, especially *On the Kabbalah and Its Symbolism* (New York: Schocken Books, 1965).

6. Adorno uses the terms "Hölderlinian caesura" and "the expression-less," without crediting the terms to Benjamin, in his letter of December 27, 1925, to Berg, reporting on the Berlin performance of *Wozzeck.* Theodor W. Adorno and Alban Berg, *Briefwechsel 1925–1935* (Frankfurt am Main: Suhrkamp, 1997), 51.

7. These lines, intentionally or unintentionally, echo Nietzsche's insight that the Apollonian visuality of the tragic and of music merely serves as a prophylactic against the blinding light of the sun—the famous passage about the healing black spots created by the sun.

8. Theodor W. Adorno and Walter Benjamin, *Briefwechsel 1928–1940* (Frankfurt am Main; Suhrkamp, 1994), 158n.Benjamin refers to the performance in a letter of 1935 on the occasion of Berg's death. One of the few books dedicated to Adorno's Viennese years is Heinz Steinert's *Adorno in Wien: Über die Unmöglichkeit von Kunst, Kultur und Befreiung* (Vienna: Verlag für Gesellschaftskritik, 1989), but it appeared too early to cover the more recently published Adorno-Berg correspondence. On Schönberg's musical work, see Hans Heinz Stuckenschmidt, *Schoenberg: Leben, Umwelt, Werk* (Munich: Piper, 1989).

9. A second version of the essay appeared in 1927. See Theodor W. Adorno, "Schönberg: Serenade, op. 24 (I)," in *Gesammelte Schriften,* 18:324–30.

10. Adorno und Berg, *Briefwechsel,* 39.

11. Adorno und Berg, *Briefwechsel,* 39.

12. Adorno und Berg, *Briefwechsel,* 39. Kolisch was the brother of Schönberg's second wife and would end up teaching in the music department of the University of Wisconsin.

13. Adorno und Berg, *Briefwechsel,* 39.

14. Cited in a text by Schönberg, graciously made available to me by the Arnold Schönberg Center in Vienna.

15. See the entry "musica ficta" in *Webster's New World Dictionary of Music* (Indianapolis: Wiley, 1998).

16. Theodor W. Adorno, *Negative Dialectics* (New York: Continuum, 1994), 362.

17. On Schönberg's triskaidekaphobia, see, for example, *Webster's New World Dictionary of Music*, 467.

18. Arnold Schönberg, *Moses und Aron: Oper in drei Akten* (Mainz: B. Schott's Söhne, 1957), 7.

19. "Niemals kam dein Wort ungedeutet ans Volk"; "Bilder führen und beherrschen dieses Volk, das du befreit hast" (Schönberg, *Moses und Aron*, 31).

20. Theodor W. Adorno, "Sacred Fragment: Schönberg's 'Moses und Aron,'" in *Quasi una Fantasia*, 225–48.

21. See Adorno, *Negative Dialectics*, 361. For Adorno's comments on *The Survivor of Warsaw*, see his 1962 text "Engagement," in Adorno, *Noten zur Literatur*, vol. 11 of his *Gesammelte Schriften*, 409–30.

22. Adorno, "Engagement," 409–30.

23. Adorno, "Jene zwanziger Jahre," *Kulturkritik und Gesellschaft*, vol. 10/2 of his *Gesammelte Schriften*, 499–506.

24. Adorno, *Negative Dialectics*, 361.

25. "Etwas von dem Grauen wird weggenommen" (Adorno, "Engagement," 423).

26. Adorno, "Jene zwanziger Jahre," 505.

9

Thomas Mann

Pro and Contra Adorno

HANS RUDOLF VAGET

The elective affinities of music and philosophy that provide the focus of this volume preoccupied Thomas Mann all his life. Mann never tired of contemplating their voluptuous spiritual union in the thought of Romanticism, or of commenting on their strained marriage throughout the nineteenth and much of the twentieth centuries. Initially Mann regarded music merely as the most distinctive achievement of German culture; in his *Reflections of a Nonpolitical Man,* he celebrated its incomparable profundity and defended its purportedly nonpolitical nature. He then came to realize, however, that the pervasive cult of music in Germany carried the seeds of an unsuspected evil, for the extraordinarily privileged status to which music had been elevated instilled in many music-loving Germans a fatal dose of hubris, which drew Germany into a Faustian pact with demonic forces that promised to secure her musical supremacy and, more darkly, translate that musical supremacy into political hegemony.

More than anyone else, Mann's philosophical mentor, Friedrich Nietzsche, exalted the "mystery" of music's union with philosophy, for that union—in wondrous analogy to the original union of music and philosophy in classical Greece—had resulted in the rebirth of tragedy in the work of Richard Wagner.[1] Strictly speaking, this was music's second marriage to philosophy: a re-union of previously well-attuned but long since estranged partners. As is often the case when ulterior motives enter into such arrangements, that second marriage, consummated under German skies, was soon in dire need of counseling. Ironically, it was Nietzsche himself, the eager matchmaker, who had to assume the responsibilities of marriage counselor. He acquitted himself of that task with grim delight, producing ever new variations on the theme of "Nietzsche contra Wagner" and calling for an end of the troublesome liaison by declaring in near desperation: "il faut mediterraniser la musique" (music should be mediterranianized).[2]

What was that problematical ulterior motive of the marriage of music and philosophy? Politics!—as Nietzsche surmised and as Mann came to witness and experience. It is crucial to note here that when Nietzsche affirms the mysterious unity of music and philosophy he pointedly speaks of "German music" and "German philosophy." In other words, far from being a universal condition, the elective affinity between music and philosophy appears to be, in Nietzsche's mind, an affinity distinctly characteristic of German history. It grew from the particular historical conditions in which both music and philosophy found themselves as they unfolded simultaneously in the second half of the eighteenth century. At that juncture, Nietzsche observes, German culture achieved a "blessed self-rediscovery after powerful influences had for a long time compelled it . . . to servitude under their form."[3] It is obvious what Nietzsche has in mind here: the long *obéissance* to French culture in the early modern period that inspired the warning of Wagner's Hans Sachs against "welschen Dunst mit welschem Tand" (against the influence of French and Italian culture). Such servitude came to an end when philosophy and music were wedded. Only then, according to Nietzsche, did the German spirit "dare to stride boldly and freely ahead of all other nations without being attached to the lead strings" of France.[4]

The long-term political ramifications of the union of music and philosophy became apparent in the first half of the twentieth century when Houston Stewart Chamberlain, Adolf Hitler, Alfred Rosenberg, and many others, especially German musicologists, routinely invoked the purported superiority of German culture to justify Germany's claim to political hegemony.[5] The only field in which such reasoning could be expected to have any credibility was music, for it was in music, not in literature, not in the visual arts, that Germany had achieved a universally acknowledged preeminence thanks to what Nietzsche referred to as the awesome "solar orbit [leading] from Bach to Beethoven, [and] from Beethoven to Wagner."[6]

No two figures in recent German history have been shaped by music and philosophy more profoundly than Theodor W. Adorno and Thomas Mann. As the recent flood of publications marking the centennial of his birth has reminded us, Adorno stands before us as the last and most prodigious representative of that glorious lineage adumbrated by Nietzsche. In contrast to Mann, however, he appears never to have felt any compunction seriously to problematize the notion of supremacy so deeply ingrained in German philosophizing about music. On the contrary, his writings on music from Bach to Berg, combined with his very influential teaching, have served as perhaps the most sophisticated philosophical justification of the perpetuation of the hegemonic claim implicit in the very concept of German music.

Mann, too, remained beholden to the emotional world of German music, but soon after taking a stand in support of the embattled Weimar Republic, in 1922, in a characteristically Nietzschean turn to a triumph over self, he began to question Germany's fixation on German music. *The Magic Mountain*, for example, displays significantly enlarged musical horizons encompassing French and Italian music as well. More importantly, Mann shows here a heightened sensitivity to the political implications of the German cult of music, for in this novel, we can detect a clear realization that German music from Schubert to Wagner exerted a powerful enchantment of the soul with potentially sinister consequences.[7] Two decades later, in *Doctor Faustus*, Mann returned to this theme to orchestrate it on a much grander scale: the crisis of German music in the post-Wagnerian era was to foreshadow Germany's road into the cultural and moral catastrophe of National Socialism. As Mann saw it, that catastrophe came about not despite Germany's vaunted cult of music, as the naively humanistic cliché would have it, but rather because of it.

Soon after he began writing *Doctor Faustus*, when the conception of this ambitious novel was still in flux, Mann had the extraordinary good fortune of making the acquaintance of Adorno, who enabled him to extend his psychohistorical probings into the musical modernism of Arnold Schönberg and Alban Berg. There can be no question that much of the novel's musical sophistication is owed to Adorno. But this assistance must not obscure the fundamental conceptual differences between Mann and his new musical advisor, even if, during their work together, both had good reasons to paper over such differences. But, as I shall suggest, a clash over the all-important question of the novel's ending was programmed and in fact inevitable.

Tellingly, nothing even remotely resembling a friendship evolved from this celebrated collaboration, profuse expressions of mutual veneration in their letters to the contrary notwithstanding. In this regard Adorno was to share the bitter fate of his orthodox Marxist rival, Georg Lukács, whose intellectual love affair with the author of *Buddenbrooks* and *Tonio Kröger* was equally frustrated by Mann's evasiveness and reluctance to engage his staunchest Marxist admirer in sustained intellectual exchange.[8] The Mann-Adorno relationship in the post-*Faustus* period thus became a lopsided affair, with the balance of the emotional and intellectual investments clearly coming from Adorno, Mann's junior by almost thirty years. This becomes evident from their recently published correspondence, and even more so from Adorno's homage to Mann, written in 1952 to welcome him to a reading in Frankfurt, in which Mann is seen as liberated Germany's foremost writer and (with uncharacteristic hyperbole), as the only German writer in possession of the full radiance of authenticity.[9] Mann generally responded to Adorno in considerably more measured tones. Nonetheless, Adorno's recent biographers remain intent on prolonging the wishful mythmaking that has sprung up in certain quarters of their industry. Thus, Detlev Claussen, as the subtitle of his biography suggests, portrays his hero as "a last genius" *(ein letztes Genie)* and suggests that working on *Doctor Faustus* brought about a very close personal relationship between the two men of genius.[10] As we shall see, their intellectual temperaments precluded any such thing.

From the beginning, discussion of the Mann-Adorno relationship has been largely dominated by the irksome question of intellectual property. And indeed, the question of the precise extent of Adorno's contribution to *Doctor Faustus* has to this day lost none of its urgency. But treating that question should be a mere steppingstone to the larger and more rewarding task of retracing their intellectual physiognomies and of laying the groundwork for a comprehensive evaluation of Mann's and Adorno's contributions to Germany's confrontation with its past and to a critical assessment of the role of music, or rather, of the cult of music, in the pre-history of the "German catastrophe."

However, the impact of Adorno's hand on *Doctor Faustus* cannot be considered in isolation; it is intimately tied to the notorious Schönberg affair. Arnold Schönberg's anger at the use of his revolutionary method of composition in Mann's novel compelled the author, beginning with the third German edition in 1951, to append a note at the end of the book declaring that "the method of composition presented in Chapter XXII, known as the twelve-tone or row-technique, is in truth the intellectual property of a contemporary composer and theoretician, Arnold Schönberg."[11] It now seems likely that Schönberg's monumental displeasure was in fact caused not by Mann but rather by Adorno.

At the time of the writing of *Doctor Faustus,* Schönberg was on perfectly friendly terms with Mann, to whom the composer dedicated, in 1945, a double canon for string quartet on the occasion of the author's seventieth birthday.[12] Then, in an initial letter to the *Saturday Review of Literature,* Schönberg accused Mann of having "taken advantage of [his] literary property."[13] He freely admitted, however, that he had not read the novel. Schönberg's real irritation, it seems, was directed at Adorno, to whom he had taken an intense personal dislike long before exile led them both to Los Angeles, the "Weimar on the Pacific," where they lived in close proximity but without real closeness.[14] Schönberg came to believe that his philosophically presumptuous prophet actually failed to grasp the essence of his new music.[15] He was dismayed at having his innovation described as the "system of the twelve tones," when correctly it should be described as the "method of composing with twelve tones." The fine line between the two formulations was of the utmost importance to Schönberg, for it underscores the crucial element of creativity—the creative use of a particular method. He readily admitted that Adorno knew everything there is to know about twelve-tone composition but added that he had "no real understanding of the creative process."[16] As Walter Levin has suggested, Schönberg's allegation—that Adorno, consenting to Mann's association of twelve-tone composition with poison and syphilis, was echoing certain Nazi denunciations of atonality as the product of a decadent Jewish mind—borders on paranoia. Levin also reminds us that Schönberg never overcame his jealousy of the critical and even popular success of Adorno's teacher, Alban Berg.[17] What all this amounts to is a deflection of blame from Mann to Adorno, from the creative artist to his uncreative "informer"—a term that unmistakably brands Adorno a traitor.[18] Schönberg apparently convinced himself that the depressingly familiar demonizing of twelve-tone music was in the final analysis the responsibility of Adorno: the result of a betrayal from within the very ranks of the "new music."

Given the personal dynamics of the Schönberg-Adorno-Mann constellation, the reconciliation between the composer and the novelist proved to be a relatively easy matter. After their notorious exchange of open letters in *The Saturday Review of Literature,* Mann wrote privately to Schönberg to reassure him: "Even if you insist on being my enemy, you will not succeed in turning me into yours." Schönberg responded: "If the hand I believe I see held out is the hand of peace . . . then I shall be happy to grasp it immediately. Let us bury the hatchet . . . and be content with this peace: You have reconciled me." To which Mann replied: "Wherever and whenever we meet again in this life it will be a joy and honor for me to shake your hand."[19] However, Schönberg's conciliatory attitude did not then and would never extend to Adorno; they remained unreconciled. It must have pained the author of *The Philosophy of Modern Music* to learn that Schönberg, shortly before he died, had decreed that Adorno be barred from access to his papers.[20]

Mann was acutely aware that his collaboration with Adorno constituted an extraordinary case of intellectual appropriation. In a letter to his collaborator, he freely admitted that his appropriation bordered on "brazen thievery."[21] He understood well the need for a public acknowledgment of the considerable debt he owed Adorno, his "privy councilor" in all questions concerning modern music.[22] In the summer of 1948, therefore, he decided to interrupt work on his new novel, *The Holy Sinner,* in order to write *The Story of a Novel: The Genesis of* Doctor Faustus. When he asked Adorno for biographical information, he pretended that he had started his autobiographical account on a whim.[23] But there can be no doubt that Mann was driven by an inner need to unburden himself of an unavoidable public confession and thus prevent the kind of clash that had stained his relations with Schönberg.

The Story of a Novel features a deft and sympathetic portrait of his "privy councilor" and a generous appreciation of his extraordinary status as a philosopher and music theorist. At a time when Adorno was little known in Germany and in the United States, this tribute from Mann meant an enormous boost. Here Mann details Adorno's role in the genesis of the novel: their encounters; their exchanges of books and manuscripts (including the yet unpublished *Philosophy of Modern Music*);

their consultations in person and by letter; and above all their joint conception of Leverkühn's last, most advanced works, including many stunning, unmistakably Adorno-inspired stylistic and technical details. Ironically, it was Adorno who convinced Mann not to present Leverkühn's
last work as a fragment—the same Adorno who as a matter of principle
privileged the form of the fragment and deemed all wholeness false.

But a strange domestic accident befell Mann's *Story of a Novel*. Katia,
his wife, and Erika, his daughter, both of whom disliked Adorno and
found "unbearable" Mann's revelations, objected that he had given
his musical advisor far too much credit.[24] One must remember that
Mann had come to rely on his daughter's judgment and had entrusted
her, after he completed *Doctor Faustus,* with the task of excising what she
deemed dispensable. Thus Mann agreed to cut more than 120 lines
from *The Story of a Novel,* thus significantly diminishing Adorno's role in
the genesis of the work.[25] Still, Adorno was delighted at the literary
monument that Mann had fashioned for him despite the fact that it had
been heavily censored in what was yet another melancholy case of
truthfulness sacrificed on the altar of family peace.

It is fair, then, to conclude that Adorno's part in *Doctor Faustus*
was larger than Mann's published account of its genesis would have us
believe. But was it large enough to support the notion, dear to many
commentators, that Adorno should be considered a coauthor?[26] In his
recent biography of the Frankfurt philosopher, Stefan Müller-Dohm
carries this notion to an extreme by suggesting that what the author of
The Philosophy of Modern Music experienced with Mann was even worse
than what he experienced with Hanns Eisler in the notorious case of
Composing for the Films.[27] Although Adorno claimed to have been respon-
sible for approximately 90 percent of that text, the book appeared with
only one author named: Hanns Eisler. But the two books can hardly be
compared. *Komposition für den Film* is a theoretical treatise; separate authors for separate parts of the book could have easily been indicated—
as they could not have been in a work of fiction. Mann, as he explained
to Adorno, could never have sprinkled the text with footnotes saying,
"This I got from Wiesengrund-Adorno."[28] Adorno seems to have been
pleased with his covert and, in a few cases, overt presence in the novel.
As for the film book, Adorno willingly dissociated himself from that collaboration when Eisler began to attract the attention of the House Com-
mittee on Un-American Activities and appeared to be content with remaining unnamed as Eisler's coauthor.

To preserve a realistic perspective in this whole tangled matter, it should be remembered that Adorno was not involved in the early planning stages. Mann met Adorno after the completion of chapter 4, and he began to consult with him at the writing of chapter 8. At that stage many decisions concerning the design and the political drift of the book had already been made. Initially Mann turned with musical queries to his long-time advisor Bruno Walter, who shrewdly recommended that he read *The Memoirs of Hector Berlioz*.[29] Mann dutifully read the book, and the traces of that reading found in the life and the work of Mann's fictitious composer, though often overlooked, are part of a significant pre-Adorno layer of *Doctor Faustus*. Two weeks before he began writing the novel, Mann quizzed Schönberg about music and about certain aspects of a composer's formation.[30] And he would continue to consult Schönberg—on one crucial occasion, about the composition of Leverkühn's apocalyptic oratorio—even "behind Adorno's back."[31]

Still more remarkable is Mann's position vis-à-vis Igor Stravinsky, Adorno's bête noire in *The Philosophy of Modern Music*. Although Mann at that time was not aware of the second part of the book (which is devoted to a critique of Stravinsky), we may safely assume that he knew from their frequent consultations of Adorno's disdain for the Russian modernist. But he turned a blind eye to Adorno's aversion to Stravinsky. Adorno's vilification of the Russian composer embarrassed even Stravinsky's rival, Schönberg, who found it simply "disgusting."[32] As his diaries show, when they met socially in Los Angeles, Mann enjoyed Stravinsky's urbanity and wit. As a matter of course, he read the Russian composer's autobiography and promptly adopted a characteristic episode from Stravinsky's studies with Rimsky-Korsakov in Saint Petersburg and incorporated it into Leverkühn's studies with Kretzschmar.[33] Again, unperturbed by Adorno's musical preferences, Mann described the orchestration of Leverkühn's second opera, *Saint Gregory*, in terms constituting a covert homage to the composer of the overtly Faustian *L'Histoire du soldat*.[34]

As these examples show, Mann subscribed to a pragmatic eclecticism and opted to remain demonstratively outside Adorno's sharply defined musical universe. Contrary to the intimations of some commentators, Mann had from the beginning a clear and definite conception of the structure and political thrust of his novel.[35] When he met Adorno it dawned on him: "This [is] my man."[36] What he meant was a supplier of ideas and a source of expert knowledge. Drawing on experts, rather

than solely on his imagination, had been his practice with *Buddenbrooks,
The Magic Mountain,* and the *Joseph* novels. Inviting Adorno formally to
collaborate on *Doctor Faustus,* with thirty-three of the novel's forty-seven
chapters completed, Mann took great care to define the scope of his
partner's input. Adorno would help him to complete not the novel
as such but the delineation of Leverkühn's musical works: "Would
you think about the problem, along with me: how the work—I mean
Leverkühn's work—can more or less be described; what sort of music
you would write if you were in league with the devil."[37] This is precisely
what Adorno did: he helped Mann to imagine Leverkühn's last works—
the oratorio *Apocalypsis cum figuris,* the Violin Concerto, the String Trio,
and the crowning symphonic cantata, *The Lamentation of Doctor Faustus*—
and flesh them out in stunning technical detail, with actual musical
sketches and examples.[38] In none of Leverkühn's earlier works, of
which more than twenty are mentioned, did Adorno have a hand. Rolf
Tiedemann, the general editor of Adorno's collected works, tries to
separate the mythmaking from the facts and concludes—correctly, I
believe—that Adorno's contributions to *Doctor Faustus,* weighty though
they undoubtedly were, represent only some and not necessarily the
most important elements that went into the making of *Doctor Faustus.*
The "privy councilor's" role as a contributor must be regarded as clearly
circumscribed.[39]

If Adorno's part in *Doctor Faustus* was limited, he at least did not need
to worry about competition from other experts who might trouble the
waters, for Mann never wavered in his commitment to Adorno. Here I
refer to an underexposed and rather embarrassing incident in the genesis of the novel. In the April 1946 issue of *Die Neue Rundschau,* Mann pre-
published some excerpts from the early parts of the novel, including the
famous description of Beethoven's Piano Sonata, Opus 111, in chapter
8, which represents the first significant contribution from his new musical advisor. Indeed, at this early moment, Mann took pains to acknowledge Adorno's presence, albeit obliquely, by graciously inserting his
patronym, "Wiesengrund," into the musical description.[40]

Unfortunately, as a result of Mann's misreading of Adorno's hand-
writing, the description of the sonata's second movement contains a
nonsensical expression: "das Fugengewicht der Akkorde" (the fugal
weight of the chords), which should be "das Eigengewicht der Akkorde"
(the proper weight of the chords).[41] When Alfred Einstein, the eminent
music critic and scholar, at that time teaching at Smith College in

Northampton, Massachusetts, read this, he wrote to Mann to express his admiration for his analysis of Opus 111, at the same time querying what the expression *Fugengewicht der Akkorde* might actually mean. Einstein furthermore pointed out that, contrary to what Mann had written, Heinrich Schütz had never composed for the organ, and he suggested clarifying a somewhat garbled passage concerning Praetorius, Froberger, Buxtehude, and Bach.[42] This must have been embarrassing to the perfectionist in Mann, even though his diary remains silent on this point. He knew his sympathetic critic from his years in Munich, where Einstein, until 1927, had been music critic of the *Münchner Post*. Mann had a high regard for this man, whose monograph on Mozart he reread shortly before his death. Einstein's letter contained the following passage: "Please don't take me for a Beckmesser. But in a novel about a musician, especially one by Thomas Mann, everything must be correct, and I would be proud if I could be in a position to prevent (further) inaccuracies, such as I have just identified."[43] Adorno or Einstein—that must have been Mann's question at least fleetingly. But he determined to stick with the music philosopher who lived nearby, was easy to reach, and shared his passionate preoccupation with Wagner.

There is yet another facet of the Mann-Adorno relationship to be considered here: Adorno's somewhat hazy stature as a creative musician. It seems that Mann was well aware of Schönberg's disdain for Adorno's music, as we may gather from remarks in *The Story of a Novel*. For instance, when Mann refers to one of Adorno's characteristically apodictic pronouncements to the effect that Wagner was often a "bad composer," he adds with superb irony and after a pregnant dash: "I have no way of judging Adorno's compositions."[44] Nor did Mann refrain from touching this wound in a portrait of his musical advisor in *Doctor Faustus* itself. One of the masks in which the devil appears to Leverkühn is that of Adorno, described here as "an intellectualist, who writes of art, of music, for ordinary newspapers, a theorist and critic, who is himself a composer, insofar as all his intellectualizing allows him actually to write music."[45] Call it sarcastic, call it unkind or merely factual, such barbs are indicative of an intellectual sovereignty and a sense of superiority in the crucial category of creativity that obviated any deference on Mann's part outside the narrow field of the "new music." Adorno for his part proved to be a good sport and signed, years later, one of his letters— with a chuckle, one would imagine—"your old devil," thereby signaling that he had not forgotten.[46]

In the face of this playful but positive evidence, it seems rather fanciful to maintain, as Michael Maar does, that the quoted passage from the novel's central conversation with the devil in chapter 25 was intended to refer not to Adorno but rather to Gustav Mahler.[47] But by no stretch of the imagination can one see Mahler in Mann's portrait of a theorist whose larger musical creativity is throttled by his theorizing—a point Marr conveniently ignores. However, this covert—or rather, overt— presence of his musical advisor at the very center of the novel did not hinder Mann from brazenly denouncing as "utterly absurd" any association between the "devil" and Adorno when this juicy piece of literary gossip first surfaced in 1950 in Hans Mayer's book on Thomas Mann.[48]

If Mann exploited Adorno for a bit of devilry, he nonetheless maintained his collaboration with the younger man—surely one of the most stellar in German literary history—because of their mutual interests and a common grounding in the vaunted tradition of the German *Bildungsbürgertum* (the educated middle class). Recognizing such communality came easier for Adorno, who had a long-standing case of hero worship for the author of *Death in Venice*. Mann, on the other hand, was surprised whenever he discovered signs of affinity, especially in the field of music, in which he was widely associated with Wagner, while his young admirer was generally perceived as the champion of the musical avantgarde. Thus when Mann first read Adorno's famous analysis of Wagner, he was struck by a "critical rebelliousness just this side of rejection" quite like that of his own essay *The Sufferings and Greatness of Richard Wagner*.[49] Likewise, when he read the prepublication manuscript of *The Philosophy of Modern Music*, he detected in it "the strangest affinity to the idea of my book" and a "startling pertinency to the world of my novel."[50]

The affinity that so surprised Mann can perhaps be best illustrated through the lens of another, equally famous book, *From Caligari to Hitler*, by Siegfried Kracauer, who was Adorno's philosophical mentor.[51] Not coincidentally, *Doctor Faustus* and *From Caligari to Hitler* were both begun during the last years of World War II, and both appeared in 1947. Each in its own way, these books bear the stamp of the exile's heightened and sharpened critical animus against the homeland. Kracauer's book is a comprehensive attempt at a deep reading of the films produced during the Weimar Republic as harbingers of Germany's turn toward Hitler and National Socialism. The differences between the two projects are obvious. Kracauer was looking at popular culture with the critical tools of the social sciences and discovered in Weimar cinema a collective susceptibility to Hitlerism. Mann turned to high culture, to the "most German of the arts," and invented a composer whose works, though entirely fictitious, possess a striking historical verisimilitude throwing into relief a mentality that seems to foreshadow Germany's collective embrace of National Socialism.[52] Whatever their differences, both books share a fundamental theoretical premise, the conviction that the embrace of Nazism is prefigured in the cultural texts of the preceding period and that these texts, properly read and contextualized, can yield unique psychological insights into the thinking that propelled Germany toward cultural and moral catastrophe.

The intellectual proximity of these two books becomes even clearer in the light of an essay by Adorno, Kracauer's erstwhile philosophical apprentice and now Mann's musical advisor. Written in English in the months immediately preceding and following the defeat of Nazi Germany in 1945 but not published at the time, this somewhat sketchy but highly revealing text has remained in the shadow of the three famous works of that period: *The Dialectic of Enlightenment, The Philosophy of Modern Music,* and *Minima Moralia,* Adorno's most widely read book in Germany. The essay of which I speak, "The Musical Climate for Fascism in Germany," is a companion piece to *Doctor Faustus* in that it, too, proposes to map in Kracauerian fashion "the fascist tendencies within German music, and musical life, before Hitler." In words that might well have been underwritten by Mann, Adorno here argues that there exists "a structural relationship between Fascism and culture," and that a true understanding of the "most terrifying anti-cultural phenomena of our time" is, in the last analysis, predicated on our awareness of their "cultural roots."[53] There is no more sophisticated and incisive exhibit in support of Adorno's argument than *Doctor Faustus* itself.

This, however, should not be construed as a recommendation to view Mann's novel as a work of the Frankfurt School. To realize this fully we need merely note the many differences separating Adorno from Mann that account for much of the subliminal aesthetic, ideological, and political tensions tearing at the fabric of this intricately woven text. It is precisely such tensions that lend *Doctor Faustus* its incomparable intellectual vibrancy and mark it as an eminent site of German cultural memory. To begin with, it is fairly obvious that, musically as well as philosophically, Mann could not have held a candle to Adorno. In his autobiographical sketch that Adorno prepared to assist Mann in writing *The Story of a Novel,* he states: "I studied philosophy and music. But instead of committing myself to either field I practiced both since I felt all my life that, actually, I was pursuing the same thing, no matter how much they were apart."[54] To be sure, Mann adapted this striking self-characterization for Leverkühn, his fictional alter ego, substituting divinity for philosophy, but in his own life, Mann had, of course, done no such thing.

As in Adorno's case, the love of music was instilled in Mann by his mother, who sang to him while accompanying herself on the piano. In his adolescence Mann took violin lessons and learned, Hanno Buddenbrook–like, to improvise on the piano. Paltry though this may sound, he nourished his passionate interest in music throughout his life and was thus able to turn his very limited abilities into an inexhaustible source of both formal and thematic literary inspiration. He became familiar with the core repertory of German music from Bach to Strauss and Pfitzner but confessed to Adorno, with respect to Schönberg and his school, a merely superficially "'initiated' ignorance."[55] Despite such deficiencies, Mann's intellectual curiosity about modern music found praise from Adorno: "Although your ears have been turned to Wagner all your life," he wrote in his homage of 1952, "you did in the end, your heart filled with terror and love, engage with the grimness and darkness of the new music."[56]

Adorno, on the other hand, had studied music seriously, first in his native Frankfurt, then in Vienna, with Alban Berg. He began composing at age fifteen and was, at age twenty-two, a published composer.[57] But composing proved to be an arduous and, in the end, frustrating task that resulted in the lasting trauma of dilettantism.[58] Mann's music-making, figuratively speaking, had early on become a trademark of his work. He pointedly, and coquettishly, told his advisor: "I have a certain reputation for my ways with music."[59] When Adorno complimented him about some unostentatiously brilliant narrative touches, Mann replied: "That sort of thing I know how to do"—an assertion that in my view applies fully to his literary uses of music, especially opera.[60] Indeed, Mann's representations of opera mark a distinct advance over his nineteenth-century models Flaubert and Tolstoy; they set him apart from all other writers.[61] Paradoxically, then, even in the field of music, in which the difference in the level of expertise is most glaring, we can detect no sense of inferiority on the part of Mann.

With respect to philosophy, however, Mann liked to describe himself as a "reverent disciple" of Nietzsche and Schopenhauer—something that suggests a more subtle knowledge of the discipline but that should not blind us to the fact that Mann was of a profoundly non-, if not anti-, philosophical bent.[62] Mann philosophizes the way his amiable confidence man, Felix Krull, plays tennis: cheekily, as he himself confesses, "with a bold, though troubled determination" recklessly "to stand my ground in a game that I had watched and absorbed but in which I had in fact never taken part."[63] Mann's skeptical attitude toward philosophizing is perhaps best revealed in a letter of 1916: "I shall never be the slave of my thoughts, for I know that nothing merely intellectual is true; only form is unassailable."[64]

Nonetheless, it appears that Adorno, professor of philosophy and a dyed-in-the-wool Hegelian, was fascinated by what he viewed as the link between Mann's work and philosophy. He acknowledged that Mann through his very example as an artist had put right much of the distortions to which Nietzsche had been subjected in Germany not by whatever he had written about that philosopher but rather by what he had set free, through the example of his artistry, of the "truth content" of Nietzsche's thoughts.[65] In a similar vein, Adorno revealed a rarely noticed but perhaps crucial aspect of his admiration when he characterized Mann as an author who remained true to all forms of desire, thus hinting at the pervasive presence of homoerotic desire in his work and thereby signaling the centrality of sexuality in his own.[66]

The vexing oscillation between distance and closeness that dizzies and teases the student of the Mann-Adorno relationship can perhaps most succinctly be illustrated by one of Adorno's most characteristic figures of speech: "mit den Ohren denken" (to think with your ears).[67] This striking formula suggests something of the formidable rigor of his approach to music; it also encapsulates the singular marriage of philosophy and music, the joining of philosophical and aesthetic interests, constituting the true essence of his thought. Mann the elegant stylist probably would not have approved of the expression, but it does nonetheless suggest something of the serious inquisitiveness about music that we find in both Mann's own essays and his fiction. The joining of aesthetic experience and critical reflection, even when it occurs in someone of merely average intelligence, such as Hans Castorp in *The Magic Mountain,* is a constant in Mann's work. The much more ambitious project of *Doctor Faustus,* which may be described as a deep reading of German music and a critical reflection on its historical ramifications, is also closer to Adorno's notion of "thinking with your ears" than it may at first appear.

Nowhere is Mann's response to Adorno more lively and engaged than in the case of Wagner. As a matter of course, both writers rejected the Wagnerian dogma of the superiority to music and literature of the synthesis of the arts known as the *Gesamtkunstwerk*. Mann read the four original chapters of Adorno's critical study of Wagner in 1944 and, after the appearance of the completed version in 1952, the entire book. He complimented the author on his "stupendous" and endlessly fascinating *In Search of Wagner*, which offered brilliant proof of what he had been maintaining all his life — that the work of Wagner constituted the greatest challenge to all aesthetic criticism.[68] Like Mann's, so also was Adorno's position one of enthusiastic ambivalence, but within that common ambivalence were important nuances of difference. All things considered, one has to say that the impulse to reject was stronger on Adorno's side, while on Mann's side, ultimately, the impulse to defend prevailed.

Adorno believed that subjecting Wagner's operas to an incisive aesthetic and ideological critique was tantamount to mapping the primordial landscape of Fascism.[69] Mann was most receptive to this view of Wagner, as is evident from his much-quoted (though usually misunderstood) remark that "there is a good deal of 'Hitler' in Wagner."[70] But while Adorno linked Fascism primarily to Wagner's operas and theories, Mann tended to connect the person of Hitler to the person of Wagner, both, for example, for having a need to have a say in everything.[71] The philosopher was drawn to Wagner because he came to see the music dramas as a coherent philosophy of history, while the author of *Buddenbrooks* and of *Tristan* was indebted to Wagner for the countless "wonderful hours of deep and solitary happiness amidst the theater throng, hours filled with shudders and brief moments of bliss, with delights for the nerves and the intellect alike, and sudden glimpses into things of profound and moving significance, such as only this incomparable art can afford."[72] Given such an anchoring of passion for Wagner in aesthetic experience, it is entirely understandable that Mann should have never ceased to feel inspired by Wagner, who remained for him the very exemplar of artistic achievement on a monumental scale. Conversely, given the anchoring of Adorno's preoccupation with Wagner in the philosophy of history, it is quite logical that his anti-Wagnerian animus would grow in response to the growing need for an interpretation of a history that seemed to be rushing toward catastrophe. Adorno was powerfully drawn to what he viewed as Wagner's Hegelianism of the Left. But since this element of progressiveness was wedded inextricably to an overpowering and seductive Romanticism, Adorno came to fear in Wagner—as Richard Klein has persuasively argued—a mortal threat to the entire project of critical theory.[73]

In view of their differently balanced ambivalence toward Wagner, it was inevitable that the symphonic conclusion of *The Ring of the Nibelung* would prove a stumbling block, and indeed, their contrasting readings of this conclusion had momentous implications for *Doctor Faustus*. To Adorno the message of redemption and renewal sounded at the very end of *Götterdämmerung* was nothing more than the "ultimate phantasmagoria"—an insincere gesture that merely masks the underlying sense of utter nothingness.[74] Mann, on the other hand, linked the Wagnerian idea of "redemption through love" to Goethe's *Faust* and steadfastly maintained that "the final words of *Faust* and what the violins sing at the close of *Götterdämmerung* are one and the same, and what they sing is the truth: 'Das Ewig-Weibliche zieht uns hinan' (The eternal-feminine draws us forward and upward)."[75] Nothing could contrast more starkly than the negative air of Adorno's reading and the positive spin of Mann's.

Clearly Mann had his problems with negativity. Thus, in his highly complimentary letter about Adorno's *In Search of Wagner,* Mann confronts his partner with a gnawing mental reservation that, having surely simmered for some time, hints at a discrepancy of their basic political outlooks. Mann indicates his delight at Adorno's observation that in Wagner's work elements of the what-is-to-be emerge from a world in collapse but then puts his finger on a crucial point of difference: "If only, my dear sir, you would ever say a single positive word about the truly desirable kind of society that you seem to postulate!" Mann suspects that Adorno's social critique, especially as encapsulated in *Minima Moralia,* implies a kind of refined and cleansed communism, and he does not hesitate to reject it, because "communism is unthinkable without despotism."[76] It appears, then, that Mann never grasped the crucial and indispensable function of negativity in Adorno's thinking, for that negativity bestows on his musical and literary analyses and on his philosophizing in general their unique force. To Mann, it seems, negativity simply meant the absence of what might be viewed as positive.

Whatever the world of Wagner may have been to Adorno—and this in itself is a highly complicated matter—the world of Wagner was to Mann, as he confessed in *Reflections of a Nonpolitical Man,* quite simply and "literally the homeland of his soul."[77] And so did it remain, especially after reading Adorno on Wagner: "The triad world of the *Ring* . . . is at bottom my musical homeland. . . . And yet at the piano I never tire of the *Tristan* chord."[78] In a similar vein, he wrote to his son Michael, a professional musician, about his attitude toward the music of the Schönberg school apropos of *Doctor Faustus:* "I would never write such music; I felt happier when I described . . . the Leonora Overture, the Prelude to *Die Meistersinger,* Act III, and even [Saint-Saëns's] aria 'Mon coeur s'ouvre à ta voix' than when I described those dodecaphonic oratorios."[79]

It is a testimony to Adorno's remarkable veneration of Mann that he, the uncompromising advocate of the avant-garde, never gave in to the temptation of calling Mann a *Banause*—a musical reactionary. Perhaps aware of the author's revealing self-characterization in *Lotte in Weimar,* Adorno knew that Mann's aesthetic physiognomy as a whole was not to be equated with his rather conventional musical taste. In that novel Mann has his fictitious Goethe elucidate his own aesthetic preferences as follows: "Boldness, yes, audacity, boldness is all, the one indispensable thing—but quiet, decorous, wedded to the proprieties, velvet-shod with irony."[80]

To complete this inventory of the pros and cons of the Mann-Adorno relationship at the time of *Doctor Faustus,* we must now briefly account for their quite different attitudes toward Germany and America. Exile in America affected them rather differently. Adorno was unknown when he came to the United States in 1938 and never came to hold an academic position that would have integrated him into the fabric of American life. Mann, too, arrived in 1938, but as a recent Nobel laureate and as "the greatest living man of letters," as he was routinely referred to, he was widely regarded as the uncrowned king of the German exile community and as Hitler's most articulate opponent. His attitude toward his host country changed dramatically from the Roosevelt era to the Truman era, but Mann was clearly intent on maintaining a balanced and nuanced view of the American political landscape. His basic sense of fairness is best summed up in a comment of 1948 when he conceded that, politically speaking, the weather had turned bad, but that the general climate was still favorable.[81] Adorno, it seems, never distinguished between weather and climate, between the current administration and the political culture, because he opposed the system as a whole, not just its present form.

Adorno's view of America found its most characteristic expression in the signature critique of the culture industry in *The Dialectic of Enlightenment,* which comes close to equating America with Hollywood. It seems hardly accidental that for his philosophical aphorisms, *Minima Mo-ralia*, written in Los Angeles, he chose as an epigraph "Das Leben lebt nicht" (Life is not alive)—an enigmatic but ominous quotation from Ferdinand Kürnberger, author of *Der Amerika-Müde* (The One who is tired of America [1855]) and one of the church fathers of German anti-Americanism. The same ideologically grounded prejudice—grounded in the belief that fascism was the inevitable and culminating phase of capitalism—rendered him unwilling, or incapable, of recognizing in Franklin Delano Roosevelt's United States, as Mann most emphatically did, the crucial and decisive opponent of Nazi Germany.[82]

Neither of our two exiles advocated a soft peace with Germany, and neither harbored illusions about some sudden disappearance of the Nazi mentality from postwar Germany. As for Germany itself, Adorno avowed late in 1944 that under no circumstances, after the defeat, did he want to play the role of the henchman. Nor did he wish to hinder anyone, he added significantly, who might wish to exact revenge for what had happened.[83] In the 1940s no serious engagement with the problem of Germany could avoid reflecting on the horrifying evidence then emerging about Germany's attempt to destroy all of European Jewry. On this decisive point, too, Mann and Adorno display a range of common attitudes. Both men were personally affected by the anti-Semitic laws and policies of Nazi Germany—Adorno because of his Jewish father, Oskar Wiesengrund, Mann because of his Jewish wife and their six children—but both had a strangely delayed reaction to the Nazis' persecution of the Jews. It was only in the early 1940s, when reports about the Holocaust were reaching America, that Adorno and Mann began to focus on this fateful and defining moment of German history. The most plausible explanation for this delay may be sought in the tendency, widespread among the German educated middle class, to underestimate the perniciousness of anti-Semitism, but also in what appears to have been a residue of anti-Semitism in both Mann and Adorno, as reflected in their various comments on some of their Jewish colleagues, such as Alfred Kerr and Herbert Marcuse.

Both men did address the Holocaust in their work, and despite their very different approaches, some notable congruence came to the fore. Mann articulated his reaction in public pronouncements made between 1942 and 1945 and in chapter 46 of *Doctor Faustus*.[84] Strangely enough, however, in the very chapter that reports the liberation of Buchenwald, the fate of the Jews receives no special mention, just as in the novel's admirably knowledgeable depiction of Germany's musical culture, its deeply ingrained anti-Semitism receives no distinctive treatment. Mann's novel gives us a Germany without anti-Semites and a Holocaust without Jews.[85] The Frankfurt School's well-known analysis of the capitalist roots of anti-Semitism in *Dialectic of Enlightenment*, undertaken in the early 1940s, tends to make us overlook the fact that Adorno as well as critical theory as a whole "failed to anticipate or to account for the rise as well as the systematic policy of anti-Semitism" in Germany.[86] So bent were Adorno and Horkheimer on "detecting potential Fascism in the United States" that they, in effect, "minimized the importance of German anti-Semitism, even at a time when its tragic results had become common knowledge."[87] Still Adorno would probably have underwritten what in *Doctor Faustus* is stated with admirable perceptiveness and prescience—that National Socialism and the Holocaust have deep roots in German history and that our perception of "all that is German" will be affected by Germany's turn to "antihumanity."[88]

Oddly, in light of this, it was Adorno who was most eager to return to Germany and to resume his academic career. There he wrote a long and uncharacteristically upbeat report about his experience with his students in Frankfurt and encouraged Mann to return as well.[89] Mann remained adamant: "No ten horses will get me back to Germany."[90] When he did permanently leave America, in 1952, Mann settled in Switzerland. Germany was out of the question. He had concluded that the mindset that had led to his "national excommunication" in 1933, when an opportunistic alliance of Munich Wagnerians and new local Nazi leaders denounced him for allegedly un-German views of the Master, was still in place.[91]

As a coda to these observations, let us once more return to *Doctor Faustus*, and specifically to Leverkühn's *Faust* Cantata, the culmination of the philosophical and musical discourse of Mann's great novel. Very late in the game, on January 12, 1947, Mann read the penultimate chapter to his musical advisor and was astonished to hear him object to the ambivalent ending of Leverkühn's last composition, which suggests the possibility of reconciliation and grace. "No, no—no such reconciliation," Mann remembered Adorno crying out. "You must not degrade despair; it must not sound as though the arch sinner had grace and forgiveness already in his pocket."[92] To Adorno's mind, as we know from his essay "Towards a Portrait of Thomas Mann," the last pages of Leverkühn's

Lamentation had come out sounding "too positive, too unbrokenly theological. . . . They seemed to lack what the crucial passage required, the power of determinate negation as the only permissible figure of the Other."[93] Adorno had provided Mann with a detailed sketch for Leverkühn's last composition, suggesting that the negativity of it all would figure as an "allegory of hope."[94] But now it seemed that Mann had botched the job of making Leverkühn's last composition sound like a work by Adorno. This was worrisome for both of them, but especially for Mann. A discordant note at this decisive juncture would suggest a flaw in the basic design of the entire novel. Mann promised to make some changes, and when they next met, both professed to be happy with the compromise that Mann had set down. But was that true? Or is what we have here perhaps the original piece of mythmaking that has accrued to the larger story of the Mann-Adorno collaboration?

As we have seen, Adorno rejected any positive reading of the end of Wagner's *Ring*. Mann must have found reinforcement of that position when he struggled with Adorno's book on Kierkegaard, which its author had given him while he was working on chapter 20, well before the end of the novel. In the Kierkegaard book, possibly Adorno's most opaque, he puts forth a scathing critique of the Christian idea of redemption— "that sublime banality of redemption"—as a typically bourgeois self-deception. Adorno reconstructs Kierkegaard's idea of hope—a hope that rises in that "night of hopelessness before death" that we all face— only to denounce it as false. Almost compulsively, he then likens Kierkegaard to Wagner, asserting: "the twilight of Kierkegaardian hope is the sallow light of *Götterdämmerung* that proclaims the vain end of an age and the aimless beginning of a new one, but not redemption."[95]

Mann read this but chose to ignore it. Like Wagner courting listeners, Mann courted readers with the same cheerful preference for quantity over quality. Both aimed to reach not only the sophisticates but also the common sort: "I also want to be read by the intellectually challenged," as he confessed to Hermann Hesse.[96] Mann's realistic understanding of his readership told him that Adorno's idea of radical negativity as the only permissible expression of hope would simply not reach his intended audience. He thus decided to go not with Adorno but with Kierkegaard and Wagner. As Leverkühn enters his night of hopelessness before death, Mann sets down two unmistakably positive signs of hope. First, he has Leverkühn's *Lamentation of Doctor Faustus* end on a gradually diminishing "high G of a cello"—a rather transparent cipher for grace.[97] Second, he retains and reaffirms that essential Kierke-gaardian thought of "hope beyond hopelessness, the transcendence of despair"—the very idea that Adorno had rejected.[98] Their clash over Leverkühn's last composition can no longer simply be glossed over, for it confirms what unbiased observers will conclude from their wider aes-thetic and ideological differences: Adorno and Mann were on a collision course from the moment they teamed up, but since they had strong per-sonal motives to keep their aesthetic and ideological differences under wraps, the myth of their close and harmonious collaboration was al-lowed to bloom.[99]

Mann's need for a musical advisor of Adorno's stature is obvious and requires no further elaboration. Adorno's stake in the prestigious collaboration with Mann is quite a different matter and lays bare the very core of his personality. When he learned that Mann was planning a book on the genesis of the novel, he expressly asked Mann to give him credit, but the right kind of credit: "Perhaps it would not be too pre-sumptuous of me to ask you to single out my conceptual and intellectual contribution to Leverkühn's work and his aesthetics rather than merely mentioning the factual information I offered."[100] This clearly is the voice of an existential anxiety over being denied his rightful share of im-mortality. And lest Mann miss the point, he added—tongue in cheek, one would hope—"I anticipate with the greatest excitement the back-door to immortality that your novel of a novel will open for me."[101] This expression of an undisguised thirst for fame and recognition coming from someone who had so far been deprived of his chance to achieve fame in his own right offers us a glimpse of the surprising depth of Ador-no's emotional investment in his collaboration with Mann. Soon after they met, he addressed a letter to the novelist on the occasion of his seventieth birthday in June 1945. Here he confessed openly what his sense of propriety probably would not have allowed him to say in per-son: that Mann's act of turning to him, acknowledging his uniqueness, and asking him to help with *Doctor Faustus* represented for him the "real-ization of a utopia such as hardly ever comes to pass."[102]

Adorno had harbored this utopian dream for over twenty years, for one summer day in 1921, in Kampen on the island of Sylt, the eighteen-year-old Teddy Wiesengrund had been walking behind the author of *Death in Venice* for some time, imagining all the while "how it would be if [Mann] addressed [him]."[103] Eerily, the seaside setting is that of *Death in Venice,* but here the emotional dynamics are reversed: it is the precocious

youth who makes the famous writer the object of his desire. And that
desire is sublimated to a yearning for recognition and a dreamlike fore-
taste of fame. Even more eerily, it may well be that during that summer on the island of Sylt, Mann actually noticed young Wiesengrund
without, of course, recognizing him. But there is an intriguing entry in
Mann's diary that appears to refer to the presence of admirers—Teddy
Wiesengrund most likely among them. Mann notes that walking on the
beach of Kampen he had become "the object of curiosity" and of what
one might today call celebrity stalking.[104]

Given Adorno's emotional involvement in the composition of
Mann's novel, it is entirely understandable why, during their time of
collaboration, he would go along with Mann's inclination to minimize
their differences. Against this background, Adorno's confession to Katia
Mann after receiving the news of Mann's death—"I loved him very,
very much"—takes on a new depth and authenticity.[105] However, his
love for Mann suffered a severe blow in 1965 when Erika Mann, in an
act of calculated malice, included in her edition of her father's letters
one in which Mann discourages a prospective author of a study of his
work from publishing his findings about his borrowings from Adorno or
from sending the manuscript to Adorno himself, arguing that he had already acknowledged his debt in *The Story of a Novel*. He added confiden-
tially: "I have turned a very powerful spotlight on him, in the glare of
which he now puffs himself up rather unpleasantly—to the point that it
almost seems that he himself has written *Doctor Faustus*."[106] Understand-
ably, Adorno's pride was deeply wounded, for it seemed to him, as he
wrote not without a touch of melodrama, that Mann had slandered him
from beyond the grave.[107] Perhaps. But such a confession of pain invites
a psychologically more compelling interpretation—as a screen for a
much greater trauma that was inflicted on him by Schönberg's harsh repudiation of his *Philosophy of Modern Music*. With Schönberg the stakes
were much higher. For deep down Adorno must have felt that, without
Schönberg's blessing, he could not easily, and unchallenged, walk the
earth as the foremost authority, Pontifex Maximus, and supreme ar-
biter of modern music.

We may now return to the thought with which I began my remarks:
Nietzsche's assertion in *The Birth of Tragedy from the Spirit of Music* that it
was the alliance of philosophy and music that launched Germany on its
daring and perilous *Sonderweg* by empowering it not only to gain cultural
independence but also to aspire to hegemony. Much of what Mann had

to say during World War I in defense of Germany's music-centered and inherently nonpolitical, that is to say, antidemocratic, culture was derived from Nietzsche. But—and this distinguishes him from the common run of German Nietzsche followers, most of whom ended up in the camp of the Nazis—Mann continued his reflections on the Nietzschean concatenation of music and German history throughout the Weimar Republic and his exile and during World War II arrived at a reversal of his earlier position. What compelled him to revise his earlier beliefs was not only his own experience of suffering "national excommunication" in 1933 but what he had been witnessing in Germany before and after 1933: the instrumentalization of Germany's musical supremacy by the National Socialists as well as by ordinary *Bildungsbürger* to justify and to legitimate the fatherland's claims to political hegemony.[108]

Doctor Faustus is permeated by the notion of an analogy between a musical breakthrough and a political breakthrough, the one anticipating and preparing for the other.[109] What tempts and ultimately moves Leverkühn to enter into an alliance with demonic forces is indeed the idea of supremacy. Threatened by the prospect of artistic impotence in the face of an unparalleled crisis of creativity and a concomitant prospect of forfeiting his country's musical preeminence, Leverkühn opts for an alliance with demonic forces even if this means embracing barbarism. This then is the most powerful argument that the devilish voice of his innermost desires articulates: "We pledge to you the vital efficacy needed for what you will accomplish with our help. You will lead, you will set the march for the future, . . . you will break through the age itself, . . . the epoch of this culture and its cult, and dare a barbarism."[110]

Mann's fictitious composer is actually closer to Schönberg than the inventor of the "method of composing with twelve tones" appears to have realized, for the "conversation with the devil" that I have just quoted from *Doctor Faustus* uncannily echoes a famous pronouncement of Schönberg's that Mann probably knew via Adorno. The dodecaphonic method of composition, its inventor predicted confidently in 1921, "will ensure the supremacy of German music for the next hundred years."[111]

Although critical theory prided itself on having fashioned the most incisive critical tools for uncovering the hidden connections between culture and politics, one has to wonder why Adorno neglected directly to address and explicitly to thematize the nexus between the Germans' belief in the superiority of German music and Germany's striving for political domination with all the implied consequences that, in other contexts, he analyzed with great intellectual and moral authority. Beholden to a Hegelian view of history entailing the belief that, ultimately, the progress of music was predicated on the state of the development of the "musical material" and its rigorous aesthetic demands rather than on any free human agency, Adorno seems to have been unable to see, or unwilling to concede, the fateful psychological connections that Mann was drawing between German music and German history in *Doctor Faustus* and in his essays.[112] Perhaps he was unable to admit such connections because he himself had in effect become the most authoritative analyst of the canon of German music, and because his own work tended to demonstrate its superiority and historical leadership. To Mann it must have seemed not only that Adorno offered no solution to the problem that haunted him—the hidden nexus of musical and political supremacy—but also that this outstanding representative of German musical culture might actually be implicated in its fateful and calamitous hubris. This, I suspect, was the deepest reason for Mann's reserve toward his brilliant and devoted musical advisor.

NOTES

1. Friedrich Nietzsche, *The Birth of Tragedy and The Case of Wagner,* trans. with commentary by Walter Kaufmann (New York: Vintage, 1967), 121.

2. Nietzsche, *Birth of Tragedy,* 159.

3. Nietzsche, *Birth of Tragedy,* 121.

4. Nietzsche, *Birth of Tragedy,* 121. I have slightly adjusted Kaufmann's translation, rendering Nietzsche's *vor allen Völkern* not as "before the eyes of all nations" but rather as "ahead of all nations," as the context seems to suggest. In what follows, unless otherwise noted, all translations are my own.

5. Cf. Pamela M. Potter, *Most German of the Arts: Musicology and Society from the Weimar Republic to the End of Hitler's Reich* (New Haven, Conn.: Yale University Press, 1998). For a more extensive treatment of this argument, see Hans R. Vaget, "National and Universal: Thomas Mann and the Paradox of 'German' Music," in *Music and German National Identity,* ed. Celia Applegate and Pamela Potter (Chicago: University of Chicago Press, 2002), 155–77.

6. Nietzsche, *Birth of Tragedy,* 119.

7. Thomas Mann, *The Magic Mountain,* trans. John E. Woods (New York: Alfred A. Knopf, 1992), 643.

8. Cf. Hans R. Vaget, "Georg Lukács, Thomas Mann, and the Modern Novel," in *Thomas Mann in Context: Papers of the Clark University Centennial Colloquium,* ed. Kenneth Hughes (Worcester, Mass.: Clark University Press, 1978), 38–65; idem, "Georg Lukács und Thomas Mann," *Neue Rundschau* 87 (1977):

656–63; Judith Tar, *Georg Lukacs and Thomas Mann: A Study in the Sociology of Literature* (Amherst: University of Massachusetts Press, 1987).

9. For the published correspondence, see Thomas Mann and Theodor W. Adorno, *Briefwechsel,* ed. Christoph Gödde and Thomas Sprecher (Frankfurt am Main: Suhrkamp, 2002). Henceforth cited as *Briefwechsel.* For Adorno's homage to Mann, see "Imaginäre Begrüßung Thomas Manns," in vol. 20/2 of his *Gesammelte Schriften,* ed. Rolf Tiedemann (Frankfurt am Main: Suhrkamp, 1986), 467–72. Adorno wrote this text for his colleague and friend Max Horkheimer, then the rector of Frankfurt University, who, however, used his own text for the occasion. Adorno did not publish his "Begrüßung." For his effusive evaluation of Mann, see esp. p. 468: "Während auf Ihrem Namen, als dem einzigen eines heute lebenden deutschen Dichters, aller Glanz der Authentizität ruht." Adorno's *Gesammelte Schriften* will be henceforth cited as *GS.*

10. Detlev Claussen, *Theodor W. Adorno: Ein letztes Genie* (Frankfurt am Main: S. Fischer Verlag, 2003), 149. A similarly naive portrayal of the Mann-Adorno relationship can be found in Stefan Müller-Doohm, *Adorno* (Frankfurt am Main: Suhrkamp, 2003), 475–89.

11. *Doctor Faustus,* trans. John E. Woods (New York: Alfred A. Knopf, 1997), 535.

12. Arnold Schönberg, "Thomas Mann zum 6. Juni 1945," in his *Chorwerke,* Sämtliche Werke, series A, vol. 18, ed. Tadeuzs Okuljar (Mainz: Schott, 1980), xv, 190. Schönberg concludes his dedication hopefully: "wir . . . beide mögen einander noch viele Jahre gute Zeitgenossen bleiben. Herzlichst, Ihr Arnold Schönberg" (May we remain good contemporaries and generational colleagues for many years to come. Most cordially yours, Arnold Schönberg). It appears that Mann recalled this phrase when, in his postscript to *Doctor Faustus,* he characterizes the twelve-tone method of composition as the intellectual property "eines zeitgenössischen Komponisten und Theoretikers [of a contemporary composer and theoretician], Arnold Schönberg." But Schönberg, oblivious to the words of his 1945 dedication, took offense at being characterized by Mann as his contemporary and responded in his open letter about this matter (see n.13) as follows: "He calls me 'a *contemporary* composer and theoretician.' Of course, in two or three decades, one will know which of the two was the other's contemporary."

13. "An Exchange of Letters between Schönberg and Mann," *Saturday Review of Literature,* January 1, 1949; for a convenient reprint, see Patrick Carnegy, *Faust as Musician: A Study of Thomas Mann's* Doctor Faustus" (New York: New Directions, 1973), 168–73.

14. Cf. Jan Maegaard, "Schönberg hat Adorno nie leiden können," *Melos* 41 (1974): 262–64; idem, "Zu Theodor W. Adornos Rolle im Mann/ Schönberg-Streit," in *Gedenkschrift für Thomas Mann 1875–1975,* ed. Rolf Wiecker (Copenhagen: Verlag Text & Kontext, 1975), 215–22.

15. Cf. Arnold Schönberg, "Stil und Gedanke," as quoted by Walter Levin in his "Adorno's 'Zwei Stücke für Streichquartett,' Opus 2 (und Gedanken zum gestörten Verhältnis Schönberg/Adorno)," in *Theodor W. Adorno: Der Komponist*, ed. Heinz-Klaus Metzger und Rainer Riehm (Munich: Edition Text & Kritik, 1989), 78.

16. Quoted by Hans Heinz Stuckenschmidt from his own correspondence with the composer, in his *Schönberg: His Life, World and Work*, trans. Humphrey Searle (New York: Schirmer Books, 1977), 508.

17. Levin, "Adorno's 'Zwei Stücke,'" 77.

18. Levin's apt comment: "Adorno wird hier von Schönberg als 'informer' bezeichnet, im Englischen eine Mischung von Zuträger, Spitzel und Denunziant" (Here, Schönberg characterizes Adorno as an informer, which in English carries implications of spying and treason), "Adorno's 'Zwei Stücke,'" 79.

19. For a complete documentation of the Schönberg-Mann exchange, see Bernhold Schmid, "Neues zum 'Doktor Faustus'—Streit zwischen Arnold Schönberg und Thomas Mann," *Augsburger Jahrbuch für Musikwissenschaft* 6 (1989): 149–79; 7 (1990): 177–92.

20. Stuckenschmidt, *Schönberg*, 512; cf. Maegaard "Zu Theodor W. Adornos Rolle im Mann/Schönberg-Streit," 219.

21. *Briefwechsel*, 19: "Aber an dem unverfrorenem Diebstahl-Charakter der Uebernahme ändert das wenig."

22. Thomas Mann, *The Story of a Novel: The Genesis of Doctor Faustus*, trans. Richard and Clara Winston (New York: Alfred A. Knopf, 1961), 222.

23. *Briefwechsel*, 30.

24. Thomas Mann, *Tagebücher 1946–1948*, ed. Inge Jens (Frankfurt am Main: S. Fischer, 1989), 322 (October 30, 1948).

25. All the excised matter is now easily accessible in Mann's *Tagebücher 1946–1948*, 948–53.

26. Cf. Karol Sauerland, "'Er wußte noch mehr . . .' Zum Konzeptionsbruch in Thomas Manns 'Doktor Faustus' unter dem Einfluß Adornos," *Orbis Litterarum* 34 (1979): 130–45; Hansjörg Dörr, "Thomas Mann und Adorno: Ein Beitrag zur Entstehung des 'Doktor Faustus,'" *Literaturwissenschaftliches Jahrbuch* 11 (1970): 285–322.

27. Müller-Dohm, *Adorno*, 479.

28. *Briefwechsel*, 20.

29. See the letter to Thomas Mann, May 31, 1943, "Thomas Mann–Bruno Walter Briefwechsel," ed. Hans Wysling, *Blätter der Thomas Mann Gesellschaft, Zürich*, 9 (1969): 26. Cf. Hans R. Vaget, "Late Love: Thomas Mann Discovers Berlioz," in *Berlioz, Wagner und die Deutschen*, ed. Sieghart Döhring et al. (Cologne: Verlag Dohr, 2003): 133–45.

30. Thomas Mann, *Tagebücher 1940–1943*, ed. Peter de Mendelssohn (Frankfurt am Main: S. Fischer Verlag, 1982), 572 (May 5, 1943).

31. Mann, *Story of a Novel*, 152.

32. Schönberg wrote to Hans H. Stuckenschmidt, December 5, 1949: "[I]t is disgusting, by the way, how he [Adorno] treats Stravinsky. I am certainly no admirer of Stravinsky, although I like a piece of his here and there very much — but one should not write like that." Quoted in Stuckenschmidt, *Schönberg*, 508.

33. Mann, *Doctor Faustus*, 160. Cf. Igor Stravinsky, *Chronicle of My Life* (London: Victor Gollancz, 1936), 39–40. As did Rimsky-Korsakov with young Stravinsky, Kretzschmar assigns his student the task of orchestrating piano reductions of acts of operas by Grétry and Cherubini and then has him compare his orchestration with those by the composers.

34. For additional comments on the importance of Stravinsky to Mann, cf. Volker Scherliess, "Zur Musik im 'Doktor Faustus,'" in *"Und was werden die Deutschen sagen?": Thomas Manns Roman "Doktor Faustus,"* ed. Hans Wißkirchen and Thomas Sprecher (Lübeck: Dräger, 1997), 113–52, here 141.

35. Cf. Hanjo Kesting, "Krankheit zum Tode: Musik und Ideologie," in *Text und Kritik: Thomas Mann*, ed. Heinz Ludwig Arnold (Munich: Verlag Text & Kritik, 1976), 27–44; Sauerland, "'Er wußte noch mehr.'"

36. Mann, *Story of a Novel*, 43.

37. Thomas Mann, letter to Adorno, December 30, 1945, in *Letters of Thomas Mann, 1889–1955*, selected and trans. Richard and Clara Winston, introduction by Richard Winston (New York: Alfred A. Knopf, 1971), 492; *Briefwechsel*, 18–20.

38. This includes two composition sketches for the apocalyptic oratorio and the Faust cantata, published now in *Briefwechsel*, 158–61.

39. Rolf Tiedemann, "'Mitdichtende Einfühlung': Adornos Beiträge zum Doktor Faustus—noch einmal," *Frankfurter Adorno Blätter* 1 (1992): 9–33.

40. Mann, *Doctor Faustus*, 59. Very regrettably, John E. Woods in his translation of the novel sacrifices the covert biographical reference to T. Wiesengrund-Adorno by rendering *Wiesengrund* literally as "meadowland" rather than leaving the name untouched.

41. Cf. Scherliess, "Zur Musik," for a good facsimile of Adorno's notes on op. 111—a better one than the one reproduced in *Briefwechsel*, 156.

42. Mann's brief correspondence with Alfred Einstein was published by Bernhold Schmid, "Alfred Einstein im Briefwechsel mit Thomas Mann," in *Musik in Bayern: Halbjahresschrift der Gesellschaft für Bayrische Musikgeschichte* 46 (1993): 5–18.

43. Schmid, "Alfred Einstein," 8–9.

44. Mann, *Story of a Novel*, 44–45.

45. Mann, *Doctor Faustus*, 253; translation slightly altered.

46. *Briefwechsel*, 43.

47. Michael Maar, "Teddy and Tommy: The Masks of 'Doctor Faustus,'" *New Left Review* 20 (March/April 2003): 113–30.

48. *Briefwechsel*, 72, 76; cf. Hans Mayer, *Thomas Mann: Werk und Entwicklung* (Berlin: Verlag Volk & Welt, 1950), 370.

49. Mann, *Story of a Novel*, 94–95; translation altered.

50. Mann, *Story of a Novel*, 43, 45.

51. For a useful review of the Adorno-Kracauer relationship, cf. Claussen, *Theodor W. Adorno*, 70–71, 107–8, 114–16.

52. Mann, *Story of a Novel*, 123.

53. Theodore Adorno, "What National Socialism Has Done to the Arts," *GS* 20/2:413–29; idem, "The Musical Climate for Fascism in Germany," *GS* 20/2:430–40.

54. *Briefwechsel*, 33.

55. Mann, letter to Adorno, December 30, 1945, in *Letters of Thomas Mann*, 495; *Briefwechsel*, 23.

56. Adorno, "Imaginäre Begrüßung Thomas Manns," in *GS* 20/2:470.

57. For a conveniently accessible list of Adorno's compositions, see Rainer Riehm, *Theodor W. Adorno: Der Komponist*, 144–46.

58. Cf. Adorno's letter of October 3, 1963, to René Leibowitz: "Es bedarf ja wohl keiner langen Erklärung, daß ich durch mein biographisches Schicksal, und sicher auch gewisse psychische Mechanismen, in meinem Leben nicht entfernt das als Komponist realisiert habe, wovon ich nach wie vor überzeugt bin, daß ich es hätte realisieren können, in meiner ganzen Existenz ein Trauma bildet" (There is no need for a detailed explanation of the fact that—because of the twists and turns of my biography, and certainly also because of certain psychological complexities—I have, as a composer, not nearly realized what I am still convinced I am capable of accomplishing; and of the fact that this constitutes a trauma in my entire existence), *Frankfurter Adorno Blätter* 7 (2001): 61.

59. *Briefwechsel*, 20.

60. Theodor W. Adorno, "Toward a Portrait of Thomas Mann," in his *Notes to Literature*, ed. Rolf Tiedemann, trans. Sherry Weber Nicholson, 2 vols. (New York: Columbia University Press, 1992), 2:13, translation altered.

61. Cf. Hans R. Vaget, "Thomas Mann at the Opera," in *Word and Music Studies: Essays in Honor of Steven Paul Scher and on Cultural Identity and the Musical Stage*, ed. Suzanne Lodato et al. (Amsterdam: Rodopi, 2002), 159–80.

62. Thomas Mann, *Reflections of a Nonpolitical Man*, trans. and with an introduction by Walter D. Morris (New York: Frederick Ungar, 1983), 54.

63. Thomas Mann, *Confessions of Felix Krull, Confidence Man*, trans. Helen Lowe-Porter (New York: Vintage Books, 1969), 335; translation altered.

64. Letter to Paul Amann, February 25, 1916: "Nie werde ich der Sklave meiner Gedanken sein, denn ich weiß, daß nichts nur Gedachtes und Gesagtes wahr ist, und unangreifbar nur die Gestalt." Thomas Mann, *Briefe an Paul Amann, 1915–1952*, ed. Herbert Wegener (Lübeck: Schmidt-Römhild, 1959), 40; translation altered.

65. Adorno, "Imaginäre Begrüßung Thomas Manns," in *GS* 20/2:471.

66. Adorno, "Imaginäre Begrüßung," 472.

67. Adorno, "Kulturkritik und Gesellschaft," in *GS* 10/1:11. Cf. *Mit den Ohren denken: Adornos Philosophie der Musik,* ed. Richard Klein and Claus-Steffen Mahnkopf (Frankfurt am Main: Suhrkamp, 1998).

68. *Briefwechsel,* 121.

69. Adorno, "Selbstanzeige des Essaybuches 'Versuch über Wagner,'" in *GS* 13:504.

70. Thomas Mann, letter to Emil Preetorius, December 6, 1949, in his *Pro and Contra Wagner,* trans. Allan Blunden, with an introduction by Erich Heller (Chicago: University of Chicago Press, 1985), 210. Mann's aperçu is actually a paraphrase of a Nietzschean remark about Charles Baudelaire: "There is a good deal of Wagner in Baudelaire." Friedrich Nietzsche, *Sämtliche Werke, Kritische Studienausgabe in 15 Bänden,* ed. Giorgio Colli and Mazzino Montanari (Munich: DTV, 1980), 11:601.

71. Mann, *Pro and Contra Wagner,* 210.

72. Mann, *Pro and Contra Wagner,* 46–47.

73. Richard Klein, "Zwangsverwandtschaft: Über Nähe und Abstand Adornos zu Richard Wagner," in *Richard Wagner und seine Zeit,* ed. Eckehard Kiem and Ludwig Holtmeier (Laaber: Laaber Verlag, 2003), 183–236, here 189.

74. Theodor W. Adorno, *In Search of Wagner,* trans. Rodney Livingston (London: NLB, 1981), 149.

75. Thomas Mann, "Richard Wagner and the 'Ring of the Nibelung,'" in his *Pro and Contra Wagner,* 171–94, here 194.

76. Mann, letter to Adorno, October 30, 1952, *Briefwechsel,* 122.

77. Regarding the world of Wagner and its meaning for Adorno, cf. Carl Dahlhaus, "Soziologische Dechiffrierung von Musik: Zu Theodor W. Adornos Wagnerkritik," *International Review of Music, Aesthetics, and Sociology* 1/2 (1970): 137–47; Max Paddington, *Adorno's Aesthetics of Music* (Cambridge: Cambridge University Press, 1993), 242–55; Klein, "Zwangsverwandtschaft." Regarding Mann's attitude, see his *Reflections of a Nonpolitical Man,* 55.

78. Mann, *Story of a Novel,* 95.

79. Thomas Mann, *Briefe, 1948–1955 und Nachlese,* ed. Erika Mann (Frankfurt am Main: S. Fischer, 1965), 17.

80. Thomas Mann, *The Beloved Returns: Lotte in Weimar* (New York: Alfred A. Knopf, 1940), 328.

81. Cf. Hans R. Vaget, "Schlechtes Wetter, gutes Klima: Thomas Mann in Amerika," in *Thomas-Mann-Handbuch,* ed. Helmut Koopmann, 3rd rev. ed. (Stuttgart: Alfred Kröner Verlag, 2001), 68–77.

82. Cf. Peter Uwe Hohendahl, *Prismatic Thought: Theodor W. Adorno* (Lincoln: University of Nebraska Press, 1995), 21.

83. Adorno, "Nachtrag zu den 'Minima Moralia,'" in *GS* 20/2:812.

84. For the public pronouncements, see Thomas Mann, "The Fall of the European Jews," in *Gesammelte Werke*, 13 vols. (Frankfurt am Main: S. Fischer Verlag, 1990), 13: 494–98; "Deutsche Hörer," September 27, 1942, in *GW* 11: 1050–53; January 14, 1945, in *GW* 11:1106–8.

85. For a more detailed comment on this aspect of the novel, cf. Hans R. Vaget, "Fünfzig Jahre Leiden an Deutschland: Thomas Manns 'Doktor Faustus' im Lichte unserer Erfahrung," in *Thomas Manns "Doktor Faustus" 1947–1997*, ed. Werner Röcke (Bern: Peter Lang, 2001), 11–34, especially 29–34.

86. Cf. Ehrhard Bahr, "The Anti-Semitism Studies of the Frankfurt School: The Failure of Critical Theory," *German Studies Review* 1 (1978): 128.

87. Bahr, "Anti-Semitism Studies," 133, 137.

88. Mann, *Doctor Faustus*, 300, 505–6.

89. Adorno, letter to Mann, December 28, 1949, *Briefwechsel*, 44–50.

90. *Briefwechsel*, 67.

91. Thomas Mann, "Reply to Hans Pfitzner," in *Pro and Contra Wagner*, 166.

92. Mann, *Tagebücher, 1946–1948*, 953.

93. Adorno, "Towards a Portrait of Thomas Mann," 17–18.

94. *Briefwechsel*, 160–61.

95. Theodor W. Adorno, *Kierkegaard: Construction of the Aesthetic*, trans., ed., and with a foreword by Robert Hullot Kentor (Minneapolis: University of Minnesota Pres, 1989), 110; translation altered.

96. Thomas Mann, letter to Hermann Hesse, April 1, 1910, in his *Briefe I: 1889–1913*, selected and ed. Thomas Sprecher, Hans Rudolf Vaget, and Cornelia Bernini, *Grosse Kommentierte Frankfurter Ausgabe* (Frankfurt am Main: S. Fischer Verlag, 2002), 21:448.

97. Mann, *Doctor Faustus*, 515.

98. Mann, *Doctor Faustus*, 515.

99. For a recent example of such a reading, see Evelyn Cobley, "Avant-Garde Aesthetics and Fascist Politics: Thomas Mann's *Doctor Faustus* and Theodor W. Adorno's *Philosophy of Modern Music*," *New German Critique* 86 (2002): 43–70.

100. *Briefwechsel*, 34–35.

101. *Briefwechsel*, 35.

102. *Briefwechsel*, 17.

103. *Briefwechsel*, 17.

104. Thomas Mann, *Tagebücher 1918–1921*, ed. Peter de Mendelssohn (Frankfurt: S. Fischer Verlag, 1979), 545.

105. Mann, *Tagebücher 1918–1921*, 153.

106. Thomas Mann, letter to Jonas Lesser, October 15, 1951, in his *Briefe, 1948–1955*, 226.

107. Adorno, "Marginalien zu Theorie und Praxis," *GS* 10/2:761.

108. For a more comprehensive argument, see Vaget, "National and Universal."

109. Cf. Jens Rieckmann, "Zum Problem des Durchbruchs in Thomas Manns 'Doktor Faustus,'" *Wirkendes Wort* 29 (1979): 114–28.

110. Mann, *Doctor Faustus*, 258–59.

111. Quoted, among many other sources, in Willi Reich, *Schönberg oder der konservative Revolutionär* (Munich: DTV, 1972), 139: "Ich habe eine Entdeckung gemacht, durch welche die Vorherrschaft der deutschen Musik für die nächsten hundert Jahre gesichert ist."

112. Thomas Mann, "To the Editor of *Common Sense*," in his *Pro and Contra Wagner*, 196–203; idem, "The War and the Future," in his *Order of the Day: Political Essays and Speeches of Two Decades* (New York: Alfred A. Knopf, 1942), 238–56.

IO

The Composer as Dialectical Thinker

Hanns Eisler's Philosophical Reflections on Music

ALBRECHT BETZ

Translated by Jost Hermand

"He was an intellectual who happened to be a musician," said Hanns Eisler's first American admirer.[1] But because Eisler, active as an innovative composer in many musical genres, was a musician through and through, we cannot—in contrast to his one-time friend Theodor W. Adorno—expect a coherent philosophy of music from him. Instead, what we can expect are philosophically informed observations about the music of his time and about the historical evolution of music in light of larger social developments.

When Eisler, in his final years, referred to himself as an "old Hegelian," he did not intend to be merely ironic. But what special feature of Hegelianism did he have in common with two of the most important German philosophers of music in the twentieth century, Adorno and Ernst Bloch, with whom he was—if only temporarily—in close contact? What special interest in Hegel's theory of music did they share?

To begin with, it is important to consider how Hegel's aesthetic differs from that of Kant. First of all, Kant's distinction between the naturally beautiful and the artistically beautiful was of little interest to Hegel since the naturally beautiful possesses no idea or spirit. For Hegel, therefore, only that which is made by human beings for other human beings can be considered as art. In other words: art must communicate. This assertion appears in Eisler's intellectual repertoire as a weapon used to fend off any attempt to lend an independent quality to the musical material. Second, in contrast to Kant, Hegel's philosophy of music is based on a historicization of aesthetic categories that always links the development of artistic forms to the development of society. In so doing, his philosophy connects the evolution of art with societal conflicts during various historical periods. This complicated way of viewing the past, the present, and a possible future became, for Eisler, an unquestionable postulate at the very core of his Marxist commitment. A child of the "Age of Extremes," to borrow Eric Hobsbawm's term, Eisler strove throughout his life to reconcile this Hegelian approach with the artistic claims of the Schönberg school.

As peculiar as it may seem, a strict historical periodization is precisely what is missing in Hegel's aesthetic, an absence that can be attributed to his lack of intimate knowledge of the general development of music. Eisler, however, sought to compensate for this shortcoming by bringing the whole of Hegel's philosophy into play. Of paramount importance to Eisler was the Hegelian notion of "contradiction," which Eisler wielded as an ideological weapon. The motor of dialectical progression, or, as Bloch called it, the negation, is what generates the "unrest" that so appealed to Eisler's concrete social commitment and to his rebellious temperament.[2] While prizing the concern with content that serves as a basis for Hegel's aesthetic categories along with Hegel's view of content as pointing toward a historical meaning, Eisler nevertheless disregards statements in Hegel's aesthetic reflections that refer to the "Romantic" as the basis of everything musical and indicate that music forms a connection between the acoustical and an absolute "inwardness." This thesis was disregarded by Eisler, who rejected the cooptation of music for soulful comfort and compensation.

One Hegelian distinction with regard to the concept of inwardness, however, did appeal to Eisler, a distinction that is encapsulated in the following passage: "To understand an object in its inwardness can mean, on the one hand, to understand this object not in its outward appearance, but in its non-material or spiritual meaning; but, on the other hand, inwardness can also mean to express a content in such a form, as it becomes one and the same with the subjectivity of a particular feeling. Both forms of inwardness are possible in music."[3]

In this way, Hegel views music as an internal movement of feelings, a manifestation of the "soul" perhaps, but not a manifestation of the "spirit." It is, therefore, not only possible but also usual that music expresses an indeterminate feeling. This applies especially to instrumental or "independent" music, as Hegel calls it. Given that Hegel's primary interest is centered on content, it is not surprising that his remarks concentrate mainly on "dependent" music, that is, music that is connected with texts. To put it another way, content, for Hegel, always represents the unity of form and material, that is, the material that has been shaped into form with compositional techniques. Only by deploying these techniques, according to Hegel, will it be possible to bring to the fore in all their complexity contradictions such as the contrast between consonances and dissonances that would enable music to express the depth and full significance of spiritual contents.

The real sense of music, however, can only be achieved in vocal music or, more precisely, through the relationship of music to the written text. This is so, "because the text," as Hegel writes, "creates out of itself particular images and snatches consciousness away from the dreamlike elements of substanceless feelings."[4] Hegel continues with a passage that Eisler accepted unconditionally and employed in his vocal compositions:

> Art consists . . . mainly in giving itself totally to the meaning of the respective words, situations, plots, and so on, and thereafter attempts to find—on the basis of an inner soulfulness—a musical expression for this meaning. That is the manner in which all great composers work. They do not add something foreign to the words, but they also do not totally neglect the free flow of sounds, the structure of the composition, which is there not only because of the text but also has a value in itself.[5]

Hegel continues in the same vein:

> It is therefore a harmful bias to maintain that the nature of the text would be of no importance to the composition. On the contrary, the most important works of music all are based on extraordinary texts that the composers selected with deep seriousness or wrote themselves. For no artist should be indifferent toward the subject matter that he treats in his works. And this even applies to the musician, especially if the texts he chooses already predetermine the epic, lyric, or dramatic form of the content with which he is engaged. The main demand, which is important in regard to a good text, is that its content have an important

substance. Out of something that is in itself flat, trivial, simplistic, or absurd, you can never create [*herauskünsteln*] something musically serious or deep.[6]

If we were to replace the "or" in the sentence about "the most important works of music" with an "and" ("that the composers selected with deep seriousness *and* wrote themselves"), we would already be dealing with Eisler's highly conscious methods with regard to selecting texts. One thinks of the utmost care he exercised in shortening texts by Friedrich Hölderlin, omitting certain mythological allusions, compressing the texts so that they contained only those statements he considered relevant for his time, and intensifying musically those dimensions in the texts that otherwise might remain obscure to a superficial or uneducated reader.

Eisler, on the one hand, accorded the highest esteem to Hegel's emphasis on the importance of content, which he regarded as being of utmost importance to his own concept of music, while, on the other hand, disregarding other all-too-obvious shortcomings in Hegel's philosophy that he felt were irrelevant to his own concept of composition and to his commitment to content. Hegel's overlooked shortcomings include the following: (1) the failure, in contrast to his chapter on the other arts, to delineate the historical development of music as an art form; (2) insufficient analysis of musical material such as the relations between homophonic and polyphonic music or the contrast of major and minor keys; (3) an ahistorical generalization of the dominance of melody over harmony and rhythm, alongside an exclusion of non-European music; (4) a tendency to reconcile underlying contradictions in favor of classicist-harmonious value judgments without anticipating the role of nonbeautiful elements in future avant-garde theories and movements; and (5) the failure to produce a convincing synthesis of the pure inwardness and subjectivity of music.[7]

Such partial objections, however, did not concern Eisler, who was interested in the grand historical and dialectical nature of Hegel's aesthetics. This interest is most obvious in the critical years of World War II, which he spent mainly in exile in California together with Adorno, Brecht, and others. Contrary to the impression afforded by the expression "Weimar in Hollywood," relations among those who had been forced to leave Germany after 1933 were characterized by strife, resentment, frustration, and all the other evils that accompany involuntary isolation. The most quoted remarks about this situation are from Brecht's *Arbeitsjournal,* in which he speaks sarcastically of a "Hollywood Hell," of those who nearly prostituted themselves in the service of a devilish marketplace, and of the Frankfurt "Tuis," his derogatory word for intellectuals, with their overly sophisticated half-Marxism.[8] The fact that some of Brecht's snide remarks also take aim at Eisler, with whom he shared the closest political and aesthetic affinity, can be understood in the context of Eisler's sometimes-wavering loyalty to Brecht's stringent demands. In the same way that Walter Benjamin oscillated between Brecht and Scholem during the 1930s, Eisler moved between the poles of Brecht and Adorno during the early part of the 1940s. Suspecting that his old comrade in arms may have fallen back into late bourgeois subtleties, Brecht assumed that Eisler would be drawn back into the Schönberg circle's "esoteric" music and relinquish his older concept of "intervening" or "activating" *(eingreifende)* music.

During these years, Adorno himself moved between Max Horkheimer and Eisler, the latter guaranteeing him a closeness to Schönberg by virtue of his high-ranking status (second only to Anton Webern and Alban Berg) among Schönberg's disciples of the 1920s. Nevertheless, out of the midst of this aesthetic, political, and psychological web of contradictions, a number of cooperative works of the first order emerged in various constellations: Brecht's and Eisler's *Galilei, Simone Marchard,* and *Schwejk;* Eisler's and Adorno's *Composing for the Film;* and Adorno's and Horkheimer's *Dialectics of Enlightenment.* In addition, Eisler's *Fourteen Ways to Describe the Rain* (film music as chamber music) is dedicated to Schönberg, and Brecht's *Hollywood Songbook* consists primarily of poems composed for Adorno. While Adorno's *Philosophy of Modern Music* and *Composing for the Film* can be read as an extended digression from the *Dialectics of Enlightenment, Composing for the Film* also grew out of Eisler's collaborations with Brecht on theater productions and out of the New York film music project that was the successor to Adorno's radio music project (both sponsored by the Rockefeller Foundation). As with the other works mentioned here, neither *Composing for the Film* nor the *Dialectics of Enlightenment* could be published before 1945 because of the war. The film music project, investigating possible relationships between music, original sound, synthetic sound, and the moving image, proceeded from a working hypothesis that radically "new" music, especially that which applied twelve-tone rows, could have a significantly greater impact in films than traditional music, which Eisler felt was deteriorating into repetitive clichés. In the final passage of this project, which was completed in October 1942, Eisler addresses an all-too-neglected discrepancy: the historically derived opposition between seeing and hearing.

> People adapt to the rational and ultimately highly industrial bourgeois order of things through the use of their eyes, since these are accustomed to understanding reality right from the start as a reality of things, in fact, basically of consumer goods; this adaptation was not provided to the same degree as by the use of the ears. Compared with seeing, hearing is "archaic" and has not kept up with technology. It could be said that to respond basically with the unselfish ear rather than with the alert, appraising eye is in some way contrary to the late industrial epoch. For this reason there resides in aural perception as such, to an incomparably greater extent than in the optical, an element of the collective. At least two of the most important factors in occidental music, harmonic and contrapuntal polyphony and its rhythmic articulation, directly indicate a multiplicity after the model of the ecclesiastical community of former times. This direct relationship to the collective, which adheres to the phenomenon, appears to be associated with spatial depth, the feeling of something all-embracing that draws individuals into itself, a feeling characterizing all music.[9]

Eisler also identifies the cynical abuse by the culture industry of this element of collectivity in the standard film music of Hollywood. This abuse encourages the perpetuation of modes of feeling that have long been superannuated, supplies acoustical reinforcement to the visual illusion, and melodiously mixes nebulous yearning with slick jollity; this is done by means of set pieces derived from late-bourgeois music. This process makes such music politically dangerous, even if only in an indirect way. While reinforcing the vague feelings that audience members have brought along with them, it confirms individual relationships and beyond these the social structures, just as they are. Such music makes for a lack of awareness and hinders change. It aids the constant rehashing of the threadbare scheme of "through-darkness-into-light" as the "tense" feature film with a happy ending. Any possible objections are silenced by the impressive level of technical perfection—always the highest possible—with which the whole show is produced: this gives it the false appearance of something interesting, something that obeys its own logic and thus seems in some way reasonable.

To expose such contradictions, a dialectical optic—schooled on Hegel—was necessary. Only in this way could Eisler and Adorno arrive at insights that expressed their shared disgust with the overwhelming culture industry. As Eisler said to Brecht when, after years of separation, they met again in Los Angeles, "Hollywood is the classical locus in which to write elegies. Being in Hollywood, you simply have to describe it."[10] The whitewashed idyll of California, accompanied by the harsh demands that come with offering one's services to the film industry, on the one hand, and the murderous battles in Eastern Europe that reached a climax in Stalingrad, on the other: what a dreadful dialectic indeed.

To the German exiles, Hollywood seemed to exist in a state of eternal presence under the smiling sun of alluring advertisements, a cultural landscape dominated by the relentless demand to succeed and to accumulate wealth. They regarded this situation as a temporary state of affairs that could be endured by creating works for the "time after," gifts in the luggage to be opened upon their return, as it were.

This was the contradictory setting in which Eisler worked on his *Hollywood Songbook* in 1942/43, about the same time Adorno wrote his *Reflections from Damaged Life,* to which he gave the title *Minima Moralia.* Next to the *Hollywood Elegies,* based on texts by Brecht, the most important subcycle in this songbook is the one based on songs by Hölderlin. In 1943, when the National Socialists celebrated the one-hundredth anniversary of Hölderlin's death, using his works as a glorification of sacrifice for the fatherland, it was Eisler's enlightened intention to work against each and every mythologization or misuse of great works of art for irrational purposes. As such, he engaged with Hölderlin's dictum: "For, our song is nothing mighty / But it belongs to life." Music for him was an experience of rational thinking, an expression of subtle perceptions of that unhappy consciousness caused by exile. And where else but in Hollywood could a modern artist experience a more aporetic existence, obliged to express artistic subjectivity under conditions that are more and more adverse to the unfolding of individuality. And here, at the epicenter of the dream factory, Eisler worked on crystal-clear musical creations that were meant as an act of resistance against the clichés, among them the musical ones, with which the ruling culture industry, in an act of deliberate deception, sought to numb its mass audience with all the means of technical perfection and the constant repetition of sameness into a state of mind that excluded the possibility of resistance and thereby of social change.

Equally important for the dialectical constellation of 1943 was, for Eisler, the question of how to be *for* and *against* his own country, Germany, whose majority did not resist its oppressors. How was it possible to support the allies while in Eastern Europe entire generations of Germans were dying in the war effort? How could one hope for victories of the Red Army in order to defeat fascism while Eisler's German and Austrian fellow countrymen sacrificed themselves or were sacrificed for the wrong cause? How could one endure the situation in which one German city after the other—and how many memories were connected with each one—was turned into a heap of rubble while at the same time realizing that this was necessary for the defeat of Nazism? With images of burning cities and despair before his inner eye—a few months after Stalingrad—Eisler wondered whether an end to the war and thereby a moment of hope were imaginable?

Which Germany would emerge on the heels of more than a decade of fascist indoctrination? Here, in exile, Eisler and his friends could only rely on their memory. But after a possible return to Germany, their identity also would require recognition by others. Which listeners in a postwar German society would be able to understand such sophisticated creations as the "Hölderlin Fragments"? In his claim to convey—via the ear—political insights and at the same time to purge the old-fashioned clichés of inwardness, Eisler studiously avoided the treacherous fullness of sound. In so doing, he declared his belief in Hegel's concept of art as something objective, even concrete, that conveys higher forms of knowledge. In this conviction he was not far from Adorno, who writes in the *Philosophy of New Music:* "The New Music incorporates its contradiction to reality into its own consciousness and into its artistic form. By so doing it sharpens itself to become knowledge. Traditional art has already approached becoming such knowledge as it has revealed the contradiction of its material, thereby bearing testimony to the contradictions of the world around it. Its depth is related to its judgment about the existing evil. But it is the aesthetic form that enables art to make this judgment."[11] Such critical memory and self-reflections are absent in a material progression that expands without a sense of history.

Eisler's music as well as his theoretical remarks about the enlightening character of progressively oriented compositions balk against being incorporated by the culture industry. Since Adorno settled in West Germany after the war and became one of the most influential music critics in the Federal Republic of the 1950s and 1960s, while Eisler joined Brecht in East Germany, Eisler's and Adorno's erstwhile friendship gave way to ideological hostilities. A comparison with the attitude of Adorno, Eisler's friend in Hollywood and subsequently the most influential

musical theorist of West Germany, makes it clear why. It is evident that
Eisler felt compelled to reject Adorno's postwar positions: "It is one of
the peculiarities of that institute in Frankfurt that it sees all tendencies
toward dissolution as progressive, with a sort of half-baked Marxism."
Eisler reduces this attitude to the superb and intentionally very summary formulation: "They only want to be more clever than the bourgeois theorists, but they do not want to take issue with them."[12] The
principal themes of the late Adorno, the rescuing of a transformed subjectivity, the insistence on "unregimented experience," on spontaneity
and imagination, meant an act of salvaging in the name of aesthetics.
Under the trauma of the experience of fascism, Adorno, after 1945, arrived at a far-reaching equation of capitalism and socialism as systems
of total manipulation. Subjectivity (basically the Romantic bourgeois
subjectivity), threatened by "socialization," looks to art for consolation
and the prospect of immortality. The concentration of his analyses on
partial phenomena, whose rights in opposition to the "whole" are ultimately so overvalued as to turn his priorities upside down, effectively replacing his theory regarding political confrontation enacted by concrete
social subjects: the great confrontations between classes and levels of society are hidden from sight. The observer adopts the perspective of the
suffering subject and, in so doing, merely blurs the dividing line that
separates it from the suffering within itself. Such subjectivism is able to
exercise only very limited force as a dialectical weapon.

Hegel characterizes this intellectual attitude in his *Aesthetics* in the
following way. Referring to the early Romanticists, he describes it as a
"reluctance to face reality" that results in "vague longings of the soul
instead of concrete actions." He continues to argue: "This is a longing
that does not condescend to concrete forms of action, because it is afraid
of polluting itself through contact with reality, although it is aware of the
feeling of lack caused by this abstraction. Therefore this attitude leads to
the absolute negativity in which the subject related everything to itself
by destroying all concrete particularities. But because this act not only
destroys the trivial, which manifests itself in its emptiness, it also undoes
everything superb and tasteful; therefore, this all-encompassing art of
destruction . . . is at the same time a form . . . that lacks the attitude of a
firm ideological position."[13]

It is this lack that Bloch evoked when, in 1969, Adorno summoned the
police to remove those students from the Frankfurt institute who were
violently rebelling against what they perceived as his lack of political

commitment.[14] But it should nevertheless be noted that Adorno's critique bestows a new aura on German high culture of the nineteenth century, although in a highly contradictory manner. As Adorno's student Albrecht Wellmer puts it, with Adorno, "it once again became possible in Western Germany to be morally and aesthetically in the present without, however, having to hate Kant, Hegel, Beethoven, Goethe, and Hölderlin."[15] "The teachings of Critical Theory were understood at that time in a twofold manner," Adorno's biographer Lorenz Jäger writes: "On the one hand, there was the radical critique of the contemporary scene, on the other hand, they—as in the writings of Walter Benjamin— opened up new approaches to a German intellectual history that would perhaps have been buried. . . . By making Auschwitz the center of his thinking, Adorno enabled his readers and listeners to hold on to their love for the German language, philosophy, and music."[16]

After Eisler returned from exile, first to Vienna and then to the German Democratic Republic, which he chose—like many others such as Bloch, Brecht, and Heartfield—in order to place himself in the service of a new, socialist culture, he encountered a legion of difficulties. During the seemingly endless period of exile, his fears had centered mainly on the danger of an involuntary return to subjective inwardness. Then, after 1950 in the German Democratic Republic, Eisler was confronted with the obligation to make artistic compromises that are partly documents of a self-imposed compositional regression.

The possibilities of a collectively oriented vocal music seemed ruined for the near future—because of the misuse by the Nazis of this form of music. The mentality of broad sections of the general public in the German Democratic Republic was determined by outdated working conditions. How far should Eisler go in mainstreaming his innovative compositional techniques under these conditions? Should he restrict himself to the composition of *New German Folksongs?* The same holds true for his theoretical reflections. How could he integrate the sophisticated concepts he had discussed with Brecht and Adorno on the West Coast of the United States into the German Democratic Republic debates, which largely advocated a crude reflection theory *(Widerspiegelungstheorie)* and the creation of positive heroes?

One sacrifice he was forced to make was to relinquish his most important project of the 1950s, nothing less than the attempt to write a new German national opera. The cultural functionaries of the German Democratic Republic criticized his libretto for a Faustus opera before he had even produced the first sketches. Eisler had dared to portray Faust as an intellectual wavering between political fronts, thereby casting him as a paradigmatic figure of the Cold War during these years, instead of conforming to the stereotype of Faust as a national hero.[17] The hair-raising *Faustus* debate shortly before June 17, 1953, proved to Eisler that he had to cope—in his own ideological camp—with adversaries who were as incompetent as they were powerful, whose arguments were monocausal, and whose strategies were outright repressive—or undialectical, as Eisler saw it.

In light of these circumstances, we have no really important late works by Eisler if we disregard the *Serious Songs* in which he integrated some of his previous Hölderlin songs.[18] In retrospect, Eisler's most creative phase remained the period in exile, which he spent mostly in the United States. But even in his last lecture, titled "Content and Form," which he gave in 1962 at the East Berlin Academy of the Arts, he continued to rely on Hegel.[19]

NOTES

1. The New York baritone Mordecai Bauman (born 1913) was trained at the Julliard School of Music. He sang Eisler's agitational songs—accompanied by the composer at the piano—for the first time during a tour through the United States.

2. Cf. Albrecht Betz, *Hanns Eisler: Political Musician* (Cambridge: Cambridge University Press, 1982), 7–9.

3. Georg Wilhelm Friedrich Hegel, *Ästhetik*, ed. Friedrich Bassenge (Frankfurt: Europäische Verlagsanstalt, 1965), 2:304.

4. Hegel, *Ästhetik*, 2:306.

5. Hegel, *Ästhetik*, 2:306–7.

6. Hegel, *Ästhetik*, 2:313.

7. With regard to the following, cf. Herbert Schnädelbach, "Hegel," in *Musik in der deutschen Philosophie: Eine Einführung*, ed. Stefan Lorenz Sorgner and Oliver Fürbeth (Stuttgart: Metzler, 2003), 55–75, here 71.

8. See Bertolt Brecht, *Arbeitsjournal* (Frankfurt am Main: Suhrkamp, 1975), 293–362.

9. Theodor W. Adorno and Hanns Eisler, *Komposition für den Film* (Leipzig: Deutscher Verlag für Musik, 1977), 55–58.

10. Hanns Eisler, *Fragen Sie mehr über Brecht: Gespräche mit Hans Bunge* (Darmstadt: Luchterhand, 1986), 43.

11. Theodor W. Adorno, *Philosophie der Neuen Musik* (Frankfurt am Main: Suhrkamp, 1959), 43.

12. Eisler, *Fragen Sie mehr über Brecht,* 38.

13. Hegel, *Ästhetik,* 1:161.

14. In a personal conversation with the author in Tübingen on September 18, 1973.

15. Albrecht Wellmer, quoted in Lorenz Jäger, *Adorno: Eine politische Biographie* (Stuttgart: Deutsche Verlagsanstalt, 2003), 253.

16. Jäger, *Adorno,* 253.

17. See Betz, *Hanns Eisler,* 217–19.

18. Betz, *Hanns Eisler,* 234–37.

19. Hanns Eisler, *Musik und Politik: Schriften 1948–1962,* ed. Günter Mayer (Leipzig: Deutscher Verlag für Musik, 1982), 572–78.

I I

Double Mimesis

Georg Lukács's Philosophy of Music

JOST HERMAND

When addressing a topic such as music and philosophy in the thought of Georg Lukács, one must begin by dispelling certain objections and biases. Paramount among them are the following: first, can the Hungarian Georg (György) Lukács really be regarded as part of a specifically German history of music philosophy? Second, were this man's aesthetic reflections not informed by a stubbornly Stalinist perspective that is undeserving of scholarly consideration? Third, what, if anything, did this expert on the function of "realism" in literature actually know about music? And does this form of art figure prominently in his work—as in the writings of Ernst Bloch and Theodor W. Adorno—or is it of only marginal importance?

The first objection would seem to be the most serious, since Lukács was, in fact, Hungarian. However, culturally descended from the Austro-Hungarian Empire of the Hapsburg monarchy, he and other members of the Jewish cultural elite—such as his parents, who, prior to 1914, are known to have hosted Thomas Mann at their home—felt as closely connected to German culture as to that of Hungary. But this tradition was not his only link to German culture, since Lukács also spent significant portions of his life in Heidelberg, Vienna, and Berlin; sought to establish himself as a professor at a German university; wrote many of his philosophical and aesthetic works in German; and, toward the end of his life, was happy to see his book *Die Eigenart des Ästhetischen* (The specificity of the aesthetic) published first in Germany, which he regarded as the "old center of philosophical aesthetics."[1] Furthermore, who could be so narrow-minded as to see in Albert Schweitzer nothing more than a Frenchman from Alsace, in Franz Kafka merely a Jew from Prague, or in Paul Celan only a lyric poet from Bukovina—rather than regarding them all as members of a more broadly defined German culture?

Turning to the second objection, a concern with Lukács's political outlook, we find that on careful scrutiny all accusations prove to be unfounded. Whether one considers the charges originating in NATO countries where Lukács was denounced as a "Stalinist dogmatist" (Adorno) and a "preacher of terror" (Daniel Bell), or those originating in countries that belonged to the Warsaw Pact, where he was branded a "traitor" and a "revisionist" because of his support for the Hungarian uprising of 1956—such accusations ultimately amount to nothing more than journalistic fiction.[2] To be sure, from the end of World War I until his death in 1971, Lukács was a steadfast advocate of socialism, but he also was in perpetual conflict with the Communist Party, both in Hungary and in Germany, because of his stubborn insistence on a "democratic socialism," especially as articulated in his *Blum Theses* of 1928 and then again in his objections to the Stalinist orthodoxy of the Hungarian Communist Party in 1949. It was therefore only logical that during the Hungarian uprising of 1956 he would join the Imre Nagy cabinet as secretary of education, a decision that nearly cost him his life. From that point forward, he was a persona non grata throughout the Eastern bloc, which meant that he was forced to publish his writings almost exclusively with the West German Luchterhand Verlag rather than with the East Berlin Aufbau Verlag, as he had done before. What is more, the alternative characterization of Lukács as a blind defender of "socialist realism" is equally untrue and can only be understood as part of a larger Cold War strategy to discredit all proponents of socialist ideas. While Lukács did make a few tactical concessions in this regard, his major works on aesthetics all are firmly grounded in a truly Marxist understanding of a cultural heritage in terms of its dialectical appropriation and are almost entirely void of Stalinist reductionism and sociological vulgarizations.

With regard to the third objection concerning the extent of Lukács's acquaintance with music, one need only point out that a great deal of chamber music was played in his home,[3] that he had close contact with Béla Bartók, and that he possessed extensive knowledge of the writings on music by Hegel, Max Weber, Bloch, and Adorno. What is more, the notion that one must be a professionally trained musicologist in order to speak authoritatively about music is questionable. After all, an intense involvement with music is not the exclusive domain of specialized scholars. One also can ponder this phenomenon—as did Kant, Herder, Schelling, Schleiermacher, Schopenhauer, and Nietzsche—in a philosophical way. Indeed, these thinkers sometimes posed more interesting questions with regard to music than the so-called experts in the field, who often were preoccupied with analyzing the formal internal structure of individual compositions. In the end, then, the claim that Lukács possessed merely a rudimentary knowledge of music is not of grave concern.

Now that these preliminary concerns have been addressed, let us turn our attention to the only really decisive question: where does Lukács—in his specifically philosophical manner—engage at length with the phenomenon of music? He does so in the chapter titled "Music" in the second part of the first volume of *Die Eigenart des Ästhetischen,* which was completed in the second half of the 1950s after drafts had appeared in the *Deutsche Zeitschrift für Philosophie* (1952) and the *Festschrift für Ernst Bloch* (1955).[4] The volume on aesthetics first appeared in 1963 with Luchterhand Verlag, whose publisher, Frank Benseler, was a close confidant of Lukács and later published their substantial correspondence.[5] But before we examine the chapter on music in extenso, let us first consider Lukács's more general aesthetic concepts in relation to the ontological questions with which he grappled during that period.

Many will be surprised to learn that Lukács, the allegedly stubborn Stalinist, did not shy away from ontological questions. Did Lukács not view philosophical ontology, the domain of Martin Heidegger and other representative members of the existentialist camp, as a deviation from rational thinking? What was Lukács's interest in the primarily "essential"? The person who first interested him in such questions was Wolfgang Harich, his copyeditor at Aufbau Verlag, who, in the early 1950s, recommended the pertinent writings of Nicolai Hartmann to him.[6] Whereas in Hartmann's oeuvre—as in his 1951 book *Teleologisches Denken* (Teleological thinking)—being *(ens)* is seen as belonging primarily to the realm of the ahistorical, Lukács located it squarely in the sphere of concrete, everyday life. In so doing, he sought, on the one hand, to infuse his concept of a "democratic socialism" with the added impetus that derives from everyday situations, and, on the other hand, to strengthen the "subjective factor" that is inherent in societal conventions.

What is more, Lukács repeatedly refers to Marx's portrayal, in the *Paris Manuscripts*, of the unfolding of every dimension of the five senses as being among the foremost aims of human development.[7] By buttressing his ontological arguments concerning everyday life with such a Marxian view, Lukács aims to revive—after all the degradations of communism during the Stalin era—a genuinely Marxist object-subject-dialectic that would afford more self-determination to the individual in the overall course of societal development. In this context, Lukács appeals to Marx's basic ways of life *(Daseinsformen)* or determinants of human existence *(Existenzbestimmungen)* as they relate to the categories of work, reproduction, ideology, and alienation in the latter's *Grundrisse der Kritik der politischen Ökonomie* (Outlines of a critique of political economy) without, however, succumbing either to ahistoricism or to an undoing of Marxism in the form of a "bourgeois re-individualization."[8] He argues that the ethical value of individual human endeavors is in no way diminished by the fact that these endeavors ultimately are subsumed by larger societal processes. On the contrary, it is precisely the struggle against alienation that defines the human being as something other than a mere slave to objective conditions or to self-reflexive egotism. Furthermore, as Lukács makes clear in his chapter on music in *Die Eigenart des Ästhetischen*, this struggle is the critical component in the creation of art.

Although Lukács originally planned this work as a three-volume set, because of his growing interest in philosophical ontology he managed to complete only the first book. A monumental fragment, consisting of some 1,600 typewritten pages, nevertheless continues the thought process that originated in 1930/31 with his reading of the *Paris Manuscripts* and his close collaboration with the Soviet scholar Mikhail Lifschitz.[9] From that time on, Lukács remained firmly convinced that only the sublation of alienating economic conditions would set in motion a humanizing force capable of activating the dormant potentialities that lie in every human being.[10] Spurning all idealistic-voluntaristic or vulgar sociological conceptualizations of art, Lukács now focused his attention—despite the many political disturbances in Moscow during the 1930s—ever more narrowly on the dialectical character of objective conditions and their subjective transformation in the work of art. This focus caused him to reject all blind utopianism, all factographic fetishization, and every Stalinistic tendency toward glossing over contradictions in the manner of an overly optimistic socialist realism. Contrary to all such views, Lukács mobilized the "sense of continuity" that Thomas Mann, one of his ardent admirers, so appreciated in his writings in order to challenge qua art the supposed all-pervasiveness of alienating forces by showing how all great works of art encompass the "totality" of social conditions.[11]

An important aspect of this endeavor is Lukács's view that the specificity of aesthetics is the critical characteristic that distinguishes art from every other form of human expression and knowledge. Asserting the primacy of aesthetic content over aesthetic form, Lukács emphasizes that form itself always is the "form of a specific content," a content that, for him, could consist only in the mimetic representation of reality.[12] For Lukács, then, one of the most important consequences of art is its capacity for "liberating" human beings from the dominance of myth and religion.[13] In art, he claims, human beings strive to create an image of the world that reflects what they are experiencing. As such, the world of art represents, for him, not only a reflected part of reality but also the expression of an ever-shifting awareness of societal developments. Viewed as "a self-identical subject-object creation," art, for Lukács, is a "world in itself."[14] Accordingly, he maintains, under the chapter subheading "Specificity as an Aesthetic Category," that the struggle of every important work of art to comprehend the world as a "totality" produces "a value-accented middle position between subjectivity and objectivity." Viewed in an anthropomorphic way, art "liberates these two extremes from their one-dimensionality: that is, subjectivity from its enclosed particularity, and objectivity from its antihuman distance."[15] Aesthetic reflection, according to Lukács, possesses an integrative capability, an evocative power, and a cathartic potential that scientific methodology lacks. Art, therefore, constitutes a being-in-itself *(Ansichsein)* as well as a being-for-itself *(Fürsichsein)*. In other words, art infuses its images and narratives with "life" in such a way as to offer us an even deeper comprehension of reality than scientific inquiry can produce.

Suspending for the moment any possible critique, let us first concentrate on Lukács's situating of the art of music within this mimetic framework and on his definition of music both as a socially determined creation and as an expression of the self-reflecting subject's rebellion against the forces of societal alienation. At first glance, any such speculations about the mimetic character of art in the realm of music would seem to be rendered mute, since music appears to lack the capability of representing something mimetically through the epic-reflective or visual-reflective means that literature and the visual arts have at their disposal. How can a Hegelian convert to Marxism such as Lukács, who, throughout his life, was a devotee of "realistic" literature, possibly do justice to music with such speculations? Indeed, one might even question, especially in the case of instrumental music, which is not invested with the meaning that words and images impart, whether it is possible—even in a highly differentiated way—to rely on concepts of a realistic "reflection" *(Widerspiegelung)*.[16]

But let us leave such questions unanswered for the moment to avoid any hasty judgments. Instead, let us first understand the criteria according to which Lukács sought to incorporate even the very specificity of music into his aesthetic theories. After all, engaging with music as a form of aesthetic mimesis is, for any materialist among philosophers of art, always the most difficult touchstone. Lukács was only too aware of the imperatives that a true materialist be consistent on every level, leaving no blank spots on the theoretical canvas while writing *The Specificity of the Aesthetic*. His chapter on music in the second part of the first volume, therefore, willingly conforms to the systematic approach of his overall project, even accounting for architecture and ornamental design in furnishing evidence that mimesis is the basis of *all* aesthetic expressions, so-called abstract or absolute instrumental music notwithstanding.

Having ascertained that the mimetic character of music—and, indeed, *any* theory of mimesis—was being questioned by modernist theoreticians in the West (especially after the period of expressionism), Lukács claims that objective social reality had disappeared behind a solipsistic subjectivity accompanied by a high degree of self-reflexivity. This development, he asserts, necessarily would cause all expressions of subjectivity to become "isolated from concrete reality." By casting aesthetic expression into the realm of "subjective particularity," he argues, the relationship of this expression to "totality" would be lost and lead to an "impoverishment" of all matters of content.[17] What the theoreticians of modernism most vigorously rejected in theories of music, Lukács declares, are the "mutual relations between the configurations of reality and the affective reactions toward them."[18] In opposition to the modernist position, theories of music dating back to Greek antiquity, that is, to the twelfth Pythian ode of Pindar, to Plato, and to the Pythagoreans, overwhelmingly have asserted that the "mimetically represented object of music" serves as a mirror that reflects the "inner life" of its creators.[19] Even as late as the nineteenth century, when instrumental music was becoming more widespread, the romantically inclined philosopher Arthur Schopenhauer continued to speak of the "content of music" as a "reflection" not merely of "ideas" but also of "the human will."[20]

Following a discussion of Schopenhauer, Lukács shifts his focus to consider several views of music in light of the older nature philosophy. He rejects Johann Gottfried Herder's claim that early humans thought of music as being constituted by sounds derived from nature without regard to social development while, at the same time, bestowing credit on the Pythagoreans in this respect. Ultimately, however, it is Hegel who put things into their proper perspective by recognizing that the endeavors of human work are manifested in art. After all, Lukács argues, the genesis of music should always be considered in the context of the human activities with which it is connected, such as dancing in the case of dance music and singing in the case of work-related melodies that are "artistic" rather than "natural" in origin. Both forms of music are, however, eminently "mimetic" in character since, as part of the motoric rhythms of dance and the singing rhythms that ease the processes of work, they facilitate an intensified expression of human emotions.[21] Thus, as Lukács apodictically asserts, music must be understood as a "mimesis of inner life" in which sociohistorical processes and the emotions that they elicit find joint expression in artistic form.

This line of argumentation brings Lukács back to the notion of a dialectic within all forms of art that he had postulated at the beginning of his chapter on music. While the view of music as a reflection of human "inwardness" or "soulfulness" satisfied the theorists of antiquity, Lukács asserts that far more concrete definitions are required today, because, after all, "inwardness" never has existed in a "natural or unmediated form" but rather has always been the product of sociohistorical developments and ever more highly differentiated social conditions.[22] Thus, he notes that while barbaric episodes occur in the arts as well as in social and political life, even in the course of change, music never loses its concreteness. What is more, according to Lukács, this feature is shared with all important forms of art. In other words, the greatness of a work of art depends on a sublation of the "purely singular" and the "barren general" into something universal. Lukács then concludes his argument with the dictum that music arrives at a "middle position of a true, world-encompassing, human inwardness [*Innerlichkeit*] that both reflects the world correctly and reacts to it in an exemplary way."[23]

To put it somewhat less emphatically, even the feelings that modern instrumental music expresses reflect a particular moment in the history of its subjective mediation, rather than merely reflecting some arbitrary or disembodied emotions. So far, so good. But what does Lukács mean by "concreteness" *(Gegenständlichkeit)* in this context? In literature and the visual arts, concreteness—as conveyed by narratives and images—is always present, whereas in the world of instrumental music, concreteness, at least as conveyed by "realistic" representation, is apparently absent. What, then, can the term "mimesis" mean in this context? Does Lukács use the representational qualities (realistic, allegorical, or symbolic) that characterize the other arts only to subject music to the straitjacket of materialistically deduced theories? I think not. Instead, what Lukács wishes to argue is that music actually contains "reflections of reflections" rather than direct reflections themselves. He further maintains that music's seemingly unrealistic forms of expression have an undeniable sociopolitical concreteness in spite of that indirectness. In short, music, for Lukács, embodies a "double mimesis" or "mimesis of mimesis" that is not based on any obvious similarity to concrete objects. The "mimesis of mimesis," for him a subjectively mediated form of understanding the world, constitutes an understanding achieved by means of a musical language that, in spite of its supposed abstractness, is always related to specific historical conditions and, by extension, to concrete reality. Put another way, instrumental music, for Lukács, is—in contrast to all formalist approaches—not merely "resounding air" or a "chess game with tones," but rather a phenomenon that distinguishes itself through the conjunction of objective, real-world experiences with the subjective mediation of those experiences. Seen in this light, music differs from literature, painting, and every other form of art in degree, but not in principle.

More than just the expressive outpourings of any particular subject, musical forms, for Lukács, are—with or without the composer's conscious awareness—always the result of a complex "doubling of reflection," a process that cannot be separated from music's many reciprocal relations with the sociohistorical surroundings in which it originates and which make it a form of "double mimesis."[24] Two things distinguish music in this respect. As an "objectification of human emotions," music possesses an evocative power, Lukács argues, capable of effecting far greater catharsis than any literary work or visual art. After all, music, in his view, reflects the subjective experience of the world more intensely—precisely by means of its alleged nonrealism—than any other form of art, since in music "uncertain or vague concreteness" constitutes the very "basis of a greater evocational capacity of the mimetically reproduced experiences of life."[25] And with this argument—after having defined his topic at great length—Lukács finally arrives at the question of value judgments. But even here he never loses himself in abstractions, remaining historically concrete throughout. Like the early Marx, who remarked that Balzac, in spite of his conservative, even royalist convictions, had always been a great artist because of his penetrating "realism," Lukács avoids rigid partisanship in his approach to art.[26] As his aesthetic treatise shows, the significance of all great art, for him, consists first and foremost in the extent to which its representations of the world succeed in distancing themselves not only from one-sided subjectivity but from one-sided objectivity as well. Lukács argues that great art strives for a middle position that, in its artistic synthesis, provides a true reflection of the actual historical situation. He refers to this process as the "defetishizing function" of art in general.[27]

But even here Lukács never yields his historical perspective. Instead of criticizing "atonal" compositional systems, as he once had done, he now simply reconceives them as reflections of a "certain sociohistorical situation." Indeed, in this context—along with Bloch—he even quotes Adorno, who, as Lukács firmly emphasizes, always accentuates the "historical implications" of all forms of music instead of separating the uses of "musical means" from their "genesis."[28] And in this historical genesis, Lukács discerns, over the course of centuries, the occurrence of many qualitatively important developments that facilitated a broader differentiation of human emotional capabilities. No wonder, then, that Hegel, as Lukács writes, calls music—in the framework of his evolutionary concepts of history—a "typical art of the Romantic period."[29] But music developed not just in the direction of differentiation but also in the direction of the liberation of so many feelings that, after having been socially repressed in strictly regulated societies, could emerge only in an emotionally intensified form under more democratic circumstances.

The "uncertain or vague concreteness" or "suggestive abstractness" of music's content, as Lukács repeatedly refers to it, is always more distant from, but at the same time closer to, human perception than any other form of art. However, Lukács thinks two things in particular should be avoided when listening to music: allowing oneself to be drawn into a sentimental mawkishness and allowing oneself to be bombarded by works that are devoid of any spiritual meaning. The compositions that Lukács therefore favors are those with a "socially human atmosphere of destiny" *(gesellschaftlich-menschliche Schicksalsatmosphäre)* such as Mozart's *Zauberflöte,* Alban Berg's *Wozzek,* and the *Cantata profana* by Bartók.[30] Even folkloristic elements are acceptable to him, and he was not at all pleased with Adorno for referring in his collected essays on music, *Dissonanzen,* to the use of such elements in Bartók's music as "volkish."[31] But none of this should be construed as meaning that Lukács always insists on programmatic content in music, since, in this respect, he holds fast to his concept of the binding "middle" in an inseparable object-subject relationship as valid for all the arts. Unlike Schopenhauer and Nietzsche, he therefore concedes an aesthetic specificity to music without, however, granting music a special place in the kingdom of the arts. In fact, he even criticizes several Germans for their attempts to elevate music to a privileged position. And he is even more critical of any attempt to use music—because of its alleged "indeterminacy"—as a means for constructing an opposition to reason, as so clearly undertaken by Thomas Mann in his essay "Germany and the Germans" and in his novel *Doctor Faustus.*[32]

Now, having considered—in a necessarily simplified form—the main ideas presented in Lukács's chapter on music in *The Specificity of the Aesthetic,* let us turn our attention to the reception and critique of these ideas by other theorists of music and to a general evaluation of the unique features of Lukács's philosophy of music. Considering first the historical reception of his views on music and aesthetics primarily as articulated during the 1970s and 1980s, three categories of response are distinguishable: (1) The relatively objective, sometimes fairly positive reception by Hungarian music critics, as in the two essays by Dénes Zoltai; (2) the sympathetic but critical evaluation of his concepts by Günter Mayer and Georg Knepler in the German Democratic Republic (GDR); and (3) the more critical discussion of Lukács's philosophy of music by the West German music scholar Albrecht Riethmüller and a rather harsh critique by the Czech music critic Vladimir Karbusicky, who moved to West Germany from Prague in the 1970s.

With regard to the first group, it is not surprising that, in the late 1980s, a Hungarian such as Dénes Zoltai would resolutely defend Lukács against the infamous accusations in which Adorno questioned not only Lukács's socialist theories but also the works of Béla Bartók, the greatest Hungarian composer of the twentieth century, in an attempt to dislodge them both from the core of modern art and aesthetics.[33] In 1958, in the journal *Der Monat,* Adorno—while living safely in Frankfurt—ignominiously attacked Lukács, who two years earlier had risked his life in the anti-Stalinist uprising in Budapest. As Zoltai points out, Lukács, by contrast, had shown great equanimity in his treatment of Adorno in the chapter on music in *The Specificity of the Aesthetic.* And finally, Zoltai writes, it had been unreasonable on Adorno's part to characterize Lukács as a mediocre representative of antimodern tendencies in art because of his partisanship for Bartók, and to use the works of Arnold Schönberg as the sole measuring stick of a truly "modern" music. Judgments such as these seemed to Zoltai like the expressions of an orthodox cult of the so-called Second Viennese School, which, in the course of the second half of the twentieth century, had become as obsolete as the pseudo-Marxist practice of fetishizing Stalinist art, which Lukács attacked.

With regard to the second group, we will examine the key essay "On Polemics between Contrasting but Ideologically Like-Minded Critics," which Günter Mayer and Georg Knepler, the two most important musicologists of the GDR, published in the early 1970s in the volume *Dialog und Kontroverse mit Georg Lukács* (Dialogue and controversy with Georg Lukács). Here they dealt with the different but at the same time rather similar views of Georg Lukács and Hanns Eisler in regard to music theory.[34] This book appeared at a moment when—after a long period of silence about Lukács—it once again became possible in the GDR to enter into a discussion, albeit in critical form, about his aesthetic theories. As expected, both Mayer and Knepler placed themselves squarely on the side of Eisler's theories and criticized Lukács for his "fetishization of the canonical works of the classical period," although they admitted that in his philosophical speculations on the uncertain or vague concreteness of instrumental music, he was following the best traditions of Marxist criticism.[35] Mayer and Knepler were equally critical of Lukács's highly abstract language and of a one-sided ideological orientation that disregarded formal structures, especially in the realm of modern music. Their arguments may have been a bit exaggerated, but they intended to emphasize the importance of Eisler's sustained efforts to locate ways of applying music in the ongoing class struggle, an undertaking that Lukács had utterly neglected in *The Specificity of the Aesthetic.*[36]

As regards the third group, I will now offer some observations about the criticism of Lukács's book in West Germany. While Adorno's general aversion to the writings of Lukács's middle and late periods has already been mentioned, it would not be difficult to identify striking similarities in their theories about the "vague images" in instrumental music. However, in the course of the Cold War, which became ever hotter in the 1950s and early 1960s, Adorno tended to reject all forms of mimetic representation in favor of concepts of an autonomous art. Albrecht Riethmüller, by contrast, deals with Lukács's aesthetic views — after the *Wende,* or "turn," of 1989 — in a far more sympathetic way. He regrets only that Lukács's philosophy of music is suffused with too many abstract features and that it is not supported by concrete musical examples, thereby damaging his "aesthetics as well as a deeper understanding of music."[37] Moreover, Lukács's aesthetics appear to him somewhat "out of date," that is, based in the past and lacking an engagement with the "modernism" of a Pierre Boulez, a Karlheinz Stockhausen, or even his fellow socialist Hanns Eisler.[38] On the other hand, Riethmüller demonstrates a significant appreciation for Lukács's theory of reflection, that is, his theory of a "double mimesis" in music, which clearly is directed not only against the Western, formalistic concept of absolute music but also against vulgar Stalinist attempts to instrumentalize music in the service of "socialist realism."[39] Vladimir Karbusicky, conversely, minces no words in his denouncement of Lukács's "theory of reflection" as a meaningless platitude.[40] He seeks, first and foremost, to discredit this concept on the basis of its alleged association with the Stalinist artistic praxis of the 1930s, calling it ideologically "obsolete."[41] In support of his arguments, Karbusicky invokes the writings of Tibor Kneif, who in 1971 had written that the "theory of reflection" resembles a "bizarre flower of the Eastern remorseful pleasure in formlessness as well as the confessing, stammering soul of a Dostoyevskian hero" who never could play any "major role" in a "socialist aesthetics of music in the West."[42]

Given his highly controversial role as a "democratic socialist" during the Cold War, the ambivalent reception of Lukács's philosophy of music on both sides of the so-called Iron Curtain is hardly surprising. Even after Lukács's death in 1971, he remained for most musicologists — whether they belonged to the Western or the Eastern ideological camp — a suspicious outsider. Like his former friend Bloch, he supported a "Third Way" between the two political superpowers and therefore encountered difficulty with the state socialist regime in Hungary.[43]

As a result, the reception of Lukács took four forms: an embarrassed silence, a Hungarian pride in the country's greatest philosopher and in
his predilection for Béla Bartók, a pitying smile in view of the supposed
outdatedness of his ideas (contrasted with a cult of "modernism"), and a
more or less openly hostile attitude. Unfortunately, however, the deeper
truths of his arguments were seldom discussed.

Of central importance in my reconsideration of Lukács's reception is
his attempt to develop an aesthetics of music, especially instrumental
music, that would engage not only with form but also with content. This
attempt was fueled by Lukács's desire to locate, even in this form of art,
the same mimetic elements that are so readily apparent in literary works
and in the visual arts. The biases against such a view are all too well
known. As early as the eighteenth century, when instrumental music, for
the first time, came into its own following the centuries-long domination
of vocal music, most representatives of the Enlightenment repeatedly
questioned the legitimacy of this form of art, which they regarded as lacking in content. After all, they claimed, music, because of its inability to
convey liberal images and ideas, would not contribute to the "progress"
of humankind.[44] This attitude would change only as the movement that
transformed sentimentality into Romanticism elevated—in a backlash
against the so-called dry rationality of the Enlightenment—instrumental
music in all its "vagueness" to the highest status among the arts. This
transformation was especially pronounced in nineteenth-century Germany, when instrumental music—because of the clash between a highly
developed culture and an underdeveloped bourgeois liberalism—
served as a vehicle for the often-discussed flight into what Friedrich
Engels once called an "effusive misery" *(überschwängliche Misere)*.

Consequently, any theories of instrumental music that did not
conform to the Romantic idea of an "absolute" music but instead attempted to interpret that genre of music in a bourgeois-realistic, left-
liberal, or even materialistic way remained marginal in Germany for a
long time. Even in the twentieth century, when rebellious movements in
music attempted to counter these Romanticizing concepts with avant-
garde or modernistic theories, no significant change occurred. The
main reason for this was that during the Cold War, most Western philosophers of art—ideologically opposed to the vulgar sociological or
Stalinist theories of direct reflection—spurned all notions of "realism"
in favor of the abstract or the nonrepresentational. Even in the field of
music theory, which was hardly a contested battleground of the Cold

War, Westerners barely noticed the theoreticians in the East who were still striving to develop theories based on a materialistic interpretation of historical and cultural developments.[45] Who, after all, in the Western bloc of that time discussed books such as the following?: *Muzykal'naja forma kak process* (The Musical Form as Process, 1976) by Boris Assafjew, *O specifice muzyki* (On the Specific in Music, 1957) by Zofia Lissa, *Lektsii po marksistsko-leninskoi estetike* (Lectures on Marxist-Leninist Aesthetics, 1969) by Moissej Kagan, *Teorija realizma i problemy muzykam'noj estetiki* (Theory of Realism and Problems of an Aesthetic of Music, 1971) by Alexander Farbstein, *Zur Frage der ästhetischen Inahlt-Form-Relation in der Musik* (On the Question of Form-Content-Relations in Music, 1971) by Eberhard Lippold, and *Um die Sache der Musik: Reden und Aufsätze* (On the Matter of Music: Speeches and Essays, 1976) by Harry Goldschmidt. Yet these are precisely the writings that deal with theoretical concepts similar to those advanced in Lukács's chapter on music in *The Specificity of the Aesthetic* (1963). The authors of these books also strive to develop a "mimetic" interpretation of instrumental music no longer based on Stalinist theories of direct reflection. On the contrary, most of them deal with "intonations" that enter into musical compositions as personal moods, thoughts, urges, feelings, and political convictions, indeed, as any possible impulse, but which are, at the same time, always more or less intricately intertwined with the moods, thoughts, urges, feelings, and political convictions of the period in which they originate and which confer their artistic specificity on them.

Even more so than in other forms of artistic expression, everything in music is connected with everything else and is fully meaningful only to those listeners who are able not only to enjoy the soulfulness of music and the sensuality of acoustic gratification but also to hear how the composers incorporated the intonations of the world surrounding them and their reactions toward these intonations into the music. Listening to serious music is just as demanding as reading a classical drama by Schiller or looking at a painting full of cryptic symbols such as those by Caspar David Friedrich. Of course, one can also listen to a symphony by Beethoven as if one were relaxing in a bubble bath and tuning out—in a comfortable state of drowsiness—all possibilities of spiritual or soulful perception. But in so doing, would one not foreclose the many and varied associations that emerge when one reads a work of serious literature or looks at a great painting?[46] Of course, the supreme seductiveness of music makes it possible for one to lapse into mindlessness in a way that other forms of art do not. While hearing it, one can be carried away, pleasantly stimulated by its melodies, and, under certain circumstances, this is a legitimate response. But in the end, does one not reduce music—by not giving one's total attention to it—to the status of a soul vibrator or merely delightful background noise? Serious listeners attempt to think with their ears and thereby become conscious of the historicity of their own feelings as well as the feelings incorporated into the music to which they are listening. For such listeners, Lukács reminds us that even those series of beautiful sounds that, like so many works of instrumental music, seem to be devoid of any specific content are artistic expressions of more or less clearly recognizable spiritual processes. And like every cultural phenomenon, these processes can be understood only in the materialistic terms connecting them to their origins. To put it somewhat emphatically, not only one's capacity for pleasure (that is, the refinement of one's acoustic sensibility) but also one's understanding of a historically and socially mediated world are deepened by a Lukácsian understanding of music.

This is not to say that everything Lukács proposes in his philosophy of music is necessarily true. Certain elements testify to a restricted knowledge of musical theory, while others are too abstract in their philosophical bent. But his basic insight nevertheless remains important: instrumental music is more than mere resounding air, a mathematical game, or an unmediated expression of private feelings. And even if music appears to be one of these things, it is also much more, because music always objectively reflects a historical period in the same way that philosophy, as Adorno was fond of saying, always is a condensation of the ideas of a given epoch.[47] In this regard the two old Hegelians, Lukács and Adorno, have much in common, despite their clashing positions during the Cold War.

NOTES

1. See Georg Lukács's letter to Frank Benseler of November 11, 1961, in *Objektive Möglichkeit: Beiträge zu Georg Lukács' "Zur Ontologie des gesellschaftlichen Seins,"* ed. Rüdiger Dannemann and Werner Jung (Opladen: Westdeutscher Verlag, 1995), 83.

2. See Theodor W. Adorno, "Erpreßte Versöhnung: Zu Georg Lukács' 'Wider den mißverstandenen Realismus,'" *Der Monat,* no. 1 (1958): 37–49; and Daniel Bell, "Durch die Sünde zur Erlösung: Die grandiose und tragische Geschichte seines Lebens ist exemplarisch für die kommunistischen Intellektuellen dieses Jahrhunderts: Georg Lukács. Volkskommissar der ungarischen

Räterepublik, Prediger des Terrors, großer Philosoph und Lehrer," *Die Zeit* 39 (September 18, 1992): 77.

3. According to personal statements made by Hans Mayer in Madison, Wisconsin, at the beginning of the 1970s.

4. Georg Lukács, *Die Eigenart des Ästhetischen* (Darmstadt: Luchterhand, 1963), 2:330–401. See also the letter of Georg Lukács to Frank Benseler of December 11, 1959, in *Objektive Möglichkeit,* 68.

5. See *Objektive Möglichkeit,* 67–104.

6. See Werner Jung, "Zur Ontologie des Alltags: Die späte Philosophie von Georg Lukács," in *Objektive Möglichkeit,* 255.

7. Karl Marx, *Ökonomisch-philosophische Manuskripte,* in Karl Marx and Friedrich Engels, *Werke,* supplementary volume, pt. 1 (Berlin: Dietz, 1974), 541–42.

8. Regarding *Daseinsformen* and *Existenzbestimmungen,* see Karl Marx, *Grundrisse der Kritik der politischen Ökonomie* (Berlin: Dietz, 1975), 26. See also Werner Jung, *Georg Lukács* (Stuttgart: Metzler, 1989), 10–16. Regarding "bourgeois reindividualization," see Frank Benseler, "Der späte Lukács und die subjektive Wende im Marxismus: Zur 'Ontologie des gesellschaftlichen Seins,'" in *Objektive Möglichkeit,* 143.

9. Georg Lukács to Frank Benseler on December 11, 1959, in *Objektive Möglichkeit,* 68.

10. See István Hermann, *Die Gedankenwelt von Georg Lukács* (Budapest: Akadémiài Kladó, 1978), 177–78.

11. Regarding Thomas Mann's appraisal, see *Georg Lukács zum siebzigsten Geburtstag* (Berlin: Aufbau, 1955), 141.

12. Georg Lukács, *Die Eigenart des Ästhetischen* (Darmstadt: Luchterhand, 1963), vol. 12 of his *Gesammelte Werke,* 689. Henceforth cited as *GW.*

13. *GW* 12:746. See also Jung, *Georg Lukács,* 26–29.

14. *GW* 12:325.

15. *GW* 12:227.

16. On this general problem, see my *Konkretes Hören: Zum Inhalt der Instrumentalmusik* (Berlin: Argument, 1981).

17. *GW* 12:330.

18. *GW* 12:330.

19. *GW* 12:331.

20. Arthur Schopenhauer, *Die Welt als Wille und Vorstellung,* vol. I, par. 52.

21. *GW* 12:346.

22. *GW* 12:339.

23. *GW* 12:255.

24. *GW* 12:363.

25. *GW* 12:366.

26. Karl Marx and Friedrich Engels, *Über Kunst und Literatur,* ed. Manfred Kliem (Frankfurt: Europäische Verlagsanstalt, 1968), 1:581–91.

27. *GW* 12:350.

260

28. *GW* 12:370.

29. *GW* 12:373.

30. *GW* 12:385.

31. Theodor W. Adorno, *Dissonanzen: Musik in der verwalteten Welt* (Göttingen: Vandenhoeck & Ruprecht, 1956), 105–6. See also *GW* 12:373.

32. *GW* 12:397.

33. Dénes Zoltai, "Das homogene Medium in der Kunst," in *Georg Lukács: Kultur—Politik—Ontologie,* ed. Udo Bermbach and Günter Trautmann (Opladen: Westdeutscher Verlag, 1987), 229–32; and idem, "Über die Anwendbarkeit der Ästhetik in den Musikwissenschaften," in *Zur späten Ästhetik von Georg Lukács,* ed. Gerhard Pasternak (Frankfurt am Main: Vervuert, 1990), 151–62.

34. Günter Mayer and Georg Knepler, "Zur Polemik zwischen gegensätzlich Gleichgesinnten," in *Dialog und Kontroverse mit Georg Lukács,* ed. Werner Mittenzwei (Leipzig: Reclam, 1975), 358–95.

35. Mayer and Knepler, "Zur Polemik," 370.

36. Mayer and Knepler, "Zur Polemik," 373.

37. Albrecht Riethmüller, "Die Musik an der Grenze der ästhetischen Mimesis bei Georg Lukács," in *Zur späten Ästhetik von Georg Lukács,* 163.

38. Riethmüller, "Die Musik an der Grenze," 164.

39. On this, see also Albrecht Riethmüller, "Die Musik als Abbild der Realität: Zur dialektischen Widerspiegelungstheorie in der Ästhetik," *Archiv für Musikwissenschaft,* Supplement 15 (1976): 82–85.

40. Vladimir Karbusicky, "Acht destruktive Thesen als Würdigung Lukács,'" in *Zur späten Ästhetik von Georg Lukács,* 196.

41. Karbusicky, "Acht destruktive Thesen," 199. Here Karbusicky refers mainly to the writings of David Tamarschenko that were published in 1931 and 1936 in Moscow and Leningrad.

42. Quoted in Karbusicky, "Acht destruktive Thesen," 200.

43. On the theory of the "Third Way," see my *Zuhause und anderswo: Erfahrungen im Kalten Krieg* (Cologne: Böhlau, 2001), 7–26.

44. See Hermand, *Konkretes Hören,* 21–31.

45. See the chapter "Materialistische Musiktheorie," in Hermand, *Konkretes Hören,* 113–31.

46. On this, see my "Beethoven oder Bonaparte? Vom Anderen und vom Selbst in der 'Sinfonia Eroica,'" in *Beredte Töne: Musik im historischen Prozeß,* by Jost Hermand (Frankfurt am Main: Peter Lang, 1991), 65–66.

47. See Jost Hermand, "Der vertonte Weltgeist: Theodor W. Adornos Beethoven-Fragmente," in *Musik im Spektrum von Kultur und Gesellschaft: Festschrift für Brunhilde Sonntag,* ed. Bernhard Müßgens et al. (Osnabrück: Epos music, 2001), 151–66, and in *Beethoven: Werk und Wirkung,* by Jost Hermand (Cologne: Böhlau, 2003), 207–23.

CONTRIBUTORS

ALBRECHT BETZ is professor of German and comparative literature at the University of Aachen, Germany. He is the author of, among other books, *Ästhetik und Politik: Heinrich Heines Prosa* (1971), *Hanns Eisler: Musik einer Zeit, die sich eben bildet* (1976; translated into four languages), *Exil und Engagement: Deutsche Schriftsteller im Frankreich der dreißiger Jahre* (1986), and *Der Charme des Ruhestörers: Heine Studien* (1997).

LYDIA GOEHR is professor of philosophy and aesthetics at Columbia University, New York. She is the author of *The Imaginary Museum of Musical Works: An Essay in the Philosophy of Music* (1992) and *The Quest for Voice: Music, Politics, and the Limits of Philosophy* (1998). She is currently completing a book titled *Notes to Adorno*. She is the coeditor, with Daniel Herwitz, of *The Don Giovanni Moment: Essays on the Legacy of an Opera* (2006).

BEATRICE HANSSEN is professor of German at the University of Georgia, Athens. She is the author of *Walter Benjamin's Other History: Of Stones, Animals, Human Beings, and Angels* (1998) and *Critique of Violence: Between Poststructuralism and Critical Theory* (2000), and coeditor of *The Turn to Ethics* (2002), *Walter Benjamin and Romanticism* (2002), and *Walter Benjamin and the Arcades Project* (forthcoming).

JOST HERMAND is the William F. Vilas Professor Emeritus of German at the University of Wisconsin–Madison and an honorary professor at Humboldt University, Berlin, Germany. The author and editor of numerous books, his works on music include *Konkretes Hören: Zum Inhalt der Instrumentalmusik* (1981) and *Beredte Töne: Musik im historischen Prozeß* (1990), as well as essays on Adorno's Beethoven fragments, Brecht as a composer, and Eisler's *German Symphony*. Among his most recent books are *Beethoven: Werk und Wirkung* (2003) and *Nach der Postmoderne: Ästhetik heute* (2004).

DAVID FARRELL KRELL is professor of philosophy and the founding director of the Humanities Center at DePaul University in Chicago. He is the author of a dozen books, including *The Tragic Absolute: German Idealism and the Languishing of God* (2005), *The Purest of Bastards: Works of Mourning, Art, and Affirmation in the Thought of Jacques Derrida* (2000), and *Contagion: Sexuality, Disease, and Death in German Idealism and Romanticism* (1998).

LUDGER LÜTKEHAUS is a well-known freelance writer and journalist who teaches German literature at the University of Freiburg, Germany. Among his books on modern literature, philosophy, and psychology are *Hegel in Las Vegas: Amerikanische Glossen* (1992), *NICHTS: Abschied vom Sein: Ende der Angst* (1999), and *Schwarze Ontologie: Über Günther Anders* (2002). He is also the editor of the German edition of Schopenhauer's collected works.

MARGARET MOORE is a doctoral candidate in philosophy at Temple University.

REBEKAH PRYOR PARÉ is a doctoral candidate in German literature and musicology at the University of Wisconsin–Madison.

GERHARD RICHTER is associate professor of German at the University of California, Davis. He is the author of *Walter Benjamin and the Corpus of Autobiography* (2000), *Ästhetik des Ereignisses: Sprache—Geschichte—Medium* (2005), and *Thought-Images: Frankfurt School Writers' Reflections from Damaged Life* (in press). He is also the editor of *Benjamin's Ghosts: Interventions in Contemporary Literary and Cultural Theory* (2002) and *Literary Paternity, Literary Friendship* (2002).

HANS RUDOLF VAGET is the Helen and Laura Shedd Professor Emeritus of German Studies and Comparative Literature at Smith College, where he taught from 1967 to 2004. He has published widely in the field of German studies, focusing on Goethe, Wagner, and Thomas Mann as well as on music history and film. A 1994 recipient of the Thomas Mann Medal for his edition of the correspondence of Mann and Agnes E. Meyer, he is also one of the chief editors of the new edition of the works, letters, and diaries of Thomas Mann.

SAMUEL WEBER teaches German and comparative literature at Northwestern University, where he is the Avalon Foundation Professor in the Humanities. In the 1980s and 1990s, he worked as a dramaturg on Wagner's *Ring* and *Parsifal* (directed by Ruth Berghaus) and on several other opera and theater productions in Germany. He recently published two books, *Theatricality as Medium* (2004) and *Targets of Opportunity: On the Militarization of Thinking* (2005). He is currently completing a study of Walter Benjamin.

INDEX